Cases in Nonprofit Management

We dedicate this book to all those who commit themselves to making the world a better place through the work of nonprofit organizations.

In addition, we offer gratitude and thanks to our family—past and present—who made us what we are and love us no matter what.

SAGE was founded in 1965 by Sara Miller McCune to support the dissemination of usable knowledge by publishing innovative and high-quality research and teaching content. Today, we publish over 900 journals, including those of more than 400 learned societies, more than 800 new books per year, and a growing range of library products including archives, data, case studies, reports, and video. SAGE remains majority-owned by our founder, and after Sara's lifetime will become owned by a charitable trust that secures our continued independence.

Los Angeles | London | New Delhi | Singapore | Washington DC | Melbourne

Cases in Nonprofit Management

A Hands-On Approach to Problem Solving

Pat Libby
Pat Libby Consulting

Laura Deitrick
University of San Diego

Los Angeles | London | New Delhi
Singapore | Washington DC | Melbourne

FOR INFORMATION:

SAGE Publications, Inc.
2455 Teller Road
Thousand Oaks, California 91320
E-mail: order@sagepub.com

SAGE Publications Ltd.
1 Oliver's Yard
55 City Road
London EC1Y 1SP
United Kingdom

SAGE Publications India Pvt. Ltd.
B 1/I 1 Mohan Cooperative Industrial Area
Mathura Road, New Delhi 110 044
India

SAGE Publications Asia-Pacific Pte. Ltd.
3 Church Street
#10-04 Samsung Hub
Singapore 049483

Acquisitions Editor: Maggie Stanley
eLearning Editor: Katie Bierach
Editorial Assistant: Nicole Mangona
Production Editor: Bennie Clark Allen
Copy Editor: Michelle Ponce
Typesetter: Hurix Systems Pvt. Ltd.
Proofreader: Wendy Jo Dymond
Cover Designer: Candice Harman
Marketing Manager: Liz Thornton

Printed in the United States of America

Library of Congress Cataloging-in-Publication Data

Names: Libby, Pat. | Deitrick, Laura J.

Title: Cases in nonprofit management : a hands-on approach to problem solving / Pat J. Libby, Laura Deitrick.

Description: First Edition. | Thousand Oaks : SAGE Publications, Inc., 2016. | ?2017 | Includes index.

Identifiers: LCCN 2015039348 | ISBN 9781483383484 (pbk. : alk. paper)

Subjects: LCSH: Nonprofit organizations—Management. | Personnel management. | Decision making.

Classification: LCC HD62.6 .L5364 2016 | DDC 658/.048—dc23 LC record available at http://lccn.loc.gov/2015039348

This book is printed on acid-free paper.

16 17 18 19 20 10 9 8 7 6 5 4 3 2 1

Brief Contents

Detailed Contents

Chapter 14: International Nonprofits 240

Cases Listed By Topic and Theme

CASE	1. Nature of the Sector: Start-ups, Mission, and Purpose	2. Board of Directors: Governance, Bylaws, Group Dynamics	3. Executive Leadership: CEO's	4. Measuring Performance: Organization, Programs, Staff	5. Strategic Decision Making: Organizational Strategy	6. Human Resource Management: Hiring, Paid Staff, Volunteer Management, Staff Management	7. Risk Management	8. Marketing and Communication: Public Relations	9. Generating Revenue: Donors, Fundraising, Grantmaking	10. Financial Management: Accountability	11. Advocacy or Lobbying: Public Officials	12. Technology	13. Grantmaking and Philanthropy	14. International	SPECIAL TOPICS a) Accountability	b) Diversity/Multicultural	c) Government	d) Organizational Policy
Case 1.1 When Mission and Money Collide	×	×	×		×			×	×	×					×		×	
Case 1.2 Why Bylaws Matter	×	×			×		×											
Case 1.3 To Starting or Aid an Existing Organization	×																	
Case 1.4 Social Enterprise Within a Nonprofit Organization	×		×		×				×							×		×
Case 2.1 Board's Role in CEO Evaluation		×	×	×		×	×								×	×		×

Case 2.2 Conflict of Interest		x			x			x		x						x			x
Case 2.3 Hiring Board Members		x	x		x	x										x			x
Case 2.4 The Rubber Stamp Board		x	x		x					x						x		x	
Case 3.1 Challenges of Executive Search		x	x			x													
Case 3.2 Toxic Leadership		x	x	x		x	x												
Case 3.3 The Board's Role in Executive Transition	x	x	x		x	x				x						x			
Case 3.4 CEO Pay		x	x	x		x		x		x						x			x
Case 4.1 Establishing Metrics				x	x				x							x			
Case 4.2 When the Program Isn't Working				x	x				x				x				x		
Case 4.3 When Outcomes Fail to Meet Benchmarks	x		x	x	x	x			x				x			x	x		
Case 5.1 Policy Disputes		x	x		x		x		x	x						x			x
Case 5.2 Generating Revenue by Selling Assets	x	x	x		x				x	x						x			x
Case 5.3 Setting Strategy		x			x					x						x			
Case 6.1 Employee Substance Abuse						x	x									x			x
Case 6.2 Volunteers Ignoring the Rules		x				x	x		x							x			x

CASE	1. Nature of the Sector: Start-ups, Mission, and Purpose	2. Board of Directors: Governance, Bylaws, Group Dynamics	3. Executive Leadership: CEO's	4. Measuring Performance: Organization, Programs, Staff	5. Strategic Decision Making: Organizational Strategy	6. Human Resource Management: Hiring, Paid Staff, Volunteer Management, Staff Management	7. Risk Management	8. Marketing and Communication: Public Relations	9. Generating Revenue: Donors, Fundraising, Grantmaking	10. Financial Management: Accountability	11. Advocacy or Lobbying: Public Officials	12. Technology	13. Grantmaking and Philanthropy	14. International	SPECIAL TOPICS	a) Accountability	b) Diversity/Multicultural	c) Government	d) Organizational Policy
Case 6.3 Policies and Procedures for Staff Members in Crisis		×	×			×	×										×		×
Case 6.4 When Volunteers Run Amok						×	×	×			×							×	×
7.1 Theft						×	×			×									×
7.2 Workplace Accidents						×	×									×			×
7.3 Stolen Information							×			×		×				×		×	×
7.4 Vulnerable Populations						×	×	×	×	×						×			×
Case 8.1 Dealing With the Press		×	×		×	×	×	×	×							×			×
Case 8.2 A Change in Policy With Unforeseen Consequences	×				×	×	×	×									×		×

TOPIC / CASE	1. Nature of the Sector: Start-ups, Mission, and Purpose	2. Board of Directors: Governance, Bylaws, Group Dynamics	3. Executive Leadership: CEO's	4. Measuring Performance: Organization, Programs, Staff	5. Strategic Decision Making: Organizational Strategy	6. Human Resource Management: Hiring, Paid Staff, Volunteer Management, Staff Management	7. Risk Management	8. Marketing and Communication: Public Relations	9. Generating Revenue: Donors, Fundraising, Grantmaking	10. Financial Management: Accountability	11. Advocacy or Lobbying: Public Officials	12. Technology	13. Grantmaking and Philanthropy	14. International	SPECIAL TOPICS	a) Accountability	b) Diversity/Multicultural	c) Government	d) Organizational Policy
Case 13.2 Foundation-Initiated Collaboration	×				×				×				×			×			
Case 13.3 Deciding When to Hire Staff	×	×			×	×				×			×			×			
Case 13.4 Donor Advised Funds			×	×	×				×	×						×			
Case 14.1 When Donors Don't Want to Fund Overhead	×	×	×			×		×	×	×				×			×		
Case 14.2 The Organic Nonprofit	×	×	×		×				×	×			×	×		×	×		
Case 14.3 Cross Cultural Clash	×				×				×					×		×	×		
Case 14.4 NGO Accountability	×				×			×	×	×						×	×		

Cases Listed by Type of Organization

Organization Type		Case
Art museum	5.1	Generating Revenue by Selling Assets
Ballet	8.3	Dealing With the Press
Community action agency	6.2	Employee Substance Abuse
Community development corp.	1.4	Why Bylaws Matter
Community development corp.	2.3	The Board's Role in CEO Evaluation
Community foundation	13.2	Donor Advised Funds
Community health clinic in Guatemala	14.1	Cross-Cultural Clash
Computer access center	10.2	Misallocation of Grant Money
Disease prevention/ awareness	8.2	Celebrity Endorsements
Domestic violence	10.1	Decision Making
Environmental	6.4	When Volunteers Run Amok
Family foundation	13.1	Deciding When to Hire Staff
Food bank	4.1	Establishing Metrics
Foster youth	2.1	Conflict of Interest
Foster youth, adoption, seniors	13.3	Foundation-Initiated Collaboration
Gang violence prevention	4.2	When Outcomes Fail to Meet Established Benchmarks
Group home	2.2	Hiring Board Members as Staff
Head Start	7.1	Stolen Information
Health clinic	3.4	Toxic Leadership
Historical association	10.3	Transparency
Homeless shelter	6.3	Volunteers Ignoring the Rules

Preface and Acknowledgments

The idea for this book came about as a result of our many years of experience teaching nonprofit leadership and management to both undergraduate and graduate students. The focus of this teaching and research was on 501(c)(3) public charities and private foundations. We found that almost all of the textbooks we read contained cases about the same organizations—stories that had been ripped from the headlines about leaders or charities that had been caught in unsavory behavior or unfortunate circumstances. The problem with those cases was that using them as teaching tools made it all too easy for students to search the Internet to find out how these situations had been resolved.

We thought why not write a book of wholly invented cases where students would need to use critical thinking skills to devise an outcome? We also wanted to write cases that could be used for an overnight homework assignment or as part of a classroom discussion or role-play. They needed to be brief, written in a narrative style, and easily digestible. We wanted to provide cases that were accessible to students regardless of how much or how little nonprofit experience they possessed and anticipated that the discussion generated by them would vary depending upon the class makeup. We threw in dialogue and a diverse set of characters to make them interesting and realistic.

Next, we organized this book by topic headings that were most common to prominent nonprofit management texts. In fact, although we provide a brief introduction to each chapter, our intention is for this book to be used as a companion to such larger texts. Our goal was not to reinvent the wheel, simply to put some shiny hubcaps on it.

The cases in this book came from three primary sources:

- First, both of us have been nonprofit practitioners for decades and have worked for, volunteered for, and consulted to organizations that have collectively experienced more than a fair share of organizational challenges. When we wrote those cases, we altered the circumstances as well as the names of people and organizations involved in order to protect everyone's privacy.

- Second, we are avid readers of *The Chronicle of Philanthropy*, *Stanford Social Innovation Review*, *The New York Times*, *The Nonprofit Quarterly*, and other publications that continually describe different types of dilemmas faced by nonprofit organizations. We fictionalized those examples as well, changing the organization name, type, or situation when we wrote the case.

- Finally, we have vivid imaginations and wrote cases describing scenarios that we knew could occur even with the best intended nonprofit manager leading the effort.

We did considerable research when we wrote each of these cases. For instance, we did Internet research to make sure that the organization names we invented did not exist in reality. We looked at the IRS form 990s of nonprofits that were similar to our imaginary organizations to make sure that our financial figures were realistic. We called colleagues and friends and reached out to nonprofit professionals we didn't know at all to ask them to read and comment on our cases when they worked for a nonprofit that was like the one we described. Our subject matter experts provided wonderful insight that enabled us to accurately write about the nuances of each organization and each situation (for example, we know for certain that the supplies we describe being provided in our beach cleanup case are the kinds of supplies that are actually given to volunteers). One of our goals was to make sure that each of our cases would ring true to someone reading the case who worked for a similar organization.

The many reviewers connected to us through our editor at SAGE, Maggie Stanley, made sure that we asked the right questions at the end of each case and that each case would be useful as a teaching tool. They noted that some questions would more readily lend themselves to either undergraduates or graduate students, and that many could be used for teaching multiple topics. For that reason, we added a matrix at the beginning of this book that indicates the overlapping topics each case touches upon to enable students and faculty to make their own decisions about where and how to use the cases.

We are indebted to all of the wonderful people listed below who kept us honest and accurate as well as to our respective family members who cheered us on throughout this process.

Sarah Adams, Voices for Children

Shelly Arsneault, California State University, Fullerton

Elaine Atencio, University of San Diego

Bob Beatty, Beatty & Company, Inc.

Alyce Belford, Mental Health Systems

Erica Bouris, San Diego IRC.

William Brown, Texas A&M University

Andy Carey, U.S.-Mexico Border Philanthropy Partnership

Debbie Case, Meals-on-Wheels Greater San Diego, Inc.

Dave Coplan, University of Pittsburgh

Diane Cox, Just in Time for Foster Youth

Anna Crotty, Crotty Consulting

Clare Crawford, Center on Policy Initiatives

Kelley Crockett, Northern Illinois University

Erin DeCurtis, Simmons College

Emmalie Dropkin, National Head Start Association

Steven Eldred, The California Endowment

Dieter Fenkart-Froeschl, San Diego Museum of Art

Inga Frikke, Shelter and Rescue Group Services, Humane Society of the United States

Richard Garner, University of San Diego

Kassie Graves, SAGE Publications

Haley Haggerstone, Surfrider Foundation, San Diego County

Jenny Jones, Nonprofit Leadership & Management, University of Florida, Gainesville

Sharon Jones-Ryan, Salvation Army Ethics Centre

Andrew Lane, Johnson Family Foundation

Peter Maribei, SOLES Global Center, PhD Student, University of San Diego

Gail Macmillan, Texas A&M University

John McNutt, University of Delaware

Danny Melgoza, County of San Diego

Marcela Merino, Fronteras Unidas Pro Salud, Tijuana, Baja California, Mexico

Debi Mishra, State University of New York at Binghamton

Larry Monteilh, Fontbonne University Saint Louis

Erin Nemenoff, University of Memphis

Casey Nguyen, Catholic Charities of San Diego

James Pappas, California Housing Partnership

Kathy Patoff, Union Bank

Desiree Pavik, Voices for Children

Bonnie E. Peterson, Valdosta State University

Emma Powell, Western Michigan University

Jane Rheinheimer, Rheinheimer Smigliani + Drake,

Theresa Ricke-Kiely, University of Notre Dame

Rosa Rojas, Ohio Dominican University

Daniel Romero, San Diego Futures Foundation

Claudia Sanchez Bajo, University of Toronto

Fernando Sanudo, Vista Community Clinic

Marika Sardar, Southern Asian and Islamic Art

Hans Peter Schmitz, Leadership Studies, University of San Diego

Eileen A. Setti, Northern Illinois University

Jennifer Shea, San Francisco State University

Liz Shear, Shear Directions

Jessica Sowa, University of Colorado, Denver

Maggie Stanley, SAGE Publications

Becky J. Starnes, Austin Peay State University

Jim Stone, Circulate San Diego

Students and Alumni of the Nonprofit Leadership and Management Program, University of San Diego

Donald Stump, North County Lifeline

Heather Sullivan, Humane Society of the U.S.

Doreen Swetkis, Evergreen State College

Laurie Taylor-Hamm, California State University, Fresno

Paul Van Dolah, Van Dolah and Associates Consulting Services

Don Wells, Just in Time for Foster Youth

Tom Winter, Abilene Christian University

Ann Wilson, Community Housing Works

Christina Wilson, Rancho Santa Fe Community Foundation

Yang Li, Beijing Normal University

About the Authors

 **Pat Libby** is a management consultant to non-profits and philanthropies. She has served as an academic, a senior executive, a board member, and a consultant to innumerable nonprofit organizations since 1978. Her consulting practice involves working with organizations to recruit executives, think and plan strategically, and find practical solutions to complex problems.

For 14 years, she served the University of San Diego as the founding director of its Nonprofit Institute. The Institute is frequently cited as one of the nation's premier academic centers dedicated to advancing the work of philanthropic organizations. In creating the Institute, Pat realized a vision for an academic center that would interweave research, theory, and practice.

Her extensive executive management experience also includes 8 years as president/CEO of the Massachusetts Association of Community Development Corporations (CDC). While there, she transformed a financially bankrupt organization into a nationally recognized model for statewide CDC associations, leveraging nearly $200 million for Massachusetts community development efforts in the process.

Pat is also the author of *The Lobbying Strategy Handbook* (SAGE, 2012), an engaging "how-to" guide for nonprofit practitioners who are seeking a simple blueprint for learning how to take part in the legislative process.

Laura Deitrick is a professor of practice in the department of Leadership Studies at the University of San Diego and the interim director of its Institute for Nonprofit Education and Research. The Institute comprises graduate programs at the masters and doctoral levels, the Caster Center for Nonprofit and Philanthropic Research that was developed under her auspices, and comprehensive community education programs serving hundreds of nonprofit practitioners each year. Her research has led to important reports on ethics, nonprofits and public education, human resource practices in the nonprofit sector, executive transition, the economics of the nonprofit sector, public confidence in nonprofits, and trends and best practices in philanthropy and grant making. She has also been a nonprofit executive director, a board member, and a management consultant.

In addition to her administrative and research roles, Dr. Deitrick is a faculty member in USD's Nonprofit Leadership and Management graduate program, where she teaches organizational theory as well as research methods, nonpropfit program design, and evaluation. Additionally, she has consulted to numerous nonprofit boards, affinity groups, and private, corporate, and community foundations on critical nonprofit issues including board governance, executive leadership development, organizational change management, and program evaluation.

1

Nature of the Sector

INTRODUCTION

Whether you call it the nonprofit sector, nongovernmental sector, third sector, or civil society, there are unique elements of "nonprofitness" that distinguish the sector from its for-profit and government sector counterparts. The sector is multifaceted and continually evolving. Our research has found that when individuals are asked to identify a nonprofit they most often mention the names of large nationally known nonprofits such as the YMCA, the Salvation Army, or the Red Cross. When they think of local nonprofits, individuals tend to most often mention nonprofits that deliver traditional social services to the needy such as food banks and homeless shelters. Yet, we know that the sector is so much more than that.

The U.S. nonprofit sector is home to more than 1.44 million registered nonprofits that contributed an estimated $887.3 billion to the U.S. economy in 2012 (McKeever & Pettijohn, 2014). From the arts to zoos, the sector encompasses an almost endless array of organizations of all different sizes ranging from purely voluntary grassroots nonprofits where no money changes hands to extremely large multimillion- (and even billion-) dollar nonprofits such as hospitals and universities. The broad spectrum of nonprofit activities and variety of organizational complexity make it all the more difficult to neatly define the sector.

In the United States, the Internal Revenue Service (IRS) defines a nonprofit as an organization that is precluded, by law or its governance structure, from distributing earnings to any individual who exercises control over that organization (directors, members, etc.). Lester Salamon (2002), a notable nonprofit scholar, includes four additional characteristics that help to broaden the definition and further distinguish the sector from that of government. He adds that nonprofits are

1. institutionalized to some extent (there is an organizational structure, goals, activities);

2. private and not part of government (even though they may receive government money);

3. self-governing (set up to control their own activities); and

4. voluntary or noncompulsory (they draw on the good-will of the people who operate and support them).

Furthermore, nonprofits have an essential reason for being, which is their mission. The mission is the central social purpose of the organization from which all of the nonprofit's activities flow and around which organization direction is set. Bryce (2000) characterizes five elements of a good mission statement that must be present in tax-exempt organizations. He suggests that a nonprofit mission must

1. be a **social contract** between the organization and its members and society at large that spells out what the organization stands for and what it seeks to achieve; it should state the common values beliefs, and aspirations of the organization;

2. have **permanence** in the sense that the mission is adopted by the board of director with a long-term vision in mind such that the mission does not need to be revisited or changed frequently;

3. exhibit **clarity** such that it clearly communicates the organization's purpose;

4. be **approved** in the sense that the mission is seen as legitimate and relevant by the board of directors and key constituencies, and in compliance with legal requirements set forth by the state, IRS, and other governing bodies; and

5. be **demonstrable,** meaning that the mission's achievement can be examined or monitored in some way with the help of performance measures.

In addition to being mission centered, most nonprofits operate within a legal framework that further shapes the form and function of the nonprofit. U.S. nonprofits are incorporated as businesses in the state or (sometime states) in which they do business and as such are subject to the corporate laws of that state. After nonprofits incorporate, they may apply for tax-exempt status at the federal level through the IRS.

In recent years, many states have adopted new laws that allow for different kinds of social purpose organizations to incorporate. These for-profit or hybrid nonprofit entities known as, among other things, benefit corporations (BCorps) and low-profit limited liability company (L3Cs), are giving social entrepreneurs a wider range of options when it comes to selecting a legal structure within which to carry out their missions. Each structure, including the traditional nonprofit structure, has constraints that impact access to capital and private investment and disbursement of earned revenue. Each structure must be considered carefully during the formation stage of the organization so that the organizational purpose may be carried out to its fullest extent.

Regardless of the corporate structure adopted, through the process of becoming a tax-exempt nonprofit, organizations will be required to establish a board of directors and to create governing documents called bylaws. While bylaws may be perceived as complicated, or even irrelevant legal documents, we suggest that nonprofit leaders think of their bylaws as the rules of the road for governing the organization. While the bylaws may not be referred to on a daily basis or at every board meeting, bylaws set forth the processes by which the organization will govern itself. Therefore, it is important for nonprofits to ensure that their bylaws reflect governing practices that support the mission and values of the nonprofit.

The cases presented in this chapter are designed to help students explore the intricacies of form and function that often present themselves when individuals come together to solve societal problems or advance a specific cause:

1. Social entrepreneurship

2. The formation of a nonprofit

3. The essence of a nonprofit

4. Why bylaws matter

REFERENCES

Bryce, H. (2000). *Financial and strategic management for nonprofit organizations: A comprehensive reference to legal, financial, management, and operations rules and guidelines for nonprofits* (3rd ed.). San Francisco, CA: Jossey-Bass

McKeever, B. S., & and Pettijohn, S. L. (2014). *The nonprofit sector in brief 2014: Public charities, giving, and volunteering*. Washington, DC: Urban Institute. Retrieved from http://www.urban.org/sites/default/files/alfresco/publication-pdfs/413277-The-Nonprofit-Sector-in-Brief

Salamon, L. (2002). What is the nonprofit sector and why do we have it? In J. S. Ott (Ed.), *The nature of the nonprofit sector* (pp.162-166). Boulder, CO: Westview.

SOCIAL ENTERPRISE WITHIN A NONPROFIT ORGANIZATION: INDEPENDENCE MATTERS

Bruno Conti liked to joke that he established Independence Matters in 1996 by accident. It was a joke because Independence Matters was born out of a work accident that left Bruno paralyzed from the waist down with no clear path about how to lead life as a disabled person. He liked to say that once he got "back on his feet" he dedicated himself to helping others who found themselves newly disabled with a roadmap for transitioning into and fully living life. The mission of the organization was "to provide support, identify solutions, and offer opportunities that enable persons with physical disabilities to participate fully in life."

Independence Matters programs included an array of social, health, recreational, and educational services. Among them, counseling and coaching of newly disabled individuals provided by a team of specially trained volunteer disabled mentors; transportation services; physician-led health services that provided information and referrals on a gamut of far-ranging health-related issues; professionally facilitated support groups for disabled individuals, their partners, and families; a fund for extraordinary medical expenses and other unanticipated expenses resulting from the disability; a wheelchair basketball team and swim program; and adaptive job training that was accompanied by a successful job referral and placement component. The nearly $7 million agency was well known throughout the community and highly respected for its work.

Bruno was proud of what he had built and of the hundreds of lives he had touched through the work of Independence Matters, but he was tired of the constant fund-raising. Relative to the programs it offered, the agency operated on a lean budget that was cobbled together year after year with a combination of grants from government agencies, private foundations, and corporations and contributions from individual donors that were netted through personal connections, annual appeals, and a golf tournament. He believed he had a talented development staff; however, he was still seen as the fund-raiser in chief for the organization. It was an exhausting and never-ending task.

Bruno shared his frustration one day over lunch with his board chair, Bob Delaney, a recently retired bank executive. "I understand feeling like you're a hamster on a never-ending wheel when it comes to keeping the place afloat," he sympathized. "And I have the utmost respect for the work you do and how vitally important it is to people in our community. As I've told you many times, I think Independence Matters literally saved my son's life when he lost his legs. You got him through his darkest hours and showed him that life was worth living. Now I have a beautiful daughter-in-law and granddaughter as a result, and I thank God every day for the part you played in making that happen. But I've been thinking, Bruno, we need to figure out a different way of raising money so that we're not so reliant on philanthropy."

"What do you mean?" asked Bruno. "Well I've been doing some reading and research, and I have an idea that I think we should explore with the board," replied Bob. "The idea is to start an arm of the agency that would retrofit the homes of people who need that type of assistance, including seniors and others who fall outside of our traditional service population. I've taken the liberty of talking to Norma Chavez, a lender in the bank's community reinvestment group, about the general concept, and she told me that she'd be willing to talk to us about putting together a special loan and grant package to get something like this off the ground if we create a viable business plan. Now that I'm retired, I have the time to work on something like this—as a volunteer of course—that is, if you and the board believe this is a concept that is worth pursuing. Norma also has strong ties with the Gunderfeld Foundation (her husband is on the board), and she told me she thought they might be willing to put in a low-interest loan and grant money for an idea like this—assuming, again, that it pencils out, and that you and the board agree that we should give it a shot."

Bruno's eyes lit up. "Bob, I think this is a fantastic idea! Let's bring it up at next week's executive committee meeting and, if they approve, move forward with a proposal to the full board to explore the feasibility of the project."

In the weeks that followed, the idea took off like a wild fire. The executive committee quickly and unanimously approved the idea as did the full board. A small committee was formed to develop the business plan, and a special grant was secured from the Gunderfeld Foundation to hire consultants with expertise to guide the plan's development and, subsequently, to assist the business in its early stages if the plan proved viable. Within a year, Independence Matters Retrofitters (IMR) was born. At the end of 2 years, it was generating $2.5 million in net revenue that was funneled back into the operating budget of Independence Matters.

Bruno and the board of Independence Matters were overjoyed with the success of the retrofit arm. IMR had a reputation for providing reasonably priced high-quality services that were specifically designed for the individual needs of each client's home. In addition, several of its staff members were former Independence Matters clients who were grateful to have steady, meaningful work; they were especially sensitive to the needs of the people they served.

As word of IMR's work spread, business grew quickly. Then Bruno and Eliezer Guzman, IMR's managing director (who was also disabled) received a special commendation from the governor, and the organization was discovered by the press. It was profiled on *60 Minutes,* which led to calls from people across the country who wanted similar services, were interested in donating money or expertise, and from other nonprofits that wanted to replicate the model. IMR had to hire a director of media and community outreach whose job it was to field these inquiries, interact with the press, arrange interviews with staff and clients, and lead tours of the operations. A line of IMR products was developed that included a number of specially designed and patented hardware items for adaptive homes as well as paraphernalia such as IMR hats, mugs, and T-shirts. Revenues boomed to $18 million annually.

Independence Matters used a small portion of the IMR revenue to expand its programs, beef up its fund-raising department (which was needed to handle the surge in donations to the organization as well as increased interest from national foundations), gave senior staff generous and significant raises, and set aside more than 2 years of operating reserves.

IMR had become so large and successful that Bruno and Eliezer decided to prepare a proposal to the board to hire a director of field operations who would fly around the country setting up nonprofit franchises of IMR. That would bring in even more revenue for the organization. It had been only 4 years since Bob had first proposed this idea to Bruno, and now it seemed like the sky was the limit on how much they could earn through this enterprise.

When Bruno and Eliezer presented the idea to the executive committee, they were surprised at the response they received. These were the questions they raised (which you should also consider):

Case Questions

1. What is the defining difference between a nonprofit organization and a social enterprise organization?

2. What are the legal and financial implications of a nonprofit wholly owned social enterprise?

3. Is IMR causing Independence Matters to drift from its core mission?

4. Are there any apparent conflicts of interest in the current setup of IMR as a program of Independence Matters?

5. Are there operating structures that could be put in place to minimize conflicts and ensure accountability?

6. Are there ethical implications for a social enterprise that generates much more revenue than is needed to fund the operations of the nonprofit parent? For instance, what about the time and energy needed to oversee both arms of this work?

TO START OR AID AN EXISTING ORGANIZATION: NO GOOD DEED GOES UNPUNISHED

Miguel Tigre knew that he was one of the lucky ones. He was born in the United States to Mexican immigrant parents who instilled in him a passion for hard work, a love of family, and compassion for others. His father worked weekdays as a baker at Panaderia La Mexicana and most weekends moonlighted as a baker for a wedding caterer. Miguel's mother had stayed home to raise the family, which, in addition to him, included his four brothers and sisters and his mother's mother, his *abuelita*. His mother kept an immaculate house and was known throughout the neighborhood for her dedication to church and tamales (some joked that making perfect tamales was her second religion).

Miguel was the oldest child. He was the first in the family to finish high school and then the first to attend college (his brother, Roberto, was now majoring in engineering at an out-of-state university; his sister, Adela, was in her first year of community college and aspired to be a nurse; and the twins, the youngest siblings, were still in middle school). The day Miguel graduated with an associate's degree in business administration was a proud day for the Tigre family. It had taken him 4 years to finish community college because of his need to balance school and work; he had helped support the family since he was 14 years old by working in a local taco shop. He loved everything about the shop: the smells, the food, and the customers. He would often tell people that he was getting two degrees, one from the college and the other from Mr. Sanchez, who was teaching him how to run a business. Then, like a dream come true, just as he was graduating from community college, Mr. Sanchez told Miguel that he was retiring and moving to Los Angeles to live with his daughter and her family. A friend of Miguel's family helped him secure a small business loan to buy the business.

Miguel had now been running Miguel's Taqueria for 2 years and had tremendous pride in his small business. He had modernized the small restaurant with fresh paint, posters, and new salsa recipes. He had a steady stream of regular customers who he knew by name (and their usual order). People loved going to Miguel's not only for the food but also to see Miguel who it seemed never left home without a smile or a kind word for everyone he met. His parents were extremely proud of him although his mother and abuela worried that he wasn't dating (and told him so frequently).

Over time, several of Miguel's customers began coming to him to ask him to translate documents they needed to sign. He was happy to help them and was always careful to be sure that they knew exactly what they were signing. Once word got out that Miguel was willing to provide this service, more and more of his customers began coming in asking for help (and he was also attracting new customers who had the same need). The neighborhood was home not only to Mexicans but also to immigrants from El Salvador, Guatemala, and assorted South American countries as well as Africans and Middle Easterners. Miguel treated everyone equally and with respect.

One Sunday afternoon he was watching football with Mohammed, a friend from community college whose family had emigrated from Syria. Mohammed had been in the shop recently and had witnessed a line of people waiting to have their documents translated. He said, "Bro, I think it's cool that you're doing that for the people, but isn't it cutting into your bottom line? What if instead of translating everything for everyone all the time you taught people how to read English so they could be doing it themselves? You could set up a class in the shop, for like one night a week, where people could learn English. You'd lose the business for that night, but I think it would probably even out because I'm thinking that you're losing business now when other customers come in and see a line out the door, and they know it will take them 20 minutes to a get a taco because you're busy doing someone's paperwork."

Miguel's eyes lit up. "That makes a lot of sense . . . man, did you see that tackle? He just got hammered."

"You know what else, "said Mohammed, "You could start a nonprofit to do that stuff. I'm on the board of my nephew's Little League and that's what they are—a nonprofit. They get all kinds of sponsors to pay for uniforms and stuff. If you become a nonprofit, I bet you could deduct the cost of the space in the shop for the night you have the class and take donations from people. Remember that guy, Dave, who was in our communications class? His brother is an attorney. I bet he could hook you up."

"Let me think about it," replied Miguel.

During the next few days, Miguel couldn't get Mohammed's idea out of his mind. The more he thought about it, the more it made sense. He went online and did a little reading about nonprofit organizations. Then he called Mohammed, who called Dave to set up a meeting with his brother, the attorney. Dave's brother said, "This is pretty straightforward. I'm happy to write up the articles of incorporation and bylaws for you for $500.00. Don't worry, though. Once you get your paperwork back from the IRS and the state, you can deduct that money." Miguel swallowed hard; $500 was serious money; he was still paying off his small business loan, and despite the influx of customers, business had been pretty flat for the past 8 months. Then he thought, "This is something that is important to do for my community. I'll figure out how I'm going to pay for it later."

He had already told his sister, Adela, about the plan, and she had agreed that she and a friend, who was studying education at the community college, would be the volunteer teachers. She was proud of Miguel for taking this on and had persuaded her friend, Miriam, to help by letting her know that Miguel was not only a nice guy, he was pretty good-looking and single. Miguel went to Big Lots and bought 20 copies of *My First Reading Book* at $4.00 each (20 people were the maximum number the restaurant could seat). When he showed the books to Miriam she said, "Those will be fine for a start, but we really need to find a book that is more suited for adult learners. Don't worry. I'll ask one of my professors for a recommendation. I'm sure she'll have some great ideas." Miguel smiled when she said that, but he was thinking, "Cha-ching. More money out the door . . ."

Adela and Miriam made a flyer to advertise the class, which would take place on Tuesday nights from 8:00 to 9:00 p.m. (his slowest night and time of the week). Miguel told them that he would have to charge a small amount in order to make up for his lost business and to help him recoup some of the money that he had laid out for the project. They all agreed that $4.00 per class seemed reasonable. He posted the flyer in his shop window, had extra copies of it on the counter, and told many of his customers about the class.

The first evening the class was held, 18 people came. All arrived at least 5 minutes before it started. Miguel was happy to see the room filled with many of his customers and their friends. Each person was given a book, paper, and pen. Miguel had bought a large flip chart, markers, and easel to use as a blackboard. It was set up on the counter where people normally placed their orders. He gave everyone a free soda, too, because he was just that kind of guy. At the end of the evening, the students looked tired but appreciative. They all shook Miguel's hand in thanks. Adela and Miriam were both exhausted and excited at the same time. Miriam's professor had told her that she could earn independent study credit for working on the project.

The following Tuesday, Miguel, Adela, and Miriam eagerly awaited the start of class. Miriam's professor had found some classroom material that was specifically geared to adult English as a second language (ESL) learners, and Miriam was excited to try it out with the class. By 8:00, only five people had arrived. Miguel and the others were disappointed; however, Miriam and Adela did their best to teach a good class.

During the days that followed, Miguel noticed that his business was slower. Many of his steady customers, the same ones who had come to the first class, weren't coming in to place their usual orders. He couldn't figure out what was going on. It didn't make any sense. Finally, late Friday afternoon, Hector Morales, one of his regulars, came in to the shop. "Hector, how are you my friend?" said Miguel with a broad smile.

"Very well, amigo," Hector replied. The two men talked for a few minutes while Miguel prepared the order to go. Because Hector was acting like his usual self, Miguel thought it was safe to ask why he hadn't come to class this past Tuesday. What Hector said surprised Miguel. "We enjoyed the class very much," he said, "and appreciate all that you, your sister, and Senorita Miriam did for us. That Sunday, many of us spoke about it to the pastor. He told us about an organization called International Rescue Committee that offers English classes. They are two blocks from here but do not charge any money. So, most of us went there. I know that many customers are ashamed now to come into your shop. You tried to do something good for them, and they turned to another place for help. I told them to come and that you would not be angry, but they are worried about offending you."

Upon hearing this, Miguel's jaw dropped open. It made perfect sense. Now he had to figure out a strategy for rebuilding his lost business and recouping the funds he had laid out for the nonprofit.

Case Questions

1. Do you think what happened to Miguel is common? What was his biggest mistake?

2. What if there was no other literacy program in the neighborhood or surrounding community?

3. What changes would you suggest to improve how Miguel went about forming his organization?

4. Make a list of the steps that must be done before starting a nonprofit organization.

5. Using the list you developed above, please list the steps in order of what needs to be accomplished first, second, third, and so on.

CASE 1.3

WHEN MISSION AND MONEY COLLIDE: WHAT IS THE ESSENCE OF A NONPROFIT?

As the longtime President/CEO of Hyland, a privately held world-renowned luxury hotel brand, Myron Morse thought he had seen it all; deceitful contractors that claimed shoddy materials were top shelf products, renegade third-world officials that halted construction unless bribed, trusted partners caught up in substance abuse. Yet, in all his years, he had never faced a situation like the one he was facing now as chairman of the board of Memorial Hospital.

Memorial was a venerable institution having served the community for more than 80 years and known widely for its outstanding research and patient care, in particular, its work in cardiovascular diseases, neurology, emergency medicine, geriatrics, and palliative medicine. With an annual operating budget that was approaching $1.3 billion, Memorial was the largest hospital in the county and preeminent in the state. Myron had served on the board for 8 years and had been honored to be selected as chairman last year (he had previously served as vice-chair along with three other board members and had been a member of the executive committee for 5 years).

The hospital was led by Dr. Dirk Figuerllo, a towering figure at close to 7 feet tall with a booming voice that added to his commanding presence. Figuerllo, often referred to as "Dr. Dirk," was a Belgium native who had done pioneering work in palliative medicine and hospice care in his native country before coming to the United States. He was internationally recognized as one of the foremost experts in the field and worked tirelessly to raise awareness of palliative medicine through advocacy with institutions such as the World Health Organization and the American Medical Association. He was an eloquent speaker on the subject who was often quoted as having said, "Honoring life by providing physical, psychological, and spiritual support to the dying and their loved ones is one of the most important acts of a civilized society. Supporting patients and their families this way, rather than with expensive, extraordinary, and often intrusive medical care during the patient's dying days, is both loving and responsible."

Dirk had been recruited to the CEO position 10 years earlier to cement Memorial's reputation as a preeminent provider of palliative care. Under his leadership Memorial enhanced its Palliative Care Center (PCC) and, in response to unabated worldwide demand, developed an active consulting and training program that provided technical assistance and support to other institutions and health care professionals that sought to replicate the model. He was not only a dedicated physician, he was also respected for his managerial talent and fund-raising skills. Under his leadership, Memorial had increased the size of its endowment from $200 million to nearly $500 million. In fact, Dirk's leadership inspired Myron to pledge $100 million to the hospital during Memorial's most recent endowment campaign. It was the largest single gift ever received by the institution.

Last week, Dirk asked Myron to meet with him privately to discuss an urgent matter pertaining to the PCC. "Myron, I don't know any other way to relate this news to you, so I'm just going to be straightforward: Memorial is under investigation by the Office of the Inspector General for falsely billing Medicare for hospice claims." Known for his expert poker skills and for his ability to be calm under pressure, Myron didn't show his surprise. "OK, Dirk," he said. "Why don't you start at the beginning and explain exactly what's going on and how we got into this mess."

With no show of remorse, Dirk began the explanation. "Medicare guidelines allow providers to receive payment for providing hospice patients up to 6 months of care. The amount Medicare pays out per patient depends upon the level of care provided and varies according to the services provided. For example, Medicare pays approximately $150 per day for routine care (a category in which very few of our patients fall) and up to approximately $900 per day for 24 hour support. Our own records indicate that approximately 13.8% of our patients during the past 5 years stayed at PCC or received PCC in-home services for more than 180 days, which is a violation of those terms. An audit of our records by the Centers for Medicare & Medicaid Services uncovered that discrepancy, which has led the government to demand repayment of what they consider to be overcharges, as well as to levy a hefty fine on Memorial. The total charges come to $142 million, which exceeds the $120 million annual operating budget of the PCC. Given our reputation in the field, I'm not sure they would have thought to audit us; however, we were exposed by a part-time internal audit manager who blew the whistle because she felt we were cheating the government."

"I understand," said Myron. "That is, I understand the Medicare rules as you've explained them to me, but how in the world did this happen? You said, our *own* records indicate that nearly 14% of our patients received services longer than was permitted. Were you personally aware that we were violating the law all this time? How could that be Dirk?"

Dirk sighed impatiently, and he became irritated. "Myron, the fact of the matter is that palliative care is a calling, a calling to provide care with dignity to the dying and to support their families during that process. Death doesn't have a stop watch. We can't judge with scientific accuracy the exact date when someone with cancer, heart disease, or Alzheimer's is going to die. Yes, I knew this was occurring with a relatively small portion of our patient population, but I also knew that it was immoral to remove critically important services from these people. We are a nonprofit hospital Myron. It is our duty and our mission to serve people in need. It just so happens that many of these longer term patients were also low income, and that is a palliative care population you don't see at for-profit hospitals because frankly, they are not profitable to serve. We are doing God's work here. You can't put a price on that."

"Well obviously the federal government has put a substantial price on that, Dirk, and it's one that we are going to have to figure out how to pay," responded Myron. "I suggest we call an emergency meeting of the executive committee to discuss how we should respond to this situation."

Three days later, the executive committee met in closed session in a hospital conference room. Attending the meeting were Jerry Goldstein, vice president of Memorial and a prominent trial lawyer; Greg Anderson, vice president of Memorial and CEO of Anderson Construction; Dr. Kenneth Gold, vice president and neurosurgeon; Harris Baum, treasurer, and private wealth manager; and Dr. Ellen Foster, secretary and retired psychiatrist. After hearing Dirk's explanation that was accompanied by detailed PCC financial statements, patient census reports, and findings from the Medicare investigation, Ken spoke.

"I cannot believe you had the audacity to make this kind of decision, to provide what was essentially illegal care—or perhaps better stated—care that was billed illegally to Medicare, to nearly 14% of the PCC patients without discussing this with the board. You said, Dirk, that this was a relatively *small* percentage of the PCC patient population; however, *small* is a relative term. The penalty we are facing isn't small at all. You're jeopardizing the reputation of the hospital and our financial viability as an institution, which is just unconscionable. I know you think that Memorial is all about PCC and spreading the word about its good works, but it's not. We're more than that. As the physician representative on this board, I like to think that we provide a lot of excellent care in other areas as well. I'm terrified that the person who leaked this information to Medicare will go to the press. Why not? It's only a matter of time."

"I have to agree with much of what Ken has said," said Ellen, although her tone was considerably calmer. "We hired you, Dirk, because you are an expert in this area. That expertise doesn't give you license to knowingly flout the law and damage the financial standing and good name of this hospital. If you had come to the board with a proposal to subsidize the care of these people who needed to be with us for longer than the guidelines allow, that would be one thing. But to do this without our knowledge. I just don't know what you were thinking."

Harris spoke next. "Gentleman, this is not the time to excoriate Dirk for his behavior. It is incumbent upon this committee to devise a plan for how we will address this situation. As I see it, there are several options before us. First, perhaps we can negotiate the amount of the penalty Medicare has levied from $50 million down to $15 or $20 million along with a long-term payment plan for the remaining charges? Jerry, my guess is that you have access to or knowledge of colleagues who may be able to assist with those endeavors. That said, even if we are successful in doing so, it will not provide an answer as to where we will get access to the funding needed to reimburse the $92 million in wrongly billed charges. We have been very fortunate with our fund-raising; however, those monies are locked into endowment accounts that cannot be used for this purpose. It is unlikely as well that our most generous supporters will be eager to dig us out of a hole. Donors want to see momentum, not regression. Therefore, although a special fund-raising campaign may appear to be a second option (one that is tethered to the first option), on the surface, it does not seem realistic. Third, and perhaps this is our best option, we can investigate selling off the PCC unit to a for-profit hospice provider that will assume the debt. Whatever we decide, we must decide quickly as, like Ken, I have to believe that the whistle blower will be sharing this information with the press in short order. "

"Harris, you're reading my mind," said Greg. "Tom Windwood is a good friend of mine. We play golf together at Brayburn twice a week in the summer. He'd chomp at the bit at the chance to buy our palliative care unit. It would be a coup for Peaceful Promise and a relatively painless way to get us out of this mess."

"That will defeat the whole purpose of what we are trying to do at this hospital!" cried Dirk. "Everyone who is in the palliative care business knows that for-profit hospices are adept at not enrolling patients that require more expensive and extensive types of care. Two separate studies—one published in *Health Affairs* and the other by the American Medical Association—document this widespread practice. The federal government is wrong—not us! We need to take a public stand to fight this injustice, not cow to it!"

"Gentlemen, please settle down," said Myron. "It is the duty of this executive committee to examine our options and to make a recommendation to the board about how we should proceed. Given the urgent nature of the situation, we must do so quickly and with utmost care to consider the consequences of our actions."

Case Questions

1. As a board member, what information would you need to make this decision? Which staff members, if any, should be involved in this decision?

2. What are the consequences to Memorial of selling the PCC unit to Tom Windwood, who heads a for-profit operation? Would you recommend the board vote to move in this direction?

3. What kind of public announcement, if any, should the board make to the press about the investigation? What should be the timing of that announcement?

4. Who within the organization should be held accountable for what occurred?

5. What kind of interaction should the board have with its donors concerning this information?

6. How should information about this inquiry be shared with the PCC staff?

7. How does this case relate to Bryce's characterizations of a nonprofit mission as described in the introduction to this chapter?

8. How might a situation like this be avoided in the future?

WHY BYLAWS MATTER: A HOSTILE TAKEOVER ATTEMPT

Jenny Jones stared out her office window in disbelief. She was stunned with what was happening to the Washington Hills Community Development Corporation (WHCDC); it was all coming at her so fast and seemingly out of nowhere.

Ten years earlier, Jenny had taken up the reins as CEO of the CDC, an organization that like many others around the country, had been founded for the express purpose of having local people determine, lead, and manage development in their predominantly low-income communities. As a longtime community activist and neighborhood development professional, she was passionate about the mission of the organization, which was to revitalize Washington Hills, a diverse inner-city low-income neighborhood, through economic revitalization and citizen empowerment projects. The slogan of the CDC was *Neighbors Empowering Neighbors,* which represented its historical roots as well as its focus on being resident-led and responsive to the expressed needs of the community.

The CDC had a distinguished history as one of the first community development corporations in the nation. It grew out of neighborhood riots in 1966 where angry protests for better housing, better schools, better jobs, and better city services turned into the ugly widespread destruction of what was an already economically devastated area. By the time the smoke cleared, Washington Hills looked like a bombed out shell.

Against all odds, a small group of neighbors led by a young minister began meeting in a church basement to devise a bold plan for revitalizing Washington Hills. There were seven of them in total: a barber, a butcher, two "homemakers" (as they were called in those days), a bus driver, a warehouse worker, and the minister, who together set a goal for building affordable housing on 20 acres in "the Hills." The U.S. Attorney General, Robert Kennedy, initiated efforts to support organizations like theirs, which led to the group being awarded an initial grant to build housing on 2 acres. It was a project that was long in the making; the 40 units of housing the CDC built took 8 years to complete but in the process created jobs, neighborhood pride, and, most important, a blueprint for revitalizing the rest of the Hills.

By the time Jenny was hired to lead the CDC, it had developed more than 1,200 units of affordable housing (both rental and homeowner-ship units), built a vibrant shopping center, opened a successful char-ter school, and operated several day-care facilities, a senior center, job training center, and a small business loan and façade improvement program. Although she was not from the neighborhood, Jenny had led a similar yet smaller organization in another city. From the start, she was drawn to the CDC because of its deeply held commitment to the principles upon which it was founded: that neighborhood revitalization should be directly overseen by and be responsive to the needs of people in the community. Although the board of directors had expanded over the years from seven to 15 members, it was still largely composed of local businesspeople and homeowners. The CDC was thriving.

If there was a downside to the CDC's success, it was the affect its work had had on the neighborhoods that abutted the Hills. Although those neighborhoods had never been as blighted as the Hills had been at its lowest point, the revitalization efforts of the CDC had led over time to dramatic renewal projects in those areas. The Pointe, for example, which was once home to a large Italian American working-class community, had seen housing prices soar to previously unimaginable levels. Bakeshops and pizza parlors had given way to sushi restaurants and yoga studios. The tax base increased, and crime decreased. While the neighborhood looked better, older residents bemoaned the lost opportunity for their children to afford homes in their beloved neighborhood. It was no longer a close-knit community and had lost much of its original character.

The West Pines, which abutted downtown and was located on the other side of the Hills, saw an even greater transformation and escalation in housing costs that displaced many working-class families in the process. The resurgence of the city's business district, port, and historic districts were putting even greater economic pressure on the remaining lower-income and working-class people in all of these areas, including the Hills, as the price of rental and homeowner housing tripled and storefront leases rose dramatically.

Although it cautiously welcomed young urban professionals to the Hills, the CDC saw its role as preserving an affordable stable community for its longtime residents. The mission of the CDC, "To advance and protect the Washington Hills neighborhood and its residents through community revitalization and empowerment efforts," was always foremost in Jenny's mind. During the past several years, she had often felt that she needed to defend it to the people who worked in the city's planning department, which was a dramatic shift from the previous administration. It seemed these planners who worked for the mayor were overjoyed and blindsided by the tax revenue that had resulted from all of the urban renewal projects throughout the city. She was growing increasingly concerned that the city was losing sight of the need to protect affordable housing. To make matters more worrisome, she didn't trust the mayor, because his election campaign had been flush with contributions from private developers.

The Hills annual meeting was a popular event where neighbors turned out to greet one another over homemade cakes and coffee, celebrate the accomplishments of the CDC (featured in a slideshow and highlighted in speeches by the CEO and Board Chair), and elect new members to the board. It was traditionally held in the high school gym since it was the most affordable place in the neighborhood that could comfortably accommodate the 350 or so people that generally attended. Anyone who was 18 years or older could be a member of the CDC by paying $5.00 and signing a pledge to uphold the mission: The founders felt that money should never be an impediment to joining the organization. The custom was for people to walk in, sign the pledge, hand in their money (many often gave much more than $5 and, in fact, this was a silent and easy fund-raiser for the CDC), and receive a ballot.

The bylaws stipulated that each of its 15 board members serve a 2-year term with approximately one half of the board (seven or eight members depending upon the year) being up for election or reelection each year. Board members were allowed to serve three consecutive terms of office for a total of 6 years. They were then required to step off the board for at least one 2-year term before being eligible to serve on the board again.

The founders felt that having half of the board in place for at least 2 years at a time would provide the CDC with stable leadership while still allow-ing room for new people with new ideas the opportunity to come onto the board every other year. Most board members, though, served 6 years before stepping down, and that was the tacit expectation of all board members when they signed on to be directors. Officers were required to be board members for 2 years before moving into those roles.

The officers of the CDC, consisting of the chairman (or chairwoman), treasurer, and secretary served as the nominating committee and, as such, were responsible for presenting the slate of board of director candidates to the membership. In addition, and in keeping with its democratic principles, the CDC also allowed the membership to nominate from the floor individuals whose names had not been placed on the ballot. In all of its years of existence, this had never occurred, although the organization always left several blank spaces on the ballot to allow for the possibility of names to be added.

One week prior to the annual meeting, Jenny learned some disturbing news from her director of housing, Richmond Lewis. Rich told Jenny that a contact of his from Bank of America had heard that Jim Stone, a well-known downtown developer and friend of the mayor, was planning to pack the CDC's annual meeting with people from outside the neighborhood who would vote for a slate of board candidates that would be nominated from the floor. All these people had to do was walk in the door, sign the pledge, pay $5.00, and they were members.

Jim knew, somehow, that the affordable housing deed restrictions on the CDC's first 40 unit apartment building were expiring in 2 years and wanted to get the CDC to sell the building to him in order to convert it into 20 units of luxury housing. Because the housing complex was located along the border of the West Pines, it was close to housing that commanded much higher prices. The rumor was that Jim and the board members on his slate would argue that the CDC should cash out of the project and use the money to do something "more productive" with it in the Hills (probably, in a part of the neighborhood that was not as "up and coming"). The truth was that if that happened, all the tenants in the building would be displaced, and new affordably priced apartments would be almost impossible for them to find. Many of those residents had lived in the complex since the apartment was built.

Given the CDC's bylaws, voting in his people wouldn't be difficult to accomplish; all he needed to do was to fill the house, get his candidates nominated from the floor, and take over control of the board since this was a year that 8 of the 15 seats would be up for election. His goal was larger than that one building; Jim wanted the CDC to focus more of its energy on projects that would accommodate the up and comers who were moving into the Hill. Rather than have the CDC continue to develop dense multiunit affordable housing, he wanted the group to focus more on developing single family for-sale homes and on creating pocket parks throughout the neighborhood. He had a luxury hotel project on the drawing board that he envisioned rising on the highest part of the Hills overlooking the West Pines, and it would work to his advantage if he presented his project as being part of the CDC's vision for the community.

Jenny was shaken to the core by this news. She never imagined that the open and democratic process that the founders and she had held dear all these years, the very process that was designed to encourage resident participation in the CDC, could jeopardize control of the organization, its mission, and its assets. She convened an emergency board meeting for that evening that was followed the next morning by an all-staff meeting. The staff members were instructed to dedicate their every waking hour between now and the board meeting to call and door-knock on all residents of the CDC's buildings, all parents of children enrolled in the charter school, all businesses involved in the loan and facade programs, all seniors at the center, and to ask all other existing CDC members to come to the meeting to vote for the official CDC-board slate. All other CDC projects were put on hold while the staff and board scrambled to reach out to everyone in their network.

The following week, nearly 700 people showed up at the annual meeting. The gym was hot from the heat of all of the bodies in the room and couldn't accommodate everyone, the crowd as spilling out onto the sidewalk. The atmosphere was tense. Reporters from TV, radio, and the local papers all came to cover the proceedings. At the end of the evening, the CDC prevailed in electing its slate of candidates.

Case Questions

1. Who within a nonprofit is responsible for reviewing its mission? Are the stakeholders with that responsibility the same regardless of the type of nonprofit organization?

2. Several board members feel strongly that the CDC's bylaws should not be changed in order to preserve the open and democratic tradition of the organization. What are the arguments for and against changing the bylaws? Do you believe they should be changed?

3. If you believe the bylaws should be changed to prevent this type of situation from happening in the future, in what ways would you recommend they be changed?

   a. Is there a way to change the bylaws and still preserve neighborhood involvement? Specifically, what do you think about the current membership system that is in place?

   b. Is it good practice for half of the board to turn over their seats at the same time? Why or why not?

   c. What role should a board nominating committee play in selecting board candidates?

4. What actions, if any, could have been taken to avoid this conflict with Jim Stone?

2

Board of Directors

INTRODUCTION

Similar to the iconic Queens Guard that diligently stands watch over Buckingham Palace in London, the governing boards of nonprofits may be considered the guardians of governance for nonprofit organizations. Today more than ever, board members and executive leaders find themselves on the front lines of a constantly changing landscape. All of this leads us to ask, what is governance, and what is the role of the nonprofit board in leading and managing third-sector organizations?

Liz Shear (2013), an expert in the field of nonprofit governance, provides this definition: "Governing boards are a legally constituted group of people, who together advance, guide, and oversee an organization's mission for the common good, on behalf of the community."

While the actual structure and composition of a governing board may vary across nonprofit organizations, all directors of governing boards have full legal responsibility for the organization. Deeply rooted in common law, these legal responsibilities are set forth in a set of three duties: the duty of care, the duty of loyalty, and the duty of obedience. While the legal provisions under each duty may vary slightly from state to state, the core concepts associated with each are presented in Table 2.1.

In addition to what board members are required to do, scholars and practitioners are also interested in how boards carry out their duties and the extent to which their actions make an organization more or less effective. The literature on boards identifies a broad range of variables that may influence effectiveness, including board composition, structure, policies, and so on, that cannot be fully captured in this introduction. However, many of them have been succinctly synthesized by Board-Source in its publication *The Source: Twelve Principles of Governance That Power Exceptional Boards*, presented in Table 2.2.

Table 2.1. Duties of Care, Loyalty, and Obedience

Duty of Care	Requires board members to exercise a reasonable level of care when governing the organization and in the stewardship of its assets. Often times this is characterized as acting in the same way as a normally prudent person would under similar circumstances. Board members who exercise the duty of care will • Follow accepted business-like practices • Ensure that the board is properly constituted • Read their materials (e.g., meeting minutes and financials) • Attend and participate in meetings • Use good judgment • Ensure proper operating policies and controls are in place • Engage in thoughtful planning
Duty of Loyalty	When making decisions or taking action, directors are called upon to prioritize the best interest of the organization over all else. Directors must avoid conflicts of interest. Board members who exercise the duty of loyalty will • Avoid taking actions where they or a close association (such as family member or business partner) will derive personal gain • Ensure that the nonprofit has adopted a formal conflict of interest policy • Review and understand the organization's conflict of interest policy • Properly vet potential transactions that involve board members • Disclose conflicts when they arise • Speak with one voice
Duty of Obedience	Requires that directors follow all laws that may be applicable to the organization even those with which they might not otherwise be familiar.

Board members must also ensure that the organization is operating in alignment with its mission, by-laws, and formal policies.
Board members who exercise the duty of care will

- Approve all major contractual obligations
- Ensure the organization complies with all government requirements for filing information
- Ensure that all employment laws are followed

SOURCE: Adapted from Worth (2014), *Nonprofit Management Principles and Practice,* (3rd ed.) Sage Publications.

Table 2.2. The Source: Twelve Principles of Governance That Power Exceptional Boards

1. CONSTRUCTIVE PARTNERSHIP
Exceptional boards govern in constructive partnership with the chief executive, recognizing that the effectiveness of the board and chief executive are interdependent. They build this partnership through trust, candor, respect, and honest communication.

2. MISSION DRIVEN
Exceptional boards shape and uphold the mission, articulate a compelling vision, and ensure the congruence between decisions and core values. They treat questions of mission, vision, and core values not as exercises to be done once, but as statements of crucial importance to be drilled down and folded into deliberations.

3. STRATEGIC THINKING
Exceptional boards allocate time to what matters most and continuously engage in strategic thinking to hone the organization's direction. They not only align agendas and goals with strategic priorities but also use them for assessing the chief executive, driving meeting agendas, and shaping board recruitment.

4. CULTURE OF INQUIRY
Exceptional boards institutionalize a culture of inquiry, mutual respect, and constructive debate that leads to sound and shared decision making. They seek more information, question assumptions, and challenge conclusions so that they may advocate for solutions based on analysis.

5. INDEPENDENT-MINDEDNESS
Exceptional boards are independent-minded. They apply rigorous conflict-of-interest procedures, and their board members put the interests of the organization above all else when making decisions. They do not allow their votes to be unduly influenced by loyalty to the chief executive or by seniority, position, or reputation of fellow board members, staff, or donors.

6. ETHOS OF TRANSPARENCY
Exceptional boards promote an ethos of transparency by ensuring that donors, stakeholders, and interested members of the public have access to appropriate

(continued)

Table 2.2. Continued

and accurate information regarding finances, operations, and results. They also extend transparency internally, ensuring that every board member has equal access to relevant materials when making decisions.

7. COMPLIANCE WITH INTEGRITY
Exceptional boards promote strong ethical values and disciplined compliance by establishing appropriate mechanisms for active oversight. They use these mechanisms, such as independent audits, to ensure accountability and sufficient controls; to deepen their understanding of the organization; and to reduce the risk of waste, fraud, and abuse.

8. SUSTAINING RESOURCES
Exceptional boards link bold visions and ambitious plans to financial support, expertise, and networks of influence. Linking budgeting to strategic planning, they approve activities that can be realistically financed with existing or attainable resources, while ensuring that the organization has the infrastructure and internal capacity it needs.

9. RESULTS-ORIENTED
Exceptional boards are results-oriented. They measure the organization's progress toward mission and evaluate the performance of major programs and services. They gauge efficiency, effectiveness, and impact, while simultaneously assessing the quality of service delivery, integrating benchmarks against peers, and calculating return on investment.

10. INTENTIONAL BOARD PRACTICES
Exceptional boards purposefully structure themselves to fulfill essential governance duties and to support organizational priorities. Making governance intentional, not incidental, exceptional boards invest in structures and practices that can be thoughtfully adapted to changing circumstances.

11. CONTINUOUS LEARNING
Exceptional boards embrace the qualities of a continuous learning organization, evaluating their own performance and assessing the value they add to the organization. They embed learning opportunities into routine governance work and in activities outside of the boardroom.

12. REVITALIZATION
Exceptional boards energize themselves through planned turnover, thoughtful recruitment, and inclusiveness. They see the correlation between mission, strategy, and board composition, and they understand the importance of fresh perspectives and the risks of closed groups. They revitalize themselves through diversity of experience and through continuous recruitment.

In addition to these 12 principles, additional lists of proper board behaviors and best practices abound, and many are readily accessible via a simple Google search. Yet, as scholars have noted, there is little evidence to suggest that there is any one right set of practices for a board to follow that will guarantee better outcomes for the organization. For example, there is great debate in the nonprofit sector about board practices ranging from topics such as the proper size and diversity of boards to imposing term limits for board members to requiring board members to make financial contributions. In each of these instances, there is simply no one correct answer that will work for every nonprofit board in every situation.

Thus, the work of nonprofit boards and the act of governance remains complicated and open to some degree of interpretation each and every time a group of citizens comes together to engage in governance. In addition to the existing board governance literature, theories about leadership, ethics, organizational behavior, motivation, group relations, and team building, among others, provide useful frameworks for assessing the myriad and complex issues often present in governing boards.

This chapter contains cases that address the following issues:

1. Conflicts of interest
2. Hiring board members
3. The role of the board in CEO evaluation
4. Rubber-stamp boards

REFERENCES

Shear, L. (2013). *The kaleidoscope of governance*. Presented at the 12th Annual Nonprofit Governance Symposium, San Diego, CA.

CASE 2.1

CONFLICT OF INTEREST: DREAM IT DO IT

Alberto Cortez had been on the board of Dream It Do It (DI), a midsize nonprofit serving foster youth for 3 years. DI served primarily as a fund-raising organization that provided scholarships and living assistance to college-bound foster youth. DI raised approximately $800,000 a year through a series of special events including a black tie dinner and auction and a golf tournament. During his time on the board, Alberto had served on several board committees, including the fund-raising committee. His fellow board members appreciated his insight and admired his ability to really leverage and stretch every dollar raised. Alberto credited his business acumen to his corporate experience in marketing and development for a major technology firm. It felt like a natural next step when, in September, the board nominated Alberto to assume the role of vice president of the board in the following fiscal year. He loved working with the organization and eagerly accepted the nomination.

In December, Alberto announced to his fellow board members that he had decided to leave his corporate job and start his own company. When asked about the new company, Alberto explained it was designed to provide direct marketing support to businesses, including website design and the creation of e-commerce platforms. The board chair congratulated him. "I admire your drive, Al. If anyone can make a go of it, I'm sure you can."

"I'm nervous but excited at the same time," he replied. "I already have a couple of clients lined up, and if things go well, I think I will be in a good position to help the organization financially, more so than in the past."

"Well, we would never turn down help from you," chimed in the chief executive officer (CEO), Betty LeMoyne. "But I'm a little worried; are you still going to have time to chair the golf tournament this spring?" she asked.

"Don't worry. I think we have that thing down to a science; it practically runs itself," Alberto assured her. Betty nodded, and they moved on to other topics.

In late February, Alberto approached Betty. "Hey, I wanted to let you know that things are really taking off with my company," he told her.

"That's great, Al." She smiled broadly. Then thinking about it she added, "You aren't going to have to leave us, are you?"

"No, of course not; don't be silly. But, I did want to talk to you about an idea I have," he replied. He went on to explain that he thought several of the products offered by his company could be helpful to the ongoing marketing and fund-raising efforts of DI. "For example, we could help to build an entire new website that could be used to promote and manage all of the events we do. We could do some of our auctions online. Maybe even sell products made by some of the kids through the website, like a regular business."

"Gosh, I don't have to tell you we have been trying to get our website functional for years."

"Well, I am ready to help today if needed, and I would give you a generous discount. Maybe you could count the dollar value of the services and give me credit toward my annual board pledge," he said.

"Why don't you draw up a scope of work and budget, and we can present it to the board next month?" she suggested. Alberto indicated he would be happy to do so.

Prior to the next board meeting, Betty briefed her executive committee about the idea and shared Alberto's proposal, which indeed did reflect a generous discount. The board treasurer, Valin Brown was the first to speak. "In concept, I love this plan. It gets us where we need to go; it's creative and cutting edge and priced well below market value . . ."

"I hear an objection coming," Betty said, filling the void.

"You are correct. I'm not sure we can pursue this because there seems to a conflict of interest since he is a board member, and he stands to benefit from this financially. I'm pretty sure the IRS frowns on that sort of thing." Other members of the executive committee shared similar concerns.

"I don't see how there is really a financial gain here since he's giving us such a reduced rate. We priced out a new website last year, and that alone cost more than what he is proposing here," Betty replied.

"I know," Valin said. "It doesn't make sense on paper. But we have to think about perception. He is stepping into an officer role as vice president of the board in July. We have to make sure we are comfortable with how this looks to outsiders. Do we want to read about it in the paper?"

"Maybe he should step off the board if we decide to do business with him like this," commented a different board member.

"Don't say that!" Betty exclaimed. "He's one of most active board members. I would rather skip the plan and keep him on the board. As board members, you are all are tasked with managing the bottom line, and this deal seems too good to pass up."

"Seems iffy to me," responded Valin.

Case Questions

1. Is there a conflict(s) of interest presented in this case?

2. Describe the ethical dilemma(s) present in the case. Would it be ethical to use Alberto's services? Why, or why not.

3. What are the IRS policies about conflicts and self-dealing on non-profit boards?

4. What policies would you recommend be adopted by DI to prevent these types of situations from arising? Explain why these policies would be an improvement over current practice.

5. Can there be a difference between an actual and perceived conflict of interest? When, if ever, is a conflict permissible?

HIRING BOARD MEMBERS AS STAFF: A FAMILY'S LOVE

As a result of the 1999 Supreme Court ruling in *L.C. and E.W. vs. Olmstead*, states are required to provide community-based services to people with developmental disabilities who, up until that time, had been housed in state-run institutions and hospitals. In response, local nonprofit organizations were established to help secure and manage homes in local neighborhoods where people with developmental disabilities could live more independently with the assistance of trained staff and health care professionals. Under this arrangement, nonprofits accessed government mandated funds to provide group home living arrangements for their clients. Not surprisingly, it was often the parents or other relatives of a developmentally disabled person who were at the forefront of establishing these nonprofits. This was the reality facing Brice and Katherine Cook, parents of a 16-year-old son, Luke, who was born with Down syndrome.

Both Brice and Katherine were established professionals in the tech field, where Brice worked in sales, and Katherine worked in new product development. Not long after Luke was born, the Cooks realized that they would need to become educated advocates to ensure that Luke received all of the services that were available to him.

Like all parents, when Luke was first born, Brice and Katherine were concerned about what the future would hold for him. "What will happen to him when we get old?" Katherine wondered, acknowledging early on to Brice, "He'll never be able to live on his own." "Well, we sure as heck are not putting him in a hospital." Brice adamantly responded. Thus, naturally, over time, the Cooks found themselves becoming more and more active advocates for the deinstitutionalization of people with developmental disabilities. Through their advocacy work, they came to know and befriend several other parents with developmentally disabled children. When the laws in the state were finally changed, everyone breathed a sigh of relief.

A few years later, as Luke was nearing adulthood, the Cooks knew that the time was coming to consider a more independent living situation for their son. However, with the advent of deinstitutionalization, they were entering waters that were still fairly unchartered. When their pediatrician, Dr. Schwartz, asked them what their plans were, Katherine said, "Well, we think Luke should live as independently as possible. We have some friends that have already been through this, and they really think Luke would thrive in a group home setting." Dr. Schwartz agreed but cautioned the Cooks. "I hear it's getting very difficult to find homes that have openings, and if you wait until Luke is in his 20s, I think it may be even harder."

Heeding Dr. Schwartz's advice, Brice and Katherine started to look at all of the available options but could not find anything that met their needs. After one particular visit, Katherine sighed. "This is so depressing. Many of these places are no better than the old mental hospitals." When the Cooks did find homes that were suitable, they were either too far away, or they were full, with long waiting lists. So, while many of their peers were making decisions about which college their child would attend, Brice and Katherine were becoming increasingly concerned about their son's future. Finally, after months of looking, they concluded that establishing their own group home was the only way they could ensure their specific desires would be met.

Feeling confident about their decision, the Cooks recruited some of the good friends they had met through the advocacy network, and they formed a 501(c)(3) corporation and named it Luke's Place. A seven-person board of directors was established to govern the nonprofit. Each board member was a parent of a resident, and Brice was named as the board chair, and Katherine volunteered to chair the operations committee. Although no one on the board was an expert in group home management or providing direct services, each member had a long history of working on behalf of their child within the existing state system. Brice, in particular, was surprised at the extent of regulation and red tape that he had to navigate to obtain the necessary licenses to allow them to operate the home. He once told Katherine, "You need to be a doctor, a lawyer, and a politician all at once to understand this system." Undeterred, and motivated by their love for Luke and other young people like him, Brice and Katherine moved the project forward.

Although the majority of her professional life had been spent working more with machines than people, Katherine took the lead in getting the group home off the ground. She contracted with a local real estate agent, and together they found a large rambling Victorian close to downtown and situated right on a major bus line. "This house is perfect!" Katherine declared. "Everything the kids need is right here . . . it will be so easy for them do their shopping and to get around town." For the first time in a year, Katherine felt some semblance of peace about Luke's future, and 8 months later, the first residents of Luke's Place moved in.

Luke's Place quickly became a model for group home living, and the home had a growing waiting list. Many of the residents worked with job coaches at local businesses. Luke himself worked at a party rental store helping to sort silverware after large events. Katherine cried when Luke showed her his first paycheck. "This is everything we hoped for him and more," she told her friends.

Despite these and other positive outcomes, the board was having more and more difficulty managing the day-to-day operations of the home. Although there were designated house managers, there was no formal executive in charge to run the nonprofit. Thus, in her board role as operations director, Katherine was called upon for everything and anything that went wrong at the house, and since the house was old, repairs were needed frequently. It was not unusual for house staff to call Katherine's cell phone several times a day. On one particularly bad day, she told Brice, "If I get called about one more running toilet, I'm going to lose my mind, not to mention my day job."

Another challenging aspect of managing Luke's Place was the constant turnover of staff, which is not unusual in group home settings. "What can you expect?" Brice asked the board. "We pay very low wages to extremely bright people, most of whom hold graduate degrees and carry large student debts. Our state contracts fix the pay rate so that we have very little wiggle room there. Anytime a better opportunity comes along, these folks almost have to jump ship. Who can blame them?"

To complicate matters, an ongoing state budget crisis wreaked havoc with the board's ability to budget and save for the future. General maintenance on the house often had to be deferred to maintain cash flow, further complicating the management of the home. During the October board meeting, Katherine exclaimed, "This is beginning to feel like a full-time job!" "It's true," agreed Betsy Swanson, a longtime friend and fellow board member. "We work on Luke's Place day and night. It takes up all my spare time. Getting all those volunteers together for that last fundraiser about killed me." She went on: "I hate to say it because I know money is tight, but we really need to consider hiring someone full time to run this operation." Everyone around the table agreed wholeheartedly.

The board spent another hour discussing the pros and cons of turning over the reins to a professional manager, but the thought of bringing in an outsider made them all extremely nervous. "No one cares about these kids like we do," said Betsy, who then turned to Katherine and said, "I think we should hire you! You do everything for this place anyway, you'd be great." In what seemed like an instant, a motion was made and seconded to hire Katherine as the first executive director of Luke's Place. Katherine and Brice both held their hands up in protest and politely asked the board to postpone the vote until the next meeting.

The board members walked as a group to their cars. On the way, the board treasurer, Maurice Wilson, said, "I'm glad we postponed. It seems to me that we should think about this further. No offense to you Katherine, 'cause you have done an awesome job with this place, but maybe we need to consider hiring someone with specific training and more experience. I don't want to discount all your hard work, Katherine; I'm just saying it might be good for us to think about."

Betsy chimed in. "Oh, Maurice, don't be silly. Name one person that could be better than Katherine? She knows everything about this place, the kids love her, and we all trust her.

As they turned out of the parking lot, Katherine said, "Geez, can you believe that? Who would have thought I could be a CEO? That's certainly not something I was thinking about." Brice replied, "Well, honey, the better question is why *not* you? Just think about all the time you have put into this and how close you could be to Luke every day. I think we seriously need to consider this."

Case Questions

1. What are the potential conflicts raised in this case? How can they be resolved?

2. What policies and procedures should the board develop for hiring staff?

3. Can you recommend the next steps that the board should take to hire its first executive director?

4. If you were Maurice Wilson, how would you get the board to seriously consider your point of view?

5. What are the ethical conflicts the board members should consider when they contemplate hiring Katherine to be the executive director?

THE BOARD'S ROLE IN CEO EVALUATION: THE LEADER WHO STAYED TOO LONG

When Walter McHenry joined the Morningside Community Development Corporation (which was mostly referred to by its nickname "Myside"), it was little more than a good idea waiting to happen. The Morningside neighborhood, marred by trash-filled lots, abandoned properties, drug-related crime, and little hope was just waiting for someone or something to rescue it. Walter who grew up in the African American neighborhood of Morningside, remembered its better days when kids rode their bikes or walked to school without fear, when families picnicked in the park on Sunday afternoons, and when Easter Sunday was just one long parade of hats and smiles. He wanted to be part of rebuilding the community so that it would be like that again. In 1975, fresh off a year's stint as a Vista volunteer, he joined the staff as a community organizer. He was the second person hired at Myside and worked tirelessly along with its founder, Joe Morgan.

In those early years Walter's work organizing the community helped Myside gain access to city funds that turned vacant lots into community gardens (along with a lot of volunteer labor). That early success led the city to provide Myside with funding to rehab abandoned homes that the organization then sold through a lottery to neighborhood residents at affordable prices. The Myside organizers put pressure on the city to repair broken sidewalks and streetlamps and put together their own graffiti patrol that was responsible for covering up new spray paint almost as soon as it appeared (an effective strategy for discouraging taggers). Little by little, and over time, the neighborhood improved. The community organizing team was seen as a highly effective and influential force—not only in the neighborhood but throughout the city.

In 1980, Walter became the executive director of Myside, which, under this leadership, grew more influential by the year. Myside's work rehabilitating one building at a time soon became much more large scale as the organization took on responsibility for restoring entire apartment buildings and for helping small businesses with loans and façade improvements that contributed to the neighborhood's revitalization.

Walter received numerous awards for his leadership and for the work of Myside. He was recruited to serve on city boards and commissions and considered an expert on urban renewal. Forty years after he started at Myside, Morningside had been largely transformed from a decaying slum into an up-and-coming hip urban neighborhood that was celebrated for its racial and economic diversity. *Forbes*, the *Wall Street Journal* and *The New York Times* had all done profiles on the transformation of Morningside, which, admittedly, was still a work in progress.

Tyrone Johnson moved to Morningside from Chicago, where he had been an active board member of a nonprofit neighborhood revitalization organization that was similar to Myside (although not as well established). He was a relatively young but accomplished architect who was passionate about restoring old neighborhoods—both physically and socially—and had bought a house in Morningside that he was painstakingly rehabbing with his wife, Charlene. Tyrone was newly affiliated with a well-respected firm that focused its work on large-scale urban renewal contracts (his job was the reason for their move). Soon after settling in, he made an appointment with Walter to introduce himself and to volunteer his services. He had read about Myside and was eager to meet this living legend. His meeting with Walter was everything he had imagined. As he later told his wife, "Charlene, this guy is the real deal. He practically built this neighborhood himself brick by brick. It's amazing to hear him talk about Myside's early days and then to look outside at the neighborhood now. He asked if I would consider joining the board, and I told him that if I am nominated, it would be an honor to serve."

A few months later at the annual meeting, Tyrone was elected to the board and met Rebecca Le, Myside's director of real estate development. He told Rebecca that he planned to be an active board member and volunteer and would help her in any way he could with Myside projects and project proposals. "My firm is supporting my volunteer time as a board member of Myside and is graciously allowing me 15 hours per month of pro bono time to help wherever I'm needed. I'm quite familiar with citing and permitting processes and through the firm, have access to good working relationships all the way up the food chain in the city's department of planning and development as well as in the mayor's office. I also worked on many affordable housing deals in Chicago and understand the financing models. Of course, I've conveyed all of this to Walter as well. I'd like to sit down with you soon to review the projects you have in the pipeline." "Wonderful," said Rebecca "Here's my card. Why don't you call me to set something up?"

The following day Tyrone called Rebecca and left a message for her with several days and times that he was available to meet. He waited a few days for her return call, and when he didn't receive it, he called again to leave her another message. A week went by, and there was still no response from Rebecca. Troubled, he called Walter's office. Carol Babida, Walter's executive assistant, answered the telephone, "I'm sorry, Mr. Johnson. Mr. McHenry is out at a meeting, and I don't expect him back today. Would you like to leave a message for him, or shall I have him call you?" Tyrone asked for Walter to call him, but again, received no response. A week later, he called back and was only able to reach Carol again. Her answer was the same as before.

Through his firm, Tyrone got word that the city was planning to auction a dilapidated hulk of an apartment building in Morningside. He was excited about the idea of Myside redeveloping the building and planned to bring it up at the board meeting that was taking place later that week. When he saw him there, Walter said, "Tyrone, it's wonderful to see you! I'm sorry I haven't had a chance to get back to you—it seems like these meetings just run one right up against another, and before you know it another week has gone by." "I know how it can be," said Tyrone (although he didn't mean it). "I'm anxious to sit down with you and/or Rebecca to talk about the Wayne Building. I'm sure you must know that the city is planning to auction it off, and it would be a terrific project for Myside. If you remember, my firm has allowed me 15 hours per month pro bono to work with you, and I would be happy to dedicate that time to assembling the proposal with Rebecca." "That would be excellent," said Walter. "I'll make sure she gets in touch with you right away."

Tyrone had a sinking feeling as the board meeting proceeded. There was no financial report, no minutes from the previous meeting, and no report on current projects. The bulk of the meeting was spent talking about the annual fund-raising dinner, which public officials had been invited to and would be honored at, how many tickets had been sold, and what the anticipated net would be. Everyone nodded and smiled when Walter spoke. It was evident in their behavior that he was adored and not to be questioned. At the end of the meeting, Tyrone asked Bob Jenkins, a longtime board member and bank vice president, if he could have lunch with him. To his relief, Bob immediately scheduled a time and place to meet.

At lunch with Bob, Tyrone related his story about not being able to get a hold of either Walter or Rebecca and about his interest in the Wayne Building (he had called Rebecca immediately after the board meeting, and three days had passed with no response). He also asked Bob if the Myside board meetings were always that loose. "Look, Tyrone," said Bob, "there's something you need to understand. Myside's glory is in its past. Walter worked like a dog for many years to create what you see today, and now he is all about burnishing his reputation and the reputation of Myside. It's a $6.5 million organization that does a good job of managing the properties it has developed and running programs that serve the community. In the early years, he made next to nothing, which is how we can justify paying him $230,000 and providing him with a company car when we all know he's not doing much work. Rebecca's job is to hold it together—not to create anything new—which is why she has not returned your calls. My bank provides Myside with a generous annual operating grant and is a major underwriter of the annual fund-raising dinner, because being affiliated with Myside makes us look good. Everyone loves Walter, he's an icon."

"But what about the Wayne Building?" asked Tyrone. "It is a once in a lifetime opportunity—not only for Myside but for this community. If we don't develop it, a for-profit developer will, and the outcome could easily change the nature of Morningside. We need to do everything in our power to make sure that doesn't happen."

Case Questions

1. What is the board's role and responsibility in CEO evaluation?

2. Do you think there is a conflict of interest present in this case? Why, or why not?

3. If you were Tyrone, what would you do? Please provide a reason for each option you select.

   a. Resign from the board?

   b. Talk to other board members about the situation?

    c. Talk to other community members about Myside?

    d. Go to the press?

    e. Take legal action?

    f. Form another organization to develop the Wayne Building?

4. What recourse does Tyrone have if he wants to report the situation?

    a. What would he report and to whom?

5. What are the possible consequences for Tyrone if he becomes a whistle-blower?

6. What are the board members' legal responsibilities in this situation?

7. What are the board members' ethical responsibilities in this situation?

THE RUBBER-STAMP BOARD: DON'T WALK—RUN!

The Bicycle and Pedestrian Coalition (BPC) was a grassroots group started by Joshua Fielding, a passionate bike rider and conservationist. When he moved to his adopted hometown to be with his girlfriend, Amy (who was now his wife), he was taken aback by how unfriendly the road-ways were to cyclists. He had been used to commuting by bike to work in New York City and couldn't believe that a city of that size treated bicyclists more civilly than this place. He and Amy had many friends who had barely escaped being injured or worse as a result of near-misses with vehicles. In fact, one friend, Bobby, a member of their bicycle club, wound up in the hospital with a broken hip after he was sideswiped by a sport utility vehicle.

After Bobby's accident, Josh decided to form a nonprofit that would raise awareness of bike safety and advocate for public improvements like bike paths and marked roadways. When he gathered together a few friends to talk about his idea and to ask whether they would be willing to be on the board, they encouraged him to broaden the mission to include walkable communities, which he readily agreed to do. The board was formed that Sunday afternoon and consisted of Josh; Bobby, an insurance agent (who was still wobbly on crutches postaccident); Emily Richards, a stay-at-home mom and friend of Amy's who was concerned about the safety of kids who walked or rode their bikes to school; Juan Gutierrez, who provided tech-support at a hospital and was a member of Josh and Amy's bicycle club; and Henok Negate, a software engineer who was also a member of the club.

Josh was a freelance website designer with a gift for stunning graphic design. He orchestrated a social media campaign for BPC that almost immediately attracted 150 members to the organization from across the city. At the end of one year, 350 people had joined BPC, and he was able to draw a small salary as a part-time executive direc-tor for the group (he still kept his role as president of the board). His salary was cobbled together from membership dues ($25 per per-son/$35 per family) and a small grant from a friend who had a family foundation.

Within 2 years, BPC had developed a reputation as a serious advocacy organization. Josh was appointed by the mayor to serve on her Quality of Life Commission that was working on a 10-year plan to improve the livability of neighborhoods across the city. He was frequently quoted in the press and featured on the local public radio station about the health and environmental benefits of more walkable and bikeable paths and roadways.

By the third year, BPC had grown enough to have Josh working full time alongside a director of education and outreach, a highly skilled urban planner, and a part-time administrative coordinator. In addition to its ongoing advocacy work with the city, BPC was working on developing a long-term plan to establish an urban trail consisting of protected bike paths and sidewalks that would ring the entire city. It also operated a pedestrian and bicycle safe-routes-to-school safety training program in cooperation with the school district that included a subsidized bike helmet program. Josh was a sought-after speaker at business improvement associations, Rotary Clubs, and university classes on urban planning, active transportation, and the environment. He received the Young Nonprofit Professional of the Year award from a local TV station.

The board of BPC met quarterly, with Josh presiding. They didn't feel the need to meet more often or really, formally, since they rode together through the bicycle club, saw each other socially, and got together at BPC sponsored community events. After all, Josh was *always* talking about BPC, so it wasn't as if they weren't informed about what was going on at the organization. Still, most quarters, three of the five members showed up to discuss the progress of the organization's work along with Josh's ideas for what seemed like an ever-expanding list of new programs. They all respected Josh and were proud of BPC. Although Emily was officially the treasurer, she always laughed that it was really weird for her to be in that role since she hated dealing with numbers. Since Josh did the bookkeeping along with the part-time admin person, no one worried about keeping track of the finances. He submitted a financial report to the board once a year and put together the IRS Form 990 for the organization.

One month, Josh called Emily, Henok, Bobby, and Juan to make sure that they could all come to the board meeting that would take place the following week. They each thought it was a little odd since Josh never seemed to care who showed up to board meetings. Even so, they trusted him completely and knew that things were going well at BPC.

Josh began the meeting with his usual broad smile and warm greeting for each of them. He told them that he was really excited about the work that BPC was engaged in and, in particular, the progress they had made on the city contract to map the walkability of four neighborhoods as part of a new initiative launched by the planning department. That contact had resulted in BPC hiring two additional part-time staff (urban planning students from the university), which was a win-win for the students and BPC; the students were gaining real-world expertise and BPC had access to reasonably priced labor (they were paid $12/hour). The problem was the contract operated on a cost-reimbursement basis, which Josh had somehow overlooked in his zeal to secure it. The city would pay BPC for the work once it was complete. BPC operated on a slim margin; the board members had not only run through its small operating reserve, it also was turned down for a grant that he had been sure it would receive. They needed to come up with $1,920 by the following week in order to pay the students for the work they had completed this month. Josh wanted the board members to reach into their own pockets and reach out to their connections to fill the gap.

"Whoa. Dude. That's a lot of money," said Henok. "You're talking nearly $500 bucks apiece from each of us, and that's only for this month. How long is the contract?"

Josh looked down. "Twelve months. It's longer than you would think because we get a lot of input from neighborhood residents throughout the process." He replied, "But the city will reimburse us on a monthly basis at the end of each month, so we really only need to front 2 months' worth of salary."

"Two months," cried Juan. "How are we supposed to come up with that kind of cash? Why didn't you tell us about any of this before?"

"Well, you are the board," said Josh defensively, "and it is your job to know these things."

Case Questions

1. Who do you believe was at fault in this scenario, and why?

2. If you were on the board of BPC, how would you respond to Josh?

3. When do you believe it is appropriate for the executive director to also serve as president/chair of the board?

4. What do you think are the key responsibilities of nonprofit boards?

5. Of those responsibilities you listed in Question 4, which do you believe that most nonprofit board members perform on a consistent basis, and which do you imagine they struggle with? Why?

6. Do you believe there is a difference between the core responsibilities of a nonprofit board at different stages in an organization's life cycle?

7. How could Josh have better aligned his staffing needs to meet the contract requirements?

3

Executive Leadership

INTRODUCTION

The leader of a nonprofit (in both paid and sometimes unpaid positions) is most often referred to as the *chief operating officer* (CEO or sometimes president/CEO) or *executive director* (ED). The terms are used interchangeably and mean exactly the same thing, although more and more leaders are opting to take the CEO title as they believe it is translates more readily to individuals outside of the nonprofit sector. Regardless of title, the CEO position at a nonprofit is complex, requiring the successful management of multiple stakeholders, many of whom, for a variety of reasons, may have competing interests (e.g., donors, community members, volunteers, corporate donors, government officials, etc.).

Further complicating the CEO role is the unique relationship that exists between the CEO and the board of directors. Striking the proper balance of power can propel the organization forward. However, a CEO with too much power can lead to a disengaged or rubber-stamp board, and, likewise, a board with too much power risks losing its ability to be strategic if it devolves into micromanaging. Therefore, building strong relationships between both parties is imperative. Providing a useful illustration, CalNonprofits CEO, Jan Masaoka, writes,

> The unique and multifaceted relationship between the board and its executive is perhaps the most important relationship leading to organizational success or failure. Like the two partners in a skating competition, each side can either bring out the best in the other or prevent the other from skating well. (2003, p. 7)

In order to achieve a positive working relationship, both parties must be clear about who is responsible for what and agree on the duties that are shared between the board and the CEO. Duties specific to the board's management of the CEO include hiring, setting CEO compensation, and ensuring regular performance evaluation. Duties that are the primary responsibility of the CEO include managing the day-to-day operations of the organization, including the hiring and management of all other staff. However, the domains of board governance and organizational management are not always mutually exclusive, and confusion can arise. To help clarify any gray areas, researchers and management consultants generally agree that a model of shared leadership is preferred. Following a model of shared leadership, the board and the CEO set mutual goals, agree on strategic directions, ensure that the CEO receives regular performance evaluations and that the board engages in some form of self-evaluation, and that clear communication processes are established. Both parties should also actively engage in succession planning.

When the time comes for a leadership change, it is the board's responsibility to select the organization's next leader. However, research has found that boards are woefully unprepared to manage executive transition. Finding the right leader for the organization entails establishing a search committee and defining a formalized process. The board may elect to use a search firm to assist them in the search. The Bridgespan Group (2009) suggests that the search committee be prepared to undertake the following activities:

1. Scope the role, and develop a good job description

2. Develop the applicant pool

3. Screen applicants

4. Conduct interviews and reference checks

5. Develop, extend, and negotiate the offer

Additionally, the search committee should make plans to welcome and properly orient their new leader.

The cases in the chapter explore prevalent executive leadership concepts including the following:

1. The board's role in executive transition

2. CEO pay

3. Challenges of executive search

4. Toxic leadership

REFERENCES

The Bridgespan Group. (2009). *Finding the right ED: Creating and managing an effective search committee.* Retrieved from http://www.bridgespan.org/getattachment/4e15beb3-2d3c-4742-a94e-26d44380dec1/Creating-Managing-Search-Committee.aspx

Masaoka, J. (2003). *The best of the Board café: Hands-on solutions for nonprofit boards.* Saint Paul, MN.: Amherst H. Wilder Foundation.

THE BOARD'S ROLE IN EXECUTIVE TRANSITION: THE EXECUTIVE WHO MOVED TOO FAST

The board of the Jefferson Youth Action Programs (J-YAP) was thrilled with the decision to hire James Donnelly as their new CEO. A recently retired AT&T executive, James had been on the board of J-YAP for many years, where he had played a leading role securing sponsorships for the organization's annual gala by tapping into his network of corporate peers. He and his wife, Beverly, had, in fact, cochaired the gala for 5 years running. Their picture appeared often in the social butterfly pages of the *Jefferson Tribune* alongside the smiling faces of their friends and colleagues who were major donors to a variety of high-profile local nonprofits. Jim was passionate about the mission of J-YAP, which was to build the leadership skills of young people ages 3 through 18 years old through social, educational, and recreational opportunities.

J-YAP operated five sites scattered throughout Jefferson County, with a combined annual operating budget of close to $18 million. Those sites included the following:

- The Gardner branch

- The Framingham branch

- The Fern branch

- The Holbrook branch

- The Mission Rails branch

The retiring CEO of J-YAP, Bob Stone, a social worker, had been with the organization for nearly 25 years. Bob kept a low profile, although he was known for being warm and approachable. He was well-respected and beloved both within the organization and throughout the community for his work developing J-YAP into the "yappy happy place for kids throughout Jefferson."

During the past 5 years, however, J-YAP struggled to meet its annual budget. As a result, some of its older facilities showed wear and tear; the pool at the Framingham branch, for example, was badly in need of repair; and a budget squeeze required eliminating program staff. The Fern branch facilities were also cracked with age, and budget shortfalls required reduced staff hours. It was not coincidental that those two branches, because of shifts in demographics that had occurred largely during the past 15 years, served primarily low-income kids and where more families paid their membership dues at the lower end of the sliding-fee-scale. No branch covered its costs with dues alone; however, the gap between dues and expenses was much greater at the Framingham and Fern sites.

At the other end of the spectrum, the Gardner site had a gleaming new facility that had been built 5 years earlier and served a largely upper-income community. The Holbrook and Mission Rails sites were not as new as Gardner; however, they were well maintained and served middle- to upper-income communities. All five sites were operating at capacity, although staff members would argue that Framingham and Fern were operating beyond their capacity because the lay-offs and reduced hours had meant that fewer staff had to oversee many more kids.

Bob had been ready to retire. He had done all he could to grow and support J-YAP and was ready for someone else to take the reins of the organization. In particular, he was ready to leave behind the perpetual headache of raising the annual budget. The last annual gala had been in his honor and had raised a record amount for J-YAP. At the end of the evening, Pearl Silver, the board chair, had introduced Jim as the new CEO to thunderous applause from the audience. "Bob was terrific all these years," Bruce Hornsby, a fellow board member, whispered to Pearl, "but I am enormously relieved we got someone who knows how to run a business to take over J-YAP. At the end of the day, it's all about running the numbers and making sure they add up. It was worth increasing the top salary to $350,000 to get that type of talent." "Amen to that," said Pearl. "Beverly will be a huge asset to us, too."

One month later, at his first board meeting as CEO, Jim presented a detailed breakdown of the financial condition of each J-YAP site to enable the board to see the discrepancies between the revenues and expenses of each operation. He chose not to have Stanley Roe, the chief financial officer (CFO), at the meeting nor Bette Ann Begelfer, the chief operating officer (COO) of J-YAP (they had always been present alongside Bob at previous board meetings). In fact, Jim told the board that he had personally prepared these financial statements as he wanted to ensure their accuracy.

Bob had always treated J-YAP as a single operating unit with the sole exception being the development of the Gardner site, as that had required a special capital campaign to build the facility. Once Gardner had been built, however, the financial statements of the branch were consolidated into a single statement along with the other sites.

The board was surprised at the stark financial differences between the sites. It was evident that the Framingham and Fern sites were not coming close to paying their own way even though both received generous allocations of block grant money from the city along with a few grants from private foundations. Several board members commented on how useful it was to receive the financial information in this format. Jim closed the meeting by saying that he was committed to finding a solution for addressing the growing financial crisis facing J-YAP and would report back on his plan at the next meeting.

Three months later, Jim walked into the board meeting with individually prepared glossy folders for each of the 13 board members. On the cover of each folder was a logo for "Club Kids" showing a picture of a smiling blond boy in a light blue polo shirt and chino pants. The shirt had a small but noticeable dark blue Club Kids logo imprinted on it. A slogan on the bottom of the cover said "Club Kids: for the next generation of leaders."

As his presentation unfolded, Jim explained that he had hired a marketing firm he knew through his work at AT&T to rebrand J-YAP as a first step to revitalizing the organization. He felt the $85,000 used for this purpose (a bargain price generously discounted by the firm) were funds well spent to bring the image of the organization into the 21st century. His idea was that each Club Kid member would receive one polo shirt each year as part of his or her membership. Club Kid merchandise, including additional polo shirts, iPhone and iPad covers, memory sticks, snacks, and so on would be sold in a *Club Kids Pro Shop* that would generate additional money for the organization and further spread the brand as the Club members went about their other activities in the community.

Brimming with confidence, Jim continued with his presentation, walking the board through the other documents in the folder. In addition to commissioning the brand work, he had contacted friends in commercial real estate who determined that selling the Framingham and Fern sites could net J-YAP $2.3 million. Jim's idea was that those funds could then be put into a new endowment fund that would be established to support the three remaining sites. Not only would Club Kids be able to build an endowment that would secure its finances well into the future, it could also rid itself of the burden of $3.5 million in annual operating expenses along with the capital improvement expenses that would be required to bring Framingham and Fern close to par with other Club Kids facilities.

He was animated when he spoke about new programming as well. He wanted to bring a cadre of corporate executives to mentor Club Kids participants at its remaining three branches (starting with the Gardner branch as he believed it would be easiest to attract these types of volunteers since the facility was near many of their homes). The mentoring program would pave the way for the Club Kids of today to become the civic leaders of tomorrow, essentially providing a pipeline of opportunity for young people. He had already run the idea by several corporate executive friends who were willing to give it a go.

After his presentation, the board was silent. Pearl was the first to speak. "Jim, it is clear that you have put a lot of thought into this plan. I'm sure you understand that the board will need time to absorb all of the information you have provided us before we can make any decision about whether and how we might move forward. Also, may I ask, did you speak with Stan and Bette Ann about your ideas?" Jim replied, "I thought it was best to leave Stan and Bette Ann out of the loop as it is clearly a new way of thinking about the work of this organization, and, because of their allegiance to Bob, I suspected they might resist these ideas." "Yes, I could see that," said Pearl. "Thank you for your presentation. Would you mind leaving now to allow the board to discuss this in executive session?" Jim was surprised. In all his years of serving on the J-YAP board, he could not recall a time when the board went into executive session. "Sure," he replied, gathering up his things, although he looked uneasy as he left the room.

After he shut the door behind him, Pearl shot Bruce a look. "Ladies and gentlemen," she said, "I think we may have a problem on our hands."

Case Questions

1. Would Jim's proposed plan alter the mission of J-YAP as you understand it?

2. What types of change management strategies should a CEO implement in situations like the one described in this case?

3. What is the board's role in guiding the integration of a new CEO within an organization?

4. How do you believe the board should respond to Jim?

5. What is the board's responsibility to the stakeholders in the community?

6. What challenges, if any, do you believe private and public sector leaders face when they transition to paid and unpaid nonprofit leadership roles?

7. Is there an ethics issue here?

CEO PAY: TOO MUCH OF A GOOD THING?

State Attorney General Valerie Nash had called her team to a special meeting. Around the table were her Chief of Staff Nancy Foster, Deputy Chief of Staff Rudy Ramirez, director of the Charitable Trust Division, Pete Sweeney, and assorted staffers from each division. Ms. Nash, at the behest of Pete Sweeney, had called the group together to discuss a series of investigative media reports about high CEO pay at some of the state's largest nonprofits and foundations. The series of reports was titled, "These Nonprofit Executives Made Over 1 Million Dollars Last Year." The weekly series featured stories about three individual nonprofits.

The first case featured the story of a private foundation CEO who was reported to earn total compensation of $1.2 million. An anonymous foundation board member was quoted in the article as saying, "Our CEO compensation is benchmarked against other CEOs at foundations of similar size. The public really shouldn't be all that concerned since the foundation does not accept tax deductible donations from individuals. We make grants based on earnings derived from the original corpus donated by our founder over 50 years ago." The report presented details of the CEO's expense account, which included reimbursement for global first-class airline travel (despite that fact that the foundation only made grants to nonprofits within the boundaries of one state), 5-star hotel stays, and restaurant bills that included $500 bottles of wine.

The second article in the series highlighted an executive at a large and well-known national charity operating in the state that provided job training to people with developmental disabilities, primarily by employing them in thrift stores. This CEO was reported to have earned $3.2 million in the last fiscal year. The article pointed out that the earnings represented about 3% of the organization's total expenses, which were in excess of $100 million per year. About 45% of the organization's $110 million revenue came from charitable contributions, government grants, and special events. The remaining revenue was generated through the earnings of the thrift stores. An unnamed thrift store employee, who was a disabled person making an hourly wage that equated to an annual salary of $29,000 per year, was featured in the article. "That seems like a lot more than I make. It don't seem fair if you ask me," she said. Following up on this observation, the article noted her pay, which was subsidized by government grants, was 110 times less than that of the CEO. Data from the organization's IRS form 990 showed that the nonprofit offered an incentive plan for members of the management team that met specific mission-related objectives. The 990 also reported that health club and social club expenses were paid by the nonprofit as they were used for business purposes.

The final story in the series featured the case of a well-known socialite who was the leader of a large and very prominent symphony who had been paid $1.7 million in the last fiscal year. Her pay was equivalent to 8% of the organization's total revenue in that year. The article also pointed out that the music director, one of the most widely recognized names in the field, earned $1.4 million a year. The story reported that 28% percent of the organization's revenue came from contributed income (including donations and grants from foundations and government), 10% from investment income, and 62% from program revenue. When asked to comment for the story, a contracted violin player with the symphony was quoted as saying, "Sort of gives new meaning to the term 'starving artist,' don't you think?" Two prominent board members defended the organization, calling out all of the economic benefit derived by the city because of the symphony. "People come from all over the world to see our productions; they spend money in our hotels and eat in our restaurants. This is all very good for our city and this state," one commented. The other board member explained that the salaries paid to top executives were commensurate with other symphony, opera, and ballet companies around the world. "To be the best at what we do, we have to compete for top talent, and that means we need to pay for it."

The series of articles generated hundreds of comments on the Web as well as multiple letters to the editor of the paper that ran the series. Most citizens expressed outrage at what they characterized as exorbitant salaries. Some called upon the government to make reforms. Still others made compelling cases about why the compensation was fair.

The purpose of the meeting called by Ms. Nash, therefore, was to discuss the need for any investigations and to explore the idea of introducing potential legislation for limiting nonprofit CEO pay in the state.

"First off, Pete, I want to know if your office thinks that anything illegal is going on here," Val said.

"We've looked into each of the charities called out in the articles," he said. "All of their filings with us and to the IRS are complete and look above board from a legal perspective. In the case of the thrift store group, they outline a pretty rigorous review process for CEO compensation. Specifically, they claim to have hired an independent firm to assess the reasonableness of their compensation for all their top managers. The firm uses survey data from organizations that are similar in terms of revenue, assets, number of employees, that sort of thing. Then their recommendations were approved by the human resources committee of the board and again by the entire board of directors in a unanimous vote. I am assuming that all of these facts can be verified through board meeting minutes."

"OK, so it looks like they are all meeting the letter of the law," Val said, "but I'm thinking we need to talk about the spirit of the law. The public outcry on this has been huge. Nancy tells me our public comment webpage page and our e-mail are exploding with messages, and public opinion is not positive."

She turned to her chief of staff. "I've got to say, people are really calling on us to reel this thing in. People don't like the idea of using tax deductible donations or government grant money to subsidize big salaries," Nancy said.

"Well, that's understandable, but where are we going to draw the line?" Pete asked. "If you make a move to propose new legislation to limit CEO pay at nonprofits, you're going to open a giant can of worms."

"I agree," said Rudy, Val's deputy chief of staff. "While it might feel right morally to set some limits, you'll be heading down a slippery slope. Pay for top execs at our nonprofit hospitals and universities will come under scrutiny. Then you will be called upon to defend the high salaries of others who get government money, like highly paid football coaches at our top public universities and defense contractors who live off government money," Rudy asserted.

"Politically speaking, this is a really gray area to get into, Val," Pete added. "Any cap you set will be seen as arbitrary. Frankly, people don't go to work at nonprofits to get rich, we all know that. But are you going to tell them they can't make a decent living just because they picked nonprofit work? I think we all need to understand that while the salary of a nonprofit exec at a multimillion-dollar nonprofit might sound high, their counterpart in the for-profit sector is still very likely making a great deal more. These are the organizations we charge with keeping our communities healthy and safe. I for one want the best and the brightest in charge of making sure that happens," Pete concluded.

Nancy concurred. "I feel a lot more comfortable with a highly skilled hospital administrator who can ensure quality service while being a good steward of public funds over someone who means well but doesn't have the knowledge or ability to balance all the competing needs. Even paying the former more, there is likely going to be significant cost savings."

Case Questions

1. What are the IRS rules for setting executive compensation at a non-profit?

2. What are the ethical dilemmas presented in the case?

3. What are Val's options?

4. Is there, or should there be, a relationship between the ability of philanthropic organizations to receive public support for their activities in the form of tax-deductible contributions and the argument that nonprofits should be required to cap wages? Does that reasoning differ if the nonprofit is a foundation that was established with private funds?

5. What are the ethical and moral reasons, if any, for wage differential to exist between nonprofit and for-profit organizations for similar work?

CHALLENGES OF EXECUTIVE SEARCH: LOST AND FOUND

"Must love dogs," joked Kathy Stuart. "The first line in qualifications section for the executive director's job announcement has to say 'must love dogs in order to be qualified for this position.'" The other members of the committee chuckled. It was the first in a series of meetings that the five-member search committee had set up to review the job description, decide on the wording of the job announcement, determine where it would be posted, and set a timeline and process for the search. They were all nervous because it was the first time any of them had been involved in leading an executive director search. The task seemed especially daunting since it involved finding a replacement for Brian Daugherty, who had led The Lost & Found Humane Society for 10 years. Brian was moving to Colorado, where his wife had landed a big job.

Kathy felt strongly that Brian should not be part of the search because she was fairly certain that there would be some internal candidates applying for the job, and she didn't want him to bias the board's decision. Brian felt a little hurt by this but respected the board's need to take full responsibility for finding his replacement. "You know I love this place, Kathy, and I'm extremely proud of what we do and how much we've grown over the past 10 years," he said. "If you change your mind and want me to help in any way, just ask. I know my job description hasn't been updated since I started working here, but it will give the committee a good jumping off point for creating the new one. You might want to keep in mind that we've grown from a $6 million shop to an $11 million operation and all that entails. That might have some bearing on the type of person you want to bring on board."

As president of the board, Kathy wanted to chair the search committee. She was joined by Linda Briggs, a technical writer and vice president of the board, and three other board members—Len Stuart, Kathy's husband and a retired military chaplain; Josie Robinson, a longtime volunteer and donor to Lost & Found, and Joe Shadroi, owner of a successful car dealership. The committee was tasked with leading the search and presenting the final candidate to the board for approval by the full 15-member body. Brian had given them a month's notice, which they appreciated, yet everyone knew the search would take much longer. Eddie McGinnis, the longtime associate director of Lost & Found, agreed to serve as interim executive director until the position was filled.

"It makes sense that the job announcement should include our mission," said Linda, "especially because of our stance on euthanizing; that's always controversial." They all agreed to include the following:

> The Lost & Found Humane Society exists to promote and provide humane protection and shelter for abandoned or lost companion animals. We seek adoptive homes for companion animals under our protective care; provide public education about the societal problem of animal overpopulation; promote the principles of responsible companion animal care; and advocate the spaying and neutering of all companion animals. Lost & Found does not euthanize except on the advice of a veterinarian in the case of critical injury, terminal illness, debilitating pain, or severe a behavioral problem in which the animal is a danger to themselves, other animals, or humans.

The rest of the job announcement was taken largely from the duties described in Brian's original job description that the committee updated to reflect the significant increase in staff, volunteers, programs, and facilities that had occurred over the past 10 years. Len agreed to work on pairing down the full job posting into a small advertisement. "Brian really has been amazing," sighed Joe. "I just don't know how we're ever going to find someone who is as talented as he is. He's a real visionary and a great manager, too. It's just incredible how far we've come under his leadership."

The committee decided to post the job on www.idealist.org, on the job search site hosted by the local nonprofit management center, and on the organization's website; to advertise it through the national Humane Society and the Society of Animal Welfare Administrators; and to announce it in the Lost & Found e-newsletter. The applications were to be sent to Geraldine Evans, the part-time human resources manager and were due by the end of the month. Before he left, Brian said to Kathy, "Look, Kathy, I know you don't want me to stick my nose into any part of the ED search, but I've got to tell you that Eddie is going to apply for the job, and I really think he deserves it. He's been here longer than I have, and I couldn't have done what I've done at Lost & Found without him. I hope you'll give him a fair shot." Kathy simply nodded in response. The truth was she had doubts about Eddie in that role. She saw him as being a good manager—a good lieutenant—but not in a role that required vision and fund-raising.

Lost & Found received 82 applications for the job, about half of which were from people who Geraldine determined weren't qualified (or at least as qualified as the remaining group). Kathy and Linda read through the 37 resumes Geraldine provided to them and chose 10 applications to share with the search committee. After reviewing and discussing the 10 resumes, the committee selected eight candidates to interview, including Eddie; after that round, they would narrow the field. Since three of the candidates were from out of town, the group decided to conduct those interviews by Skype and to do the rest in person.

On the day of his interview, Eddie wore a suit and tie. He came prepared with a handout detailing his accomplishments at Lost & Found and ideas for improving current programs. He was visibly nervous throughout the interview. Toward the end of the hour, as the interview was coming to a close, he startled several members of the committee when he said, "To be honest, the biggest thing we need to work on is living up to our euthanasia policy. We say we only euthanize in extreme cases of illness, injury, pain, or dangerous behavior, but the fact is that due to the volume of animals we receive at times, particularly right after Christmas in January and February, we sometimes have no choice but to euthanize healthy animals because we just don't have the space for them, and nobody else in the county does either. It breaks my heart. We just can't pretend that it doesn't happen; we need to develop a *much* better strategy to avoid this at all costs."

After he left the room, Kathy said with disgust in her voice, "I cannot believe he would openly criticize Brian like that. That was uncalled for." "What are you talking about?" asked Josie. "Are you referring to the comments he made about euthanizing animals? That is just fact; not criticism. I've volunteered here long enough to know that the staff and volunteers do everything in our power to prevent this from happening, but it's an impossible situation." Kathy fumed and said nothing. Joe spoke up. "I think it was an important topic to discuss although his timing was poor to bring it up during a first interview. It was not professional." Len agreed.

During the days that followed Eddie's interview, Dr. Dane Ripellino, head veterinarian at Lost & Found, made it a point to interact with as many search committee members as possible, intercepting them in the hallway when he could. Speaking to Kathy he said, "I want you to know that the staff is 100% behind Eddie becoming the new ED. We all think he's got the skill, talent, and experience to run this place. He's well respected by everyone, and he is passionate about what we do here." "That's good to know," replied Kathy. "Thank you for letting me know. Please keep in mind this is a board decision, not a staff decision."

When the eight first interviews were complete, the committee met to decide which candidates would move forward to the final round. Kathy argued against including Eddie in the group. "He just doesn't have the polish and sophistication we need, he doesn't know how to speak to donors, and he certainly hasn't exhibited professional behavior during this interview process." Linda and Josie argued to include Eddie in the final interview round. "What will that say to the other staff if we exclude Eddie from the final interview round? How can we do that to him after all of the love and energy he's put into this place? Don't you think, too, that we'll risk losing him altogether if he's not even invited for a final interview?" Kathy refused to budge. Through their silence, Len and Joe appeared to agree with Kathy.

The committee held second interviews with three candidates and selected one, Amanda Corona, to present to the board. The board met at its regularly scheduled meeting and voted to accept the recommendation of the search committee.

Eddie was devastated not to be asked back for a second interview. He called Brian to let him know what had happened (Brian was dumbfounded by the decision). He informed Dane as well, who responded, "I just don't understand how the board can make such an important decision without consulting the senior staff. This is a slap in the face not only to you, Eddie, but to all of us."

A few weeks later, Kathy assembled the staff to inform them that Amanda had been selected to be the new ED. Amanda was director of development of the zoo where she had raised significant funds from individual donors. In the press announcement, Amanda said, "The opportunity to lead Lost & Found is a dream come true. I am looking forward to building on the work and reputation of this wonderful organization."

Eddie announced his departure 3 months later. He had been selected to serve as ED of the Washington County Humane Society.

Case Questions

1. What is your opinion of the search process?

   a. What are your thoughts on the composition of the search committee?

   b. Do you think it was equitable for some first round candidates to receive a Skype interview, while others were interviewed in person? Why, or why not?

   c. Geraldine Evans was the only staff person who was somewhat involved in the search process. What role, if any, should the staff have played in the search process?

   d. What role, if any, should the exiting ED have played in the search process?

   e. Should Eddie have been granted a second interview? If so, why?

   f. How would you have designed and organized the search process?

2. How often should an executive director's job description be reviewed?

TOXIC LEADERSHIP: THE QUEEN BEE

Fifteen years ago, Julia Sullivan founded Parkview Community Health Center to help provide basic health services to low-income women in her community. Since that time, Julia's public reputation has grown exponentially, and she is looked upon favorably as a community leader. Under her direction, the health center has grown to five sites across the county of Greensville with a staff of 150 people. The daily operations of the center are overseen by Julia's executive team, which is made up of Don Tanaka, the chief operating officer; Bill King, the chief financial officer, and Sylvia Garcia, the human resources manager. Both Don and Bill have worked with Julia for more than 5 years, but Sylvia is new to the team, having just been hired. Sylvia has 6 years of management experience in the retail field and recently completed graduate school with a master's in management and a specialization in human resource management. She is enthusiastic about translating her knowledge into practice and is excited to be working at such a reputable nonprofit.

The health center is governed by a board of directors that has been handpicked over the years by Julia. As a result, the board members enjoy being together, and many are known to be personal friends. In fact, Julia and her husband often vacation with the board chair, Sandra Jaynes, and her husband, Phil. There are no term limits, and thus, several board members, including Sandra, have been with the organization since its founding. For the most part, the board is concerned with fund-raising and, as such, they spend a lot of their time promoting the health center to wealthy donors. Julia and Sandra are known to throw elegant dinner parties for board members and potential donors. Sandra fondly refers to Julia as "the Queen Bee," and rarely does the board question any of Julia's decisions.

In her first week on the job, Sylvia spends most of her time meeting with the employees in an attempt to get to know them. She notices that people seem pretty closed and somewhat reluctant to interact with her. She learns from talking to some of the office staff that Julia may not be as beloved as she had originally assumed. She comes to learn that Julia often yells at the staff in front of clients and other employees. As the human resources manager, this is of concern to her, and she raises the issue during the weekly executive team meeting. Giving her report she says, "It's been a great first 2 weeks, and I've really enjoyed getting to know some of the staff. Wow! I'm really impressed with their work ethic and commitment to the clients. But, I do have a couple of concerns that I would like us to discuss." At that point, Sylvia noticed that Don and Will both shifted a bit in their seats and looked down at the ground. Julia looked directly at Sylvia and snapped, "What sorts of things are you hearing?"

"Well, there is some concern about the way managers are talking to staff in front of clients," Sylvia responded.

"Who said that?" Julia demanded to know. "You better name names."

Sylvia was quite taken aback with Julia's tone, and sensing that she should protect that staff, she brushed the topic aside by saying, "Well, nothing was said specifically; it was just a feeling I was getting."

Julia responded. "We don't pay you to listen to your feelings or to employee gossip, Sylvia. You're here to fill out paperwork. Don't go stirring up trouble; everything is just fine here. If employees aren't happy, they can walk right out that door. There are plenty of people who would love to work here," fumed Julia. After that, Sylvia remained silent for the remainder of the meeting. "Wow," she wondered to herself, "I never saw that side of Julia before . . . who knew she was such a hothead?"

Later that afternoon, Sylvia received a visit from Don. "Hey, do you have a minute to talk?" he asked her. "Sure," she said. "Hopefully you're here to tell me I imagined that little scene during our morning meeting," Sylvia smiled somewhat wistfully.

"Well, actually," Don replied, "I'm here to give you a little advice." He went on to tell Sylvia that she should avoid ever directly confronting Julia or giving her negative feedback. "It just doesn't work. It's not worth it," Don said. "She doesn't want to hear it, and frankly, she doesn't need to listen. Everyone knows this is her show; the board does whatever she wants. They're all friends for Pete's sake! If she doesn't like you, she'll get rid of you."

"Well no one is above the law," Sylvia countered, "and I'm here to make sure that at least the employment laws get followed. From what I've heard, some of her behavior could be considered harassment. We have to protect our people and the organization." Don smiled in a fatherly way at Sylvia, "Young lady, while I appreciate your ideals, you have a lot to learn about reality, and the reality here is it's Julia's way or the highway." Don shrugged and started walking toward the door. Sylvia thanked Don for taking the time to counsel her, although her disappointment was quite apparent.

Over dinner later that night, she told her boyfriend, Jose, about the incident. "Well, what can you do?" he asked her. "This was your dream job, and there aren't too many of those out there these days."

"You're right," Sylvia said. "I'll just give it some time. How bad could it be? I mean, you can't run a successful organization like that for very long . . . somebody in the community will find out."

As the weeks went on, however, Sylvia learned more about Julia's mistreatment of employees. She overheard Julia tell the development director that she was "stupid," she heard Julia swear several times in different department meetings, and she regularly heard yelling from the CEO's office. To get herself fully up to speed in her new position, she read through past employee records and studied turn-over rates. It was then she noticed two incidences of employees who had filed complaints about Julia and were shortly thereafter terminated for seemingly nominal offenses. However, there were few details recorded, and the files did not contain the proper written warnings and documentation to support termination. "I'm getting really worried," she told Jose. "I think this place is a lawsuit waiting to happen, but I feel like there is nothing I can do."

"Can't you talk to someone above her? Someone on the board, maybe?" Jose asked.

"Well, the only person I can think of is the guy on the board who heads up their finance committee, which means he's also on the executive committee. His name is Ben McCue. I've only met him a couple of times, but he was on the hiring committee when I interviewed for this job. He seemed reasonable to me, but I don't have a good sense of how close he is to Julia."

Jose replied, "It's not worth all the stress, Syl. You're gonna make yourself sick. You gotta find a way to bring this to his attention."

The following week, Sylvia was approached by Pedro Ramos, a program manager in one of the larger satellite health centers. "That's it. I can't take it anymore!" he exclaimed as he shut her office door behind him. "Julia walked into my center, and she was steamed because I had not been able to move my schedule to accommodate a visit from a potential donor. I don't see what the big deal was," he went on. "With three people on vacation, I simply couldn't make it work. I told her we could make it happen next week, when I have a full staff again . . . then, boy, did she give it to me."

"What do you mean?" asked Sylvia.

"Well, she told me I was shortsighted. She said, 'Pedro, you just don't understand rich people . . . you're not from that world; they don't like to be told to wait!' And then, she stormed out and pretty much slammed the door. But the worst part is all of this happened in front of a full waiting room full of patients. I was so embarrassed, and I felt threatened," Pedro confessed and hung his head. "I hope you can do something to make things better around here, Sylvia. I'm not letting her force me out, like she's done to other people."

Sylvia documented Pedro's complaint, and as she closed his folder, she was overwhelmed by the feeling that she had no idea of how to do her job.

Case Questions

1. What are the major points of conflict in this case?

2. What policies need to be enacted or enforced at the organization to alleviate the problems present in the case? What specific board policies should be in place?

3. What is the best way for Sylvia to exercise leadership in this situation?

4. Is it acceptable for the staff members to approach the board chair to report a grievance?

5. What is at risk if nothing is done?

4

Measuring Performance

INTRODUCTION

Over the last decade, the demands placed on nonprofit leaders to demonstrate tangible proof of their impact on the communities they serve has been increasing. This need for nonprofit leaders to provide evidence of their success is attributable to several factors, most notably the rapid growth of the sector since the 1990s and increased competition for what is perceived as a shrinking pool of resources. In order to compete for philanthropic dollars, nonprofit leaders must show that they outperform other nonprofits providing similar services or that they have designed their programs to mimic the proven best practices of nonprofits that have demonstrated success in the same area. At the same time, the rise of entities such as Charity Navigator and other nonprofit rating services has influenced some individual donors to view charitable giving more as a philanthropic investment, and thus, nonprofits are being asked to articulate their return on investment (ROI). Additionally, government entities and foundations that are accountable to taxpayers and other constituents are asking for proof of success to justify their allocation of resources to particular nonprofits.

It is no longer enough to ask the public to trust the effectiveness of non-profits. Those who lead and manage nonprofits today are accountable for demonstrating success to a variety of stakeholders. Therefore, the processes and systems needed to show that their work is achieving its intended impact must be integral to the daily operations of the non-profit. Yet, for a variety of reasons, this is easier said than done as performance measurement in the sector is extremely complex, and reliable measurement systems remain elusive.

Before a plan for performance measurement can be established, a distinction must be made between the concepts of effectiveness and efficiency as it is conceivable that a nonprofit could be extremely efficient but not at all effective. Similarly, a unit of analysis must be determined as nonprofit performance may be measured at the organizational level (how is the organization doing overall?), at the programmatic level (is this program working?), at the board level (is the board working well?), or by departments or units within the organization (which departments use what kinds of resources?).

Regardless of the unit of analysis, nonprofits use some common tools and practices for measuring performance, including financial analysis and program evaluation. Financial outcomes are often measured by calculating different ratios that can help people understand things such as what it costs to serve an individual client or how much it costs to raise a dollar. In its simplest form, program evaluation entails collecting data about program participants or clients and accounting for what happens to them as a result of receiving services from the nonprofit.

When deciding to create a plan for any type of performance measurement nonprofit leaders must consider the following:

1. What is the purpose of the measurement?

2. What questions need to be answered, and to whom do we need to provide the information?

3. What indicators of success will be used?

4. Who will collect the data, how will it be stored, and who will analyze the information?

5. What resources will be needed to establish and maintain a performance measurement system?

6. How will the findings be presented and shared, internally and externally?

Tools such as logic models and theory of change processes are helpful for illustrating how services offered by nonprofits are linked to intended outcomes. The balanced scorecard approach, measurement frameworks like efforts to outcomes, third party program evaluations, and dashboards are methods by which nonprofits are tracking and accounting for their outcomes. Yet, many nonprofits lack the staff capacity and resources required to identify proper and useful metrics and to accurately collect data and report on findings.

In addition to the mechanics of performance measurement, there are often important ethical issues to consider. Since nonprofits are often the place where people come together to apply new and innovative solutions to seemingly intractable societal problems, much of what they do can be considered experimental. And, just like the products developed in the research-development arms of for-profit companies, sometimes new ideas don't work well. It may be that a nonprofit's program needs to be modified to reach its intended results, or that the idea isn't easily scalable, or a program may need to be rejected all together. Thus, if nonprofit leaders are held too tightly accountable to rigid or even inappropriate performance measures, they may be discouraged from being entrepreneurial in the pursuit of their missions. Or worse, individuals could be incentivized (wrongly) to set up performance measurement systems that skew results in their favor or allow for incorrect conclusions to be drawn about programmatic and organizational success.

The cases presented in this chapter provide students with an opportunity to think about the different levels at which performance may be measured in a nonprofit. Students are encouraged to consider the inherent tensions often faced by nonprofit leaders working in an age of increasing demand for accountability through the following topics:

1. Establishing reasonable metrics with a funder

2. Failing to reach agreed-upon outcomes

3. What to do when the program isn't working

CASE 4.1

ESTABLISHING METRICS: WHAT COMES OUT OF A BACKPACK

The Westhaven Food Bank (WFB) provides 87,000 pounds daily to residents in four metropolitan cities as well as three adjacent rural counties. For years, the organization has been led by Jerry Cartwright, a gregarious and well-liked member of the Westhaven community. Jerry was known for his creativity and for his ability to think up new ways of getting food to hungry people.

WFB used hundreds of volunteers every week to deliver food to other food pantries, shelters, soup kitchens, and senior centers. To keep all of their providers supplied, they relied on donations from food drives, local churches, and grocery stores. They also augmented donations by purchasing directly from vendors at a reduced cost. To cover the costs of food purchases and general operations, WFB had to raise $365,000 dollars a year.

All fund-raising efforts were led by the director of development, Jon Durnford. Jon, along with two part-time staff, maintained long-standing relationships with major funders. On any given day, Jon could be found touring potential donors through the food bank's expansive facility. Jon felt fortunate that he was able to work for a nonprofit with such a compelling cause. "It's a pretty simple sale," he constantly reminded his staff. "We get food to hungry people, and donors understand that."

One afternoon, Jerry stopped by Jon's office. He said, "I had an interesting conversation with some folks from the Patton Bank Foundation today."

"Oh really?" Jon replied, raising his eyebrows. "They're pretty new to town. I haven't had any luck getting a meeting from them. What happened?"

"I was just at the Chamber of Commerce awards lunch, and I was seated next to their foundation CEO. Her name is Kathy Nash. She was there with the director of their local bank operations, Julius Roberts," Jerry explained.

"Good fortune always smiles on you, Jerry," Jon said to his boss. "Hopefully you got them to write us a check."

"Close." Jerry smiled. "They have an idea for a program that they want to fund. The idea is something they have seen in other cities where they have branches, but it's not something they have funded before themselves."

Jerry continued. "As you and I both know, government funding provides breakfast and lunch to low-income kids at school, but we have no idea what happens to them on the weekend. In this program they were talking about, kids who qualify get a backpack every Friday that we will fill with healthy, kid-friendly food they can access over the weekend. Then, they return the backpack on Monday so we can fill it again. We set up the delivery so it is discreet, and the kids don't have to be embarrassed."

Jon really liked the idea. "Teachers have been telling us that weekend hunger is a big problem for some time. I know we've tried some things with families and schools in the past, but they just didn't fly. I think this could work if we had enough support and could work out the details with the schools."

"Great," Jerry said. "Here's Kathy Nash's card. I told her you would follow up."

Within a week, they had a meeting set up with Kathy and Julius. During the meeting, they learned more about the research Kathy had done about how the program was working in other places. Jon was particularly interested in the business model, wondering how much money it would cost to launch and sustain the program. Kathy showed him a proposed budget.

"We will cover the costs of the backpacks and some food," she said. "You will need your volunteers to stuff and deliver the bags and to pick up empty bags on Monday mornings. I've learned it works best if the food is child friendly and of course nonperishable. Other program have reported that the kids really like knowing that they can get food anytime over the weekend so they don't have to wait until they get back to school to get a meal. It really helps over long holiday weekends too," she added.

"As another part of our contribution, we will provide a core group of volunteers from our bank branches here in Westhaven to get the program going," Julius said. After some more discussion, they sealed the deal, and within a matter of months, the program was launched. Overall, the program was deemed quite successful. Jon and Kathy spoke regularly, and he kept her apprised of the positive comments and notes he had been receiving from school officials, teachers, and parents. The bank received positive coverage in the press, and true to his word, Julius provided a regular team of volunteers to support the efforts.

After 2 years of operating the program, WFB was serving 2,000 children nearly 12,000 meals every week. They served 54 schools in seven cities in the region. In the middle of that year, Kathy moved on to a job at a different foundation, and she was replaced by Margo Stevens, who was promoted to the position from within the bank. Although Margo and Jon spoke occasionally, they did not have the same close working relationship that he had enjoyed with Kathy.

Jon was especially surprised when, at the end of the third year of the program, he received a formal end-of-year grant report request from Margo's office. After reading through the request, he proceeded directly to Jerry's office. "This is crazy," he started. "I received a request to send an end-of-year outcomes report to Margo over at Patton, which is normally not a problem, but you should see some of the things they want us to report on."

"Such as?" Jerry replied.

"Well, she wants to know if, since the backpack project started, the kids are less obese and if there has been any improvement in grade-level reading, for starters," Jon answered.

"What? That's really weird," Jerry said. How could we possibly know that? We never intended for this to be an obesity program or a student achievement program. This was supposed to be about getting healthy food to hungry kids."

"I know. I've always kept Kathy in the loop and have shared all the great stories with her. I've always provided reports about the kids and schools we're serving. They never told me they wanted us to track this information. Even if we did, it would be a pretty big stretch to say that the backpack program was directly related to any changes in these metrics. I'm going to give Margo a call. I just wanted to give you a heads-up."

The phone conversation with Margo did not go well. "What do you mean you don't?" she asked. "Patton Bank needs to be able to talk about the impact of our foundation dollars in the community. It's not enough to just tell people we gave some kids some food in a backpack. I have to be able to tell our board and the bank shareholders what our investment is doing to actually improve things."

"I get that," Jon said, "but I don't think it's possible to link our program to the outcomes you have listed in your request."

"Jon," Margo replied coolly, "we've been at this with you for 3 years now. I simply can't believe you haven't tracked these data. If you hope to keep the program going you need to send me that report."

Case Questions

1. What should Jon do next?

2. Do you believe that Margo's requests are unreasonable? Why, or why not?

3. Are there ethical issues when a funding organization changes expectations when personnel change?

4. What type of outcome data would you propose the organization collect? Why those data?

5. What are some things that a nonprofit like WBF can do to collect outcome data for a program like one presented in the case?

6. What are some strategies the organization can use to negotiate with Margo?

WHEN OUTCOMES FAIL TO MEET ESTABLISHED BENCHMARKS: A PROBLEM OF SCALE

I Believe was a small nonprofit with a great track record for any organization, let alone one that was only 3 years old. It was founded by Eduardo Apparacio for the purpose of providing at-risk kids with counselling, coaching, and tutoring that would enable them to succeed in school. Eddie had spent 4 years in a notorious gang, a situation that he had miraculously managed to extricate himself from because of the dogged determination and compassion of a high school teacher, Felipe Agular, who saw through Eddie's anger and fear.

The truth was that Eddie had been promoted in school year after year despite the fact that he couldn't read. He was embarrassed to go to school because he had no way of being able to do the work that was required. Mr. Agular, Eddie's sophomore-year homeroom teacher, was somehow able to get through to Eddie, arrange for him to participate in remedial education, and eventually helped him secure a full scholarship to the state university. Eddie was not only a good student; he was exceptionally bright. He launched *I Believe* during his junior year in college and graduated with honors in a dual-track Social Work and Business program. His personal goal was to be a Mr. Agular for as many at-risk students as possible.

Eddie had a 100-watt smile and a magnetic personality to match. By networking with county officials, he managed to secure a grant to operate a pilot program to fund *I Believe* at Lincoln High School, his alma mater. Felipe Agular had retired but agreed to serve as president of the board of directors. He and Eddie worked closely on developing a psychosocial approach to working with at-risk youth (most were involved in gang-related activity). During the first 3 years, they had managed to successfully reach 47 kids altogether (8 others were not successful) who were all on their way to completing high school or had already finished (three were going to college in the fall). The county was thrilled with this record and publicly recognized Eddie for his excellent work.

Eddie was *I Believe* in that he was the only staff person. His work was guided by an active three-member board, and he was assisted by an additional four volunteers. It was a difficult balancing act to serve the kids and maintain the operations of the organization, especially since Eddie was greatly in demand as a public speaker and was responsible for raising ongoing support for the organization from local businesses and the Rotary Club. For instance, funding to supplement the county grant was needed for special tutors, field trips, supplies, office expenses, and so on.

One month at the board meeting, Felipe said, "Eddie, all of us know that you have been doing a fabulous job running this organization. We are incredibly proud of what you have accomplished. I've been thinking lately that it is time for *I Believe* to expand. You've proved that you know what you are doing with this population, why not take the program to other schools as well? I took the liberty of talking to Mark Peters, a program officer at the community foundation, and he told me that they would be willing to entertain a proposal to expand the program to two additional sites if you feel that you are ready to take that next step."

"Wow," replied Eddie, a bit stunned. "Do you think we're ready for that?"

"I do," said Felipe, and the others nodded in agreement. "Why don't I set up a meeting for you to talk to Mark and explore the possibilities?"

When Eddie met with Mark, he was amazed at how well things went. Mark was willing to entertain a 3-year proposal that would provide funding for office support as well as for additional staff to work in two new schools. The target was to reach an additional 40 kids per year.

A few months later, Eddie reported to the board that the community foundation had come through with the funding. He was elated. "Thank you Felipe." This never would have happened without your leadership." He beamed. "Now all I have to do is find the right people to do the work."

Eddie had never been involved in a hiring process before. When he wrote the grant, he worked closely with Felipe to develop the job description for each of the positions (a part-time office manager/executive assistant and two youth outreach workers). Once he secured the funding, Eddie advertised the jobs through the career department at the state university, the local community college, and at the job center that was run out of the nonprofit neighborhood development organization. He also spoke with several of his former professors to ask if they had ideas about people he should talk to about the jobs and posted the announcements on Linked-In and Facebook. His goal for the outreach workers was to hire two people who had backgrounds that were similar to his own.

As a result of his advertising, *I Believe* attracted more than 60 candidates for the outreach worker positions and 20 for the part-time office manager. Eddie decided to hire the office manager first so that he would have help organizing the paper work and interview process for the other positions. After sorting through those resumes, he interviewed three candidates and chose Berta Morales who had recently graduated from a job training program sponsored by the neighborhood development organization. He and Berta negotiated an 8:30 a.m. to 12:30 p.m. daily schedule as she had two little ones at home who were able to be cared for by her mother during those hours.

He then interviewed 20 people for the youth outreach worker positions. He couldn't believe how much time it took to meet all of these people, and he was frustrated that it was time away from mentoring his kids at Lincoln High. At least he felt he could rely on Berta to set up the interviews and check the references of the people he would eventually decide he wanted to hire. In the end, he chose Malik Allen, an African-American guy who was a few years younger than Eddie, and Carmen Finca, a Latina, who was the same age as Malik. Malik was a recent community college graduate who wanted to take a break from school before enrolling in a bachelor's program. He had grown up as a member of the Black Cobras while he was a student at Douglas High and told Eddie that he was honored to have the opportunity to straighten out gang bangers at his old school. Some of the kids there were the younger brothers of the kids he ran with at one time, and he thought that because of that, he'd be able to get through to them.

Carmen had never been in a gang herself, although she had two brothers who were heavily involved in Los Lobos (both were now in jail). She felt she understood gang culture and was eager to reach out to girls who were caught up in the culture. Eddie decided that she and Malik would work together at both Douglas High and Washington High, alternating their time between the two schools.

Once they were hired, Eddie spent a week training them in the strategies he developed with Felipe for reaching the kids. He worked with his new staff on creating an outreach plan for each school and then sent them out into the community with a great deal of confidence. He felt both were well suited to the job.

During the first several months, Malik and Carmen seemed to be working well as a team. Then their relationship began to deteriorate. Carmen complained to Berta, "I have no idea where he is or what he's doing. He's all show about helping the kids, but he's not doing what Eddie told us," she whined.

"You need to tell this to Eddie, not to me," replied Berta. "It's none of my business." Carmen didn't tell Eddie though because she was afraid she would sound like a snitch. Instead, she ran from school to school trying to do her best to mentor the kids. When Eddie brought them all together for monthly check-ins, Malik assured him that everything was going just fine even though Berta knew that it wasn't. They couldn't keep kids in the program, and it was getting a reputation for being a joke. Eight months had passed, and there were only 5 kids at both schools who were being helped by *I Believe*. They would have a nearly impossible time keeping it going over the summer as the school year came to a close.

Eddie was so focused on his work at Lincoln High, fund-raising, and public speaking that he wasn't paying close attention to the other schools. He just assumed things were going well because of the reports he was getting from the staff until he finally took the time to make a site visit at the end of the year. He was devastated to learn what was happening. To make matters worse, Mark had called asking for a report back to the foundation since it had been 1 year since he funded the project.

Case Questions

1. Why do you think the project had difficulty going to scale?

2. What could Eddie and/or the board have done to make the transition more successful?

3. What should Eddie and/or the board do now to address the situation?

4. If you were Eddie, what would you do about reporting back to the foundation? How would you present what was happening?

WHEN THE PROGRAM ISN'T WORKING: AN OUT-OF-CONTROL GROUP

Trinh Ngo loved her job at the Tri-Line, a multiservice agency that offered a variety of programs and services to low-income residents in three adjoining cities. Now 26, she had been introduced to the work of Tri-Line through a college internship program designed for public health majors. When the internship ended, Tri-Line hired her as a part-time employee and brought her on full-time after she graduated. Her job was to develop and oversee a network of 90 sexual health youth educators at 6 high schools throughout the three districts. She was passionate about ensuring that kids who grew up like she did, children of recent immigrants and others who were at risk because they lived in economically disadvantaged communities, had access to tools that could help them escape poverty and disease.

Growing up, Trinh had seen far too many girls abandon their dream of going to college because they had gotten pregnant. Three of her closest friends had waved off full scholarships to Penn, Brown, and the University of Chicago, ending up instead in dead-end service jobs where they couldn't make ends meet. One had married her boyfriend (who was also in a low-paying job); all of them still lived with their parents, who helped them care for their babies. She had also known several boys who had become infected with HIV because they were gay and didn't know who to turn to for advice within a community and culture that saw homosexuality as deeply shameful. Working through an understanding and acceptance of their sexual orientation was difficult enough without having the added stress of learning to live with HIV.

Using a train-the-trainers model, Trinh taught 16- to 18-year-olds how to be expert teachers and "go-to" resources for information on HIV/STD and pregnancy prevention as well as sexual identity. The goals of the program, called *Says Who* were to delay the start of sexual intercourse, reduce the number of students' sex partners, decrease the incidence of unprotected sex, increase condom use, and help LGBTQ youth learn about resources that would improve their self-esteem and overall mental health. The program was funded in part by a small grant from the county although the vast majority of its funding came from an annual renewing grant from The Health Justice Foundation.

Trinh had high expectations of herself, of the program, and of the students she trained. It was a difficult job going from school to school ensuring that there were enough kids who were interested in being Says Who trainers and that they were doing a good job reaching out to and being accessible to their peers. She had a never-ending stream of recruitment and training work as established trainers graduated and moved on to the next phase of their lives (the vast majority were college-bound which was something that made her quite proud). Trinh had a close working relationship with Brett Cutler, a program officer at the Health Justice Foundation, who oversaw her grant. Brett was impressed with Trinh's dedication to Says Who and had even asked her to make a presentation about the project to several trustees of the foundation. She was extraordinarily articulate as she interwove her personal story into the narrative about why this work was critically important to at-risk youth. He marveled at how much energy she had and how her enthusiasm for helping kids never seemed to wane.

Shortly after the start of the new program and academic year, Brett asked to meet with Trinh to talk about her program outcomes. "You know that I'm your biggest fan; otherwise, I wouldn't have asked you to make a presentation to our trustees," Brett said. "However, there is a new effort on the part of the foundation to ask our grantees to do a much better job measuring impact. You've been great at providing us with regular updates on how many trainers you have, on the racial and ethnic composition of those trainers, on how many workshops they provide, and on the percent of graduating trainers that go on to college, but now the foundation is asking for a whole new level of evaluation. Simply put: We'd like to know whether or not the program is meeting its stated outcomes before we provide funding for another year. As you know, Trinh, the foundation has invested a lot in this project, and we want to be sure that our investment is paying dividends by making an impact on the health of the kids we are trying to reach. Don't worry, though. We are fully prepared to pay the university to do this research so that we don't add to your workload, which I know is fuller than full. I think you'll be pleased to know that Fred Packard has agreed to do the evaluation on our behalf."

"Wow, that's a lot to take in," replied Trinh. "I'm so happy to know that you hired Dr. Packard to look at our project. He was one of my favorite professors, and I know that he really cares about low-income communities and people."

Before the evaluation work began, Fred met with Trinh to describe the process. "It's fairly straightforward, Trinh," he explained. "Four graduate students and I are going to do some pre- and post-test assessments at the beginning and end of the spring semester to see how knowledgeable the students are about sexual health issues and resources. In addition, we plan to take a look at some other success indicators. We're working on designing this instrument now. Our plan is to survey students at nine high schools—the six with which you are working and three others that we'll use as a control group. Of course, students at those control schools will be closely matched with the participants in that they will be from the same socioeconomic demographic, and their racial/ethnic composition and gender will mirror that of the students in the Says Who schools. We also plan to do some qualitative interviews with students who have participated in the Says Who training sessions to hear what they think about the program and to separately interview the trainers about their experiences. Brett told me that the foundation is anxious to get the results, so we're going to push hard to get the report back to you by the first week in August."

"This is so exciting!" exclaimed Trinh. "I can't wait to see the results. Thank you so much for working on this project, Dr. Packard."

During the second week of August, Trinh met with Brett and Fred at the foundation to discuss the findings of the research. As soon as she walked into the room, she could tell that they had been meeting for some time, and that something was wrong. Together they spent the next hour discussing the results of the research conducted by Fred and his team.

At the end of the hour, Fred said, "The bottom line, Trinh, is that we couldn't see any statistically significant difference in the assessment scores of the students who were and were not exposed to the Says Who training. In my mind, there were, however, two key findings that are worth noting. First, we know that much greater numbers of the Says Who trainers report that they plan to, or have been, accepted to college than the general student population at any of the schools we studied. That means that in at least one way, the training is having a real benefit in that it . . . actually, you are cultivating the leadership potential of those students and, specifically, instilling in them a belief that they can go to and succeed in college. We heard that time and again from the trainers—that your role in that regard was significant—and I think that is something you should be quite proud of even though it's an unintended consequence of the program. We asked them a series of probing questions about their interest in college, and it is evident that you are the key variable in that equation."

"The flip side of that same coin perhaps, is that when we conducted focus groups with students who had attended the training, an overwhelming number told us that they didn't think it was effective because 'cool' kids weren't conducting the sessions. They saw the trainers as being 'geeks' or 'nerds'—people they couldn't relate to— which is why they weren't willing to fully listen to what they were saying. The sexual practices of those who participated in the Says Who program turned out to be no different than those who did not. Similarly, it does not appear that LGBTQ students availed themselves of the services and resources that were offered."

Brett said solemnly but gently, "I know this must be quite a shock and a huge blow to your many hours of hard work, but the facts speak for themselves. For obvious reasons, the foundation can't continue to fund the project as it is, although we might be willing to entertain a different type of proposal from Tri-Line."

Fighting back tears, Trinh could only nod. She thanked them both and burst into tears once the elevator doors closed.

Case Questions

1. What types of support are needed for program managers to identify and measure outcomes?

2. What, if anything, could Tri-Line have done to support Trinh in her initial efforts? Do you see this type of thing happening at other nonprofits?

3. What, if anything, could Trinh have done to design the program in a way that it would have worked better from the beginning?

4. What should Trinh's next steps be? What kind of changes to the program, if any, should she propose? Who should she enlist to help her decide what those changes should be?

5

Strategic
Decision Making

INTRODUCTION

As stewards of the public's trust, leaders of nonprofits are required to
make sound decisions, even in the most turbulent environments. For
these leaders, decision making is made all the more challenging by virtue
of the fact that nonprofits are accountable to a wide variety of
stakeholders, many of whom may have competing interests. For example,
nonprofit leaders are accountable to their donors and their clients, but
what donors want to give or fund might not be what clients need. More
broadly, nonprofits are accountable to the government and public
because of their tax exempt status. Keeping everyone satisfied all of the
time is an all but impossible task, so the stakes are high when strategic
decisions must be made.

To whom are nonprofits accountable and for what? In general most experts agree that nonprofits should be accountable to society for pursuing their mission, operating transparently within a legal and ethical framework, being good stewards of the public's trust, and generating positive outcomes for those they serve. How, then, do we know this happens?

There are myriad ways in which nonprofit organizations demonstrate accountably or are held accountable for their actions. First and foremost, nonprofits are regulated by government, both state and federal. Nonprofits must comply with all applicable IRS regulations. Certain subsectors of nonprofits, such as health-care and education-related nonprofits, have established standards for accreditation. Internally, nonprofits may elect to self-regulate by establishing codes of ethics and adopting professional standards for their organizations. The Standards for Excellence Institute and the Association for Fund-Raising Professionals codes of ethics (see http://www.standardsforexcellencein-stitute.org and http://www.afpnet.org/Ethics) provide good examples. Nonprofits are also held accountable by third-party watchdog groups such as the media and Charity Navigator (see http://www.charitynavigator.org).

A formal strategic planning process is one tool nonprofits use to inform and guide organizational decision making. Commonly, strategic planning entails a participative process whereby the vision, mission, and values of the organization are defined, issues of strategic importance are surfaced, and the future direction of the organization is then established accordingly. Timelines for strategic plans can extend for as long as 5 years or more, although short-term or "real-time" planning is becoming increasingly popular as a way to keep up with rapidly changing environments (LaPiana, 2008). Ensuring that the proper mix of stakeholders (e.g., board members, staff, constituents) is involved in the planning process is critical to a plan's success. Likewise, nonprofit leaders must ensure that adequate resources (e.g., staff, space, equipment) are in place to carry out whatever plans are devised. Last, a successful planning process should result in a living document that informs the strategic leadership of the organization.

Different dimensions of accountability and the complexity of strategic decision making may be explored in the following cases:

1. Generating revenue by selling assets

2. Policy disputes among board members and between board and constituents

3. Strategy setting dilemmas

REFERENCES

LaPiana, D. (2008). *The nonprofit strategy revolution*. St. Paul, MN: Fieldstone Alliance.

GENERATING REVENUE BY SELLING ASSETS: A PICTURE IS WORTH A THOUSAND . . .

The Dixworth Museum was the pride of Fanning, Michigan, a popular college town located 37 miles northwest of Detroit. The Dixworth was founded in 1947 by Franklin Reginald Dixworth, who wanted to draw attention and tourists to the growing town by establishing a museum that would showcase his vast and growing art collection.

The Dixworth collection included works by the famous Spanish Renaissance artist, El Greco, along with several of his lesser-known contemporaries, ancient Greek sculptures, early American paintings, and a large and well-known collection of modern works by Dali, Picasso, Van Gogh, Gaugin, Calder, and Miro that had expanded over the years to include pieces by Rothko, Pollock, Warhol, Lichtenstein, and Stella. The collection was revered by art lovers of all types, which was exactly what Dixworth had hoped for when he established the museum for the stated purpose of "Disquieting the mundane, delighting the mind and eye, and stirring the soul and spirit with evocative and provocative art."

During his lifetime, Dixworth was a hands-on trustee with an uncanny knack for befriending and acquiring art from artists just prior to their works soaring in popularity (and price). Some said that his affiliation with unknown artists was directly related to their discovery and success. When he died in 1968, the town mourned his passing by wrapping each light pole on the road fronting the museum in black. His obituary in *The New York Times* mentioned his prodigious eye for contemporary art, extraordinary vision, and generosity. The writer included vignettes about his disarming personality that startled those who did not know him when his gentle manners and calm demeanor gave way at unexpected times to boisterous laughter. He was noted for being an adept steward of the museum, which, along with his loving family, was the centerpiece of his life. Although his two sons had been appointed to serve on the board following his death, both had died shortly thereafter in a single-engine plane crash, leaving no family tie to the museum.

In 2012, the Dixworth hired Martha Carmine as its new director. Hiring Martha was seen as a major coup for the museum. She had worked for many years alongside Glenn D. Lowry, director of the Museum of Modern Art in New York, before moving to Boston to direct the Institute for Contemporary Art (ICA) that she led for several years. Although she loved the east coast, landing the job at the Dixworth was a dream come true for Martha; even though she enjoyed her time at the ICA, she aspired to be affiliated with an institution that had a robust and renowned permanent collection. At the time of Martha's arrival, the Dixworth owned 18,000 works of art, had an annual operating budget of $11 million, an endowment valued at $80 million, and employed close to 100 staff members. The museum operated and maintained an 110,000-square-foot facility with 30,000 square feet of exhibition space spread across 25 galleries.

During her first few years at the museum, Martha dedicated herself to forming alliances with directors of neighboring museums in Detroit and in surrounding communities, getting to know her board members and major donors, and working with her senior staff to develop new programs. She knew that she was fortunate to have walked into a job with a stable board, a sizeable endowment, and a steady stream of visitors from throughout the world. She was most excited about planning for the future of the museum, work that she did in consultation with her chief operating officer (COO), Javier Navarro, with whom she met regularly to hammer out a vision of what the Dixworth could become. They often included the museum's chief curator, Johanna Tremblay, in their discussions. "I didn't come here to be a keeper of the flame," Martha would say. "I came here to carry the vision of Frank Dixworth into the 21st century."

Once she, Javier, and Johanna settled on their plan, Martha and Javier devised a strategy for selling it to the board. They would begin the campaign by discussing it with the five-member collections committee, each of whom would then play a key role convincing the other 28 board members of its value. Martha was particularly concerned about convincing Paula Rosenstein, her board chair and a retired judge, who she saw as being a steady and thoughtful leader but someone who was not particularly innovative. The judge (as she was always referred to) focused on numbers—membership, attendance, annual revenue, endowment performance—more than on the mission and the artwork. To Martha, it seemed as if the judge was more concerned with the museum as a business rather than as a mission-centered, mission-driven organization.

The collections committee was headed by Jacqueline Borck, an art collector and generous benefactor to the museum. Martha, Javier, and Johanna were sure Jackie would love the plan, and they weren't disappointed with her response. "Martha, this is exactly why we hired you!" she exclaimed. "I can't wait for the committee to hear this!"

A few weeks later, Jackie called the collections committee meeting to order. They, too, were excited by the vision presented by Martha. There was a unanimous vote to bring the plan forward at the next full board meeting. Jackie pulled Martha aside after the meeting and said, "I believe this plan represents a new future for the Dixworth. If the board gets behind it, and I sincerely hope they do, then I will pledge $25 million to the campaign. However, I don't want that publicly disclosed to the board until after their decision has been made."

The following day, Jackie crafted a memorandum from the committee (in her role as chair) to the full board that framed and summarized the materials that Martha, Javier, and Johanna had outlined in their comprehensive and (to her thinking) well-researched proposal. The proposal was titled "The Dixworth: A Future of Provocative Art."

Jackie's memo read as follows:

Dear Fellow Trustees:

Enclosed is a proposal that epitomizes the spirit and vision of Frank Dixworth, which has, since the founding of this institution, been reflected in our mission of "Disquieting the mundane, delighting the mind and eye, and stirring the soul and spirit with evocative and provocative art." This proposal builds upon his foresighted collection in a way that will ensure future visitors experience the stunning brilliance of modern and contemporary art for years to come. Voted on unanimously and enthusiastically by the collections committee, the documents contained within this folder outline a plan for maintaining the preeminence of the Dixworth in the world of modern and contemporary museums. The plan, which has been thoroughly researched by our director, chief curator, and COO over a series of months, is summarized as having the following objectives:

1. Strengthen our outstanding collection by aggressively moving to acquire works by major modern and contemporary artists not

already represented within it, including luminaries such as Jeff Koons, Damien Hirst, Robert Rauschenberg, Helen Frankenthaler, Robert Mapplethorpe, Lee Krasner, Willem de Kooning, Robert Motherwell, Ai Weiwei, Keith Haring, Annie Leibovitz, Kiki Smith, Cindy Sherman, and others.

2. Expand the footprint of the museum by building a modern wing to house these new works (please refer to the enclosed sketch of the proposed building, generously provided pro bono by Luce & Williamston, as one example of what could be built within the confines of what is now our sculpture garden).

3. Generate $300 million for these efforts by taking the following steps:

   a. Deaccessioning those pieces in our collection that are not aligned with our mission. Through this process of refining our collection, we expect to net sufficient revenue that will allow us to underwrite approximately half of the cost of this plan. Specifically

      i. One of our El Greco paintings is a companion to the *St Dominic in Prayer* piece that sold at Sotheby's for more than $14 million in 2013. Sotheby's estimates that our piece is worth between $20 and $25 million

      ii. Quiet negotiations with the Museum of The American Artist has indicated an interest in having them acquire our early American painting collection that has been valued at $10 million

      iii. Our collection of ancient Greek sculptures has been estimated by Sotheby's to fetch between $75 and $90 million

   b. Embarking upon a major fund-raising campaign to net approximately $150 million for these efforts (i.e., we would need to raise whatever cannot be covered by the sale of existing works). An anonymous donor has pledged $25 million toward this sum should the board approve this plan.

The collections committee looks forward to discussing this electrifying plan for our future, the details of which are outlined within the enclosed materials. We want to recognize and applaud the audacious vision that Martha has brought to the board. She, Javier, and Johanna have done outstanding work, conceiving, developing and researching this bold blueprint for the Dixworth.

Sincerely,

Jacqueline Borck

In the intervening days between the time the material was sent and the board meeting took place, Martha, Javier, and the members of the collections committee met with as many board members as possible to gauge their reaction to what was being proposed. Some were tight-lipped about their opinion, others were thrilled with the proposal, some voiced concerns about the cost and risk involved, others literally could not be found, and several were appalled that Martha and Javier had brought this fully fleshed-out plan to the board without having discussed it first at a more conceptual level with the trustees.

The judge opened the meeting by asking Jackie and Martha to walk the group through the plan. She then allowed the trustees to ask questions about the proposal.

The questions raised by the board (which you should consider) were as follows:

Case Questions

1. If Frank Dixworth's vision included Spanish Renaissance art, Greek sculptures, and early American paintings, should those items be deaccessioned now to accommodate a new vision/new interpretation of the original mission? Is this new vision, in fact, different from Dixworth's original vision since the mission statement remains the same? How often should the board revisit an organization's mission? Are there extenuating circumstances when the mission of a nonprofit is established by a single individual particularly when that individual dedicated such extensive resources to the organization?

2. Is it ever right for a museum to sell off its holdings in order to acquire new works? Separately, is it ever right for a museum to sell works in order to fund the operating budget?

3. If Frank Dixworth had established a permanently restricted endowment fund to pay for the maintenance and upkeep of the old Spanish master paintings, does that alter your thinking about a possible new direction for the museum? If you said "yes" to moving in the new direction, how should the board approach the idea of repurposing these endowment funds?

4. What type of risk assessment should the trustees do to make the best decision? What kind of information do the trustees need to gather to ensure this is a sound strategic and financial decision for the museum? How might the museum determine whether there is a compelling need to construct a larger gallery space? What factors should the museum trustees consider in making this decision?

5. Do you think Martha and Javier took the right approach in the way this opportunity was presented to the board?

POLICY DISPUTES: THE WRONG CLIMATE FOR DISCUSSION

Brownsworth University looked every bit the part of the elite institution that it was. The first building erected for the school 185 years earlier had been designed by the preeminent architect of that time, Charles Bulfinch. It was the quintessential New England campus, surrounded by towering trees and located within close proximity to a quaint town.

Patricia Avery had served as president of Brownsworth for 11 years. She was the university's 22nd president and its first woman president. Dr. Avery received her PhD from Georgetown University's School of Medicine, after which she had engaged in postdoctoral work in neuroscience at MIT. Working with a team of physicists, computer scientists, and mathematicians there and later at a nonprofit research institute, she launched a distinguished career developing models for predicting complex neural activities in the brain. This work was considered an important cornerstone to an eventual understanding of how brain diseases might be treated. Despite this distinguished pedigree, Dr. Avery was a plainspoken woman who was able to relate well to most others. Those who criticized her did so saying that because she worked tirelessly, she expected those around her to do the same.

Although Dr. Avery was adept at working with donors, she had difficulty mastering the art of working with a board of trustees. She felt that she had good relationships with each of the 33 members individually (at least, to the extent that she knew them) but that she could not always predict the outcome of board decisions. She reminded herself that when she was involved in scientific experimentation that she could not be certain of the outcome of that work either, regardless of how carefully the model had been constructed. Still, she felt chastened that she was not better at predicting the behavior of the group of trustees.

Dr. Avery was particularly worried about the forthcoming trustees' meeting, which centered upon a discussion of Brownsworth's investment policies. Over a year ago, a student group calling itself the Brownsworth Climate Action Coalition of University Students (cleverly nicknamed "B-CAUSe") began petitioning the administration to divest its endowment of fossil-fuel energy companies. B-CAUSe held protests and teach-ins that had been covered not only in the local press but had also reached *The New York Times* as part of an article on universities that had taken this action. Brandon Lewis, the president of the student group, was quoted as saying, "This is our South Africa, and this is our future. Just as universities across the nation divested themselves of companies doing business in South Africa during the apartheid regime, we must divest ourselves of companies that are destroying the planet." He had requested a meeting with Dr. Avery to allow the B-CAUSe steering committee to present their case, which she had granted.

Dr. Avery allowed 1 hour for the students to discuss their concerns. They were well prepared and professional, bringing along a packet of material describing the impact of climate change, listing 20 other universities that had divested from fossil-fuel energy companies, and providing language used by several universities in their resolution for an energy stock divestment policy. They noted that Stanford was the most prestigious institution to have taken this action among the group of colleges and universities to have done so. It also had the largest endowment among this cohort (Mandery, 2014). Dr. Avery listened intently and nodded in response to their comments. She concluded the meeting by saying, "Thank you for your thoughtful research and presentation. Ultimately, this is a decision that will be made by the board of trustees. I will convey your materials and concerns to our investment committee whom I assure you will give it their utmost and timely consideration." "We appreciate that, Dr. Avery," replied Brandon, "and want you to know that we will continue campus protests until this issue is resolved."

In subsequent days, Dr. Avery called her colleagues at several other schools to learn how they handled this issue at their respective institutions. She was told in no uncertain terms by her close friend, Harvard president Drew Gilpin Faust, "The endowment is a resource, not an instrument to impel social or political change" (Mandery, 2014). Lee Bollinger, her counterpart at Columbia told her that in order to take this kind of action, "The bar has to be very high, and the reason is there are lots of things that people don't like about the world" (Mandery, 2014). "Yes," she replied, "that's my thinking exactly. We already have students who want us to take sides in the Israeli–Palestinian conflict and others who will likely argue for different things if we go down this path. My sense is that if we open the door to this argument, it will never shut."

Despite this reassurance from her colleagues, she was worried about the discussion that would take place among the trustees serving on the investment committee. The committee consisted of nine members that included herself; Marcus Burgeson, the vice president of finance and chief financial officer for the university; Gil Stevens, the board chair; and six at-large board members. They would deliberate the issue and report back to the full board with their recommendations by the next full meeting of the trustees. She was fairly sure that the board as a whole would approve whatever the investment committee recommended, yet because the issue was contentious, she could not be certain.

After Dr. Avery framed the issue, Marcus explained in frank terms that making this type of policy change to Brownsworth's $1.5 billion investment portfolio would potentially cost the university at least $200 million over the next 10 years. "One of the fundamental problems we would face would be the process of removing approximately 60% of our investments from comingled funds that are part of larger index funds. While we could reinvest that portion of the endowment in alternative index funds, we face a serious risk to our return. As you can see from the chart I have prepared, the loss in the first year is projected to be $11.2 million rising to $73 million in year 5 and more than $200 million by year 10."

Paul Nierman, a seasoned investment professional, alumni, and longtime trustee, was the first to speak. "I have reviewed the materials presented by the students, and I applaud their diligent research, cogent arguments, and impassioned pleas. I am delighted that Brownsworth is continuing to produce such fine students. Their presentation reflects well on the academic environment here. That said, we cannot afford to place the university in a situation where the value of the portfolio declines precipitously as the risk rises significantly. It's fine to have ideals; however, this money is needed for down-to-earth expenses such as scholarships, faculty research, and new programs. It is a nonstarter for me."

Ellen Novak, a second trustee, spoke next. "I am all for saving the planet, but if major producers of carbon dioxide don't reduce their output, our little effort at Brownsworth will be for naught, while, at the same time, we will be hurting our wonderful school."

Gil Stevens, the board chair, spoke next. "Patricia, ahem, that is, Dr. Avery, and I had the opportunity to discuss this issue prior to our meeting today, although she did not reveal her views to me. In as much as I have deep respect for Marcus, Paul, and Ellen, I must also tell you that common sense compels me to come down on the side of the students with regard to this matter. These young people and their children and grandchildren will inherit this planet, live in it, and lead it for years after we are gone. This is not a superfluous cause ladies and gentleman, this is the world that is at stake. Brownsworth must assume the mantle of leader, innovator, and agent of change. If our portfolio declines—and I must say, Marcus, I question your dire predictions— then it is the responsibility of the board to redouble its commitment to raising funds for this institution. I like to think that I have been a generous contributor to Brownsworth, and I intend to continue to be one should the institution remain focused on its core values, which to my mind include high academic standards, ethical conduct, and forward thinking. This is the perfect opportunity for Brownsworth to embody those values with our actions." The remaining trustees in the room stood and applauded Gil's remarks.

In immediate response to Gil's remarks, Paul asked, "Gil, just to be clear, are you implying that you might curb your giving to Brownsworth if we do not adopt this divestment policy?" In response, Gil replied, "That is correct. In fact, Paul, I may cease my giving altogether."

Dr. Avery allowed the discussion to continue back and forth. The exchange was polite, yet the anger of the trustees was bubbling just below the surface of the discussion.

According to the rules of the committee, in the event of a deadlock, the president was provided with the tie-breaking vote. As the conversation went back and forth, Patricia tried to hide the emotion she felt. She kept making mental calculations. What would be the financial loss to Brownsworth if Gil withdrew his support versus the expected decline in the endowment? What would be the public relations consequences of this decision (either way it was decided)? If the decision was made not to divest, would it impact future enrollment (particularly if the student protests continued)? How would the decision—and in particular, her tie-breaking decision—affect the functioning of the board? Would there be resignations as a result of the vote?

Case Questions

1. What are the key considerations that Dr. Avery and the board need to assess as part of making this decision?

2. What, if anything, could Dr. Avery have done to mitigate the conflict among the board?

3. Please outline a series of next steps if the vote is to divest regarding communication with different campus constituencies.

4. Would those steps be any different if the vote is not to divest?

5. Is there a third option other than to divest or not divest? What do you think the university should do?

REFERENCE

Mandery, E. J. (2014, November 2). The mission campus climate debate. *The New York Times*, p. 5.

SETTING STRATEGY: FINDING YOUR ORGANIZATION'S NORTH STAR

North Star Community Support Services had been in existence for 2 decades providing a variety of social services in Greenwood County. It had a budget of $8.5 million with over 150 employees and 600 volunteers. North Star's website advertised "Four Pillars of Service," including youth development, domestic violence and family services, workforce development, and legal services. North Star received the majority of its funds through government grants and contracts, and, as a result, North Star's programs were often developed in response to available funding streams. Furthermore, despite North Star's solid reputation in the community, organizationally it was somewhat siloed and bureaucratic, in many ways reflecting the attributes of the government agencies from which it received funding.

The youth development unit provided programming to local middle school and high school aged youth, reaching more than 800 annually. Programs included before and after-school care, gang and drug diversion programs, and assistance with passing the high school proficiency exam that allowed participants who had dropped out, or who were at risk of dropping out, the opportunity to earn the equivalent of a high school diploma. The programs were offered in donated or rented space at several local school sites and community centers. Although there were similar programs operating in the region, including two Boys and Girls Clubs, the program itself maintained a relatively steady state, providing several beloved programs that community leaders and families had come to count on to keep kids safe and out of trouble. Some of these programs relied heavily on the development of over $400,000 in private funding every year and required the buy in and support from several community partners, including city administrators and school district employees and counselors to continue to be effective. However, continued cuts to the state budget forced staff to scramble for funding and increased the need for even more private fund-raising and partnerships to sustain the programs.

The domestic violence and family services unit provided in-home family support, group therapy, and parenting classes to over 1,000 families per year. All programing was administered by clinical therapists and social workers employed by North Star, many of whom were trained specifically in innovative and short-term mental and behavioral health methodologies. The program also relied on a vibrant group of counseling and social work interns from the local state university to support service delivery. Incidentally, the mental health expertise of the staff had enabled North Star to effectively address issues related to commercial sexual exploitation of children, a growing concern in Greenwood County.

North Star's legal services, the smallest unit in the organization by budget and staff, were provided by a cadre of lawyers and mediation experts who worked pro bono. The unit had a big impact and was therefore very efficient, serving 3,200 clients annually. Additionally, many of those who volunteered for the program personally made donations and directly solicited large philanthropic gifts from prominent law firms to support the program. The program was staffed by a full-time manager and two part-time office administrators who coordinated the volunteers.

The workforce development unit was by far the most developed of the four pillars as it had grown rapidly during the Great Recession with steady funding provided through the American Recovery and Reinvestment Act. North Star used these and other federal funds to enroll people in job training programs and to provide direct job placement services. As the funds flowed in, new programs were added on to existing 3- to 5-year demonstration grants. North Star had quickly become the "go-to" nonprofit in the region when it came to job placement. However, these were programs with an expensive unit cost per client, and it could take 10 to 24 months to achieve the desired outcomes of employment and employment retention.

North Star was operated under the capable leadership of a newly appointed CEO, Louisa Calderon. Louisa had enjoyed a successful career in social work, primarily in the area of youth development, working for the likes of Big Brothers Big Sisters and the YMCA. She progressed steadily professionally, and it was not long before she found herself moving out of direct service provision, taking up management positions with increasing responsibility. Prior to her position at North Star, Louisa had spent 5 years as the COO of a $5 million human services agency.

Confident in her abilities to lead an organization, she was quite pleased to be recruited for the CEO position at North Star.

When she first arrived at North Star, Louisa launched a personal listening tour, meeting with community members, politicians, church leaders, program clients, donors, and other stakeholders to learn more about the community and its needs. Additionally, Louisa engaged the board in a thorough financial review that also included a detailed financial forecast provided by a local consultant. Before long, it became obvious to Louisa that North Star was not fully aligned with the needs of the community.

At dinner on Friday night, she shared her observations with her husband: "Essentially, the organization is reactive rather than strategic. They've built almost every program based on whatever grant dollars were available at the time. It feels like a house where the owners added on to make some room for a new baby, then a few years later added on again, and then again, as their family grew. Before long, the house no longer had an intentional design, and the floor plan was a mess. That's what it feel like has happened at North Star."

"That bad, huh?" he commented.

"Don't get me wrong," Louisa said. "There is plenty of good being done and so much opportunity to do more. Everywhere I look, I see opportunities," she said.

"Think about the counseling staff," she continued. "They have real bench strength and capacity to address a wider variety of issues than we provide in our current services. We also have some real prospects to leverage or even completely offload youth programs to other partners. And we need to get ahead of the curve in terms of government funding. The recession is supposedly over, so I expect that workforce development money pot will be shrinking."

"Sounds like you have your work cut out for you, dear," he told her.

Louisa knew he was right. She spent the better part of that weekend thinking about how to move the organization forward. As her first order of business on Monday morning, Louisa announced that North Star would be embarking on a major strategic planning initiative. "I want to us to assess this place from top to bottom, look under every rock for new and exciting opportunities," she told the staff.

Case Questions

1. What are the strategic decisions facing the organization?

2. Outline the steps Louisa should take to lead an effective strategic planning process.

    a. Who should be involved?

    b. How long should it take?

    c. What resources will be needed to complete a thorough planning process?

    d. What potential challenges may need to be addressed?

    e. What are some trade-offs that may need to be considered along the way?

3. What sorts of processes can North Star adopt to help it move from reactive to strategic?

6

Human Resource Management

INTRODUCTION

Nonprofits are driven by human capital, relying much more heavily on people than machines to deliver on their social purpose missions. The Urban Institute (2014) estimates that the nonprofit sector employs approximately 10% of the workforce in the United States, and, unlike the for-profit and government sectors, nonprofit employment grew exponentially, throughout the Great Recession. Human resources in the nonprofit sector is different from other sectors as it includes both paid employees and volunteers. Therefore, to effectively manage human resources, leaders must identify the often unique factors that drive both paid employees and volunteers to work in the nonprofit sector. Maslow, Herzberg, Pink, and others (Pink, 2009; Worth, 2009) provide useful theoretical frameworks for understanding employee motivation. Many posit that individuals drawn to work in the nonprofit setting are more often than not driven by intrinsic motivation (i.e., personal connection to the mission or alignment with personal values) rather than by extrinsic rewards such as public recognition or a big paycheck. However, the recent professionalization of the nonprofit sector has helped to make working for a nonprofit less of an either-or proposition. In other words, choosing a career in the nonprofit sector does not necessarily mean forgoing a fair wage and benefits. The tendency of nonprofit workers to be intrinsically motivated coupled with the inability of many nonprofits to provide traditional rewards such as fringe benefits or bonuses, increases the complexity managers of employees and volunteers face in the nonprofit sector.

Nonprofits must design and implement employee and volunteer policies that ensure compliance with all laws, both state and federal. While employment law differs from state to state, minimally there should be written job descriptions in place for each employee and policies that address the following:

- Hiring practices that ensure legal compliance with prevailing wage laws, interview questions, background checks, reference checks, and so on
- Compensation and benefits (including workers compensation policies and Family Medical Leave)
- Employee behavior expectations (rules for conduct and disciplinary action)
- Equal employment, sexual harassment, and nondiscrimination policies
- Sick leave and vacation time
- Performance evaluation
- Recording work hours
- Explanation of exempt and nonexempt employees
- Use of technology/social media policy
- Conflict of interest and nondisclosure policies
- Work hours and time off
- Health and safety regulations, including substance abuse
- Processes for hearing grievances, performance evaluations and documentation, and dismissal

Similar to other governing or policy documents, employment policies at a nonprofit should align with the mission and values of the organization. For example, nonprofits with a mission to fight poverty may want to consider wage policies that ensure their employees earn a living wage. Boards of directors and executives should review all policies on a regular basis.

Despite the tremendous importance of human effort to the success of nonprofits, for a variety of reasons the management of human resources (HR) remains an often neglected aspect of nonprofit management, many times left to managers who wear many other hats. Furthermore, since the majority of nonprofits are small and relatively flat, employees seeking to move up a traditional career ladder often have to job hop from one organization to another, making employee turnover a recurring challenge for nonprofit leaders. Yet, the growth and professionalization of the sector demands nonprofits be able to attract and retain top talent, therefore nonprofit leaders must be prepared to adequately address a variety of human resource issues including wages, benefits, chief executive officer (CEO) pay, and executive transition.

This chapter explores the following issues in greater detail about:

1.   A staff member in crisis

2.   Employee substance abuse

3.   Volunteers ignoring the rules

4.   When volunteers run amok

REFERENCES

Pink, D. (2009). *Drive: The surprising truth about what motivates us.* New York, NY: Riverhead Books

Urban Institute. (2014). Data in action: a breakthrough in estimating nonprofit employment. Retrieved from http://www.urban.org/urban-wire/data-action-breakthrough-estimating-nonprofit-employment

Worth, M. (2009). *Nonprofit management: Principles and practice.* Thousand Oaks, CA: Sage.

POLICIES AND PROCEDURES FOR STAFF MEMBERS IN CRISIS: A TRAGEDY WITH RIPPLE EFFECTS

Jennifer Yebba loved being executive director of Buffalo Urban Gardeners (BUG). Five years earlier, she and her good friend, Jamie Otis, founded the organization with a vision of transforming blighted vacant lots into neighborhood-managed fruit and vegetable gardens.

Buffalo had so many vacant lots that city officials had readily agreed to provide BUG with a community development block grant and access to the city's heavy equipment. Soon front-end loaders and backhoes driven by municipal employees were deployed to help Jennifer and Jamie realize their dream of an urban oasis. Buffalo had seen more hard times than good and was in desperate need of neighborhood improvement and unification. In its decline, the city had also become a magnet for refugees from around the world. Jennifer and Jamie thought that gardening would be a way for neighbors to beautify the city, to get to know one another by swapping old family recipes, and to help lower-income folks save money on their food bills.

Since it was founded, BUG had worked with neighborhood residents from some of the lowest-income neighborhoods to redevelop 21 lots across the city into community gardens. These gardens were now maintained by more than 350 residents. BUG also started and coordinated food purchasing groups where neighbors jointly bought commodities in bulk and distributed them among themselves to save money. The program was so successful, the housing authority contracted with BUG to establish food purchasing groups at three family development complexes (with promises of additional contracts once those programs were successfully launched). BUG wasn't only about gardening—it was about building community, beautifying Buffalo, and providing low-income people with access to affordable food.

During the first year of the organization's life, Jennifer and Jamie volunteered their time to organize the first four gardens. Once the city and the community foundation provided funding for BUG, Jennifer became its first staff person. Jamie, who had a full-time job as a graphic designer, stayed on as president of the board, which also included four community gardeners—Edna Skrobowski, Vi Nguyen, Denise Brown, and Vanessa Sanford—who were joined by Sister Margaret from Blessed Sacrament and Ed Milczarek, a recently retired parks and recreation employee.

As BUG grew, it hired a few more staff: Manny Lopez and Willie Smith as community organizers/garden coordinators and Deb Horwitz as coordinator of the food purchasing groups. MJ Schumann was the part-time bookkeeper. Jennifer's time was spent coordinating the activities of the group, interacting with city agencies, and fund-raising. She was known throughout the city for her effervescent smile, ingenuity, and dedication to the mission of BUG. She and Jamie had been dating when they launched BUG, but he soon realized that Jennifer would always be more committed to her work than she could ever be to him. They were still close friends, and she still worked 70 hours per week.

The staff members loved Jennifer and loved working for BUG. Each was passionate about the mission and felt lucky to be paid to do this work. Manny and Willie were, after Jennifer, the longest standing employees, having worked there for about 2.5 years (they had been hired just a month a part). Deb had started at BUG as a student intern during her senior year at Buffalo State and was hired after her graduation, a little over a year ago, as BUG's food purchasing club coordinator. MJ worked for many nonprofits throughout the city, and he had worked at BUG for 2 years. The staff not only loved Jennifer; they were also close knit. Working at BUG felt a little like being part of a family.

One afternoon in mid-June, Jennifer got a call from Willie. He was sobbing so hard she initially had a difficult time understanding what he was saying to her, "L'Tanya was hit by a drunk driver. I've got to go to the hospital now." "Go," she said. "I'll meet you there." L'Tanya was Willie's wife of 10 years, the love of his life, his high school sweetheart. They married right before he left to fight in the Iraq war. They had an 8-year-old son, Willie, Jr. By the time Willie arrived at the hospital, she was dead.

Everyone at BUG was devastated. Manny spread the word to community gardeners across the city, and many came to the funeral to express their condolences. Jennifer called an emergency meeting of the board to talk about bereavement leave for Willie as there was no provision for bereavement leave in the personnel policies, and she did not want to make the decision by herself.

Sister Margaret spoke first. "As a caring community, we must give Willie a month off with pay. This is a devastating loss, and he will need time to begin to heal and rebuild his life with Willie, Jr." Denise and Vanessa nodded in agreement. "Sister," replied Ed, "I appreciate your compassion, but I know the city only allows 3 days of paid leave for bereavement, which I think is a pretty standard practice for most businesses. I can only imagine what Willie is going through right now, but I don't see how BUG can afford to give him that much paid leave. Who's going to fill in for him while he's out in the middle of our busiest season? We can't ask Manny to do the work of two people."

"I know it's much more than most organizations do or would be willing to do," said Jamie, "but BUG isn't most organizations. We are about building community and loving our neighbors. I'm willing to take 2 weeks off work to fill in for Willie. I know I won't do as good a job as he does—I'm no gardening expert—but at least I'm a familiar face to many folks in the neighborhood." "Thank you," sighed Jennifer, "that really means a lot to me that you're willing to do that for Willie and for BUG." "All right," said Ed. "I'll volunteer for a week myself if we agree to give him 3 weeks and 3 days off in total." And so it was decided to give Willie 3 weeks and 3 days of paid leave.

During Willie's leave of absence, Manny worked extra hours to coordinate Jamie and Ed's efforts and to fill in the gaps as best he could. It wasn't anything like having Willie around, but Manny felt that he needed to do everything in his power to help his buddy. Even though he was dog tired from the extra work, he stopped by Willie's house a few times a week to check in on him and Junior and to fill Willie in on what was happening at the gardens. Willie's mother and father were often there, watching Junior. Willie looked like an empty shell of himself.

Two weeks after Willie returned to work, he got into a shouting match with one of the gardeners. Mrs. Ahmed had never been easy to deal with; however, an issue with aphids on her summer squash escalated way too quickly into an ugliness that had Mrs. Ahmed, a petite elderly woman, running from the garden in fright. Mrs. Negash, one of the other gardeners, called Jennifer to report the incident. "I'm so sorry, Mrs. Negash. I will speak to Willie and come to the garden myself to apologize to Mrs. Ahmed."

That incident was the first of many to follow. Nearly every day for the next 5 weeks Jennifer got calls from gardeners who were on the receiving end of Willie's wrath. Manny tried his best to intervene when he could, but he was often working across town at another site. He was carrying more than his share of the workload, maintaining half of the existing gardens and organizing three new sites. He told Jennifer that word was spreading among the gardeners about Willie's behavior, and that there was widespread fear in the community.

Jennifer met with Willie on a weekly basis to talk it through with him. "Willie, this can't keep happening, and I know you don't want it to keep happening. The gardeners are afraid of you, and the staff is becoming afraid of you, too." When she said this, Jennifer thought of Deb, who had expressed fear of Willie's outbursts, which had happened in the office as well. Angry about something, one day he had thrown a chair across the room.

"I know that losing L'Tayna was devastating—I can't imagine," said Jennifer, with tears in her eyes. "But you desperately need professional help. We can't have you out in the community acting like this." Willie hung his head, apologized, and yet his behavior continued. Manny talked to him, too, both at work and at his house, but Willie's behavior did not change. Jennifer was beside herself. She loved Willie, yet she could not stand by and watch him destroy BUG's good work in the community.

Case Questions

1. What should Jennifer do now?

   a. What are the ethical and legal choices she faces?

      i. Should she put Willie on probation? If so, what are the steps to doing so?

      ii. Can she mandate Willie attend counseling?

      iii. Can, and should, she fire Willie? If she should fire Willie, on what grounds?

      iv. What kinds of policies can an organization put into place to address emergency leave?

      v. What kinds of policies can an organization put into place to address issues pertaining to employee conduct?

2. What actions should Jennifer take regarding BUG's relationship with the community gardeners?

3. Should Jennifer discuss this matter with the board and involve them in her decision about how to handle the situation? Why, or why not?

4. What policy changes, if any, should BUG make?

5. What are the ethical dimensions of smaller nonprofits implementing flexible employment policies?

EMPLOYEE SUBSTANCE ABUSE: THE UNEXPECTED TRUTH

It was a winter for the record books. The snow started to fall well before Thanksgiving, and by early February, it seemed like it would never stop. Cold and snow were second nature to everyone in the Tri-City area, but this winter's weather had been punishingly cruel. As a result, the strain on the Tri-City Community Action Agency's Low-Income Home Energy Assistance Program (LIHEAP) was extreme. The agency was deluged by a never-ending parade of stress and anxiety in the form of applicants who were desperate for funding to heat their homes. The stories they shared with the case managers were almost unimaginably sad as low-income families, the elderly, and disabled struggled to make impossible choices between food, rent, and fuel.

Soledad (Sol) Delgado thought she was prepared to handle the pressure when she accepted the job the previous summer as program director for Tri-City's LIHEAP as well as its weatherization unit (the latter provided free energy insulation and weather stripping to income-eligible households). A newly minted social worker with a graduate degree, she had worked previously in more junior management roles at other human service agencies. This was a major promotion for her (she had been featured in the university's alumni magazine) and one that she was eager to take on.

During her first day on the job, she was introduced to her deputy managers, Jack Marcum and Eileen Kaufman. Jack had been with the agency for almost 2 decades and was an expert on LIHEAP. He had applied for Sol's job but was not offered it because he did not have a college degree. He was, nevertheless, extremely gracious and welcoming to Sol. Eileen had been with Tri-City for 11 years. She was hospitable to Sol yet also came across as being slightly aloof. She looked tense and had a constant habit of chewing mints.

Jack and Eileen were in lateral roles, where he had primary responsibility for directly supervising the work of the weatherization teams, while she had primary responsibility for overseeing the LIHEAP intake operations and application processing. It was clear that Jack and Eileen were dedicated to doing all they could to meet the needs of Tri-City's clients.

They were compassionate, well-organized, respected by the staff they supervised, and professional in their approach to the job.

Jack and Eileen were both significantly older than Sol (he was old enough to be her father). Regardless of this age difference, they treated her with the utmost respect and were eager to talk through and adopt the suggestions she made for streamlining how the waiting room functioned and how applications were processed. She also worked with them on developing a new plan for strengthening the outreach activities of both programs to ensure that those most in need, such as homebound seniors and disabled residents, were reached. Sol had tremendous appreciation for their skills and experience; however, she recognized that she would have to work on getting each of them up-to-speed on their computer skills as both preferred and were in the habit of recording things in a handwritten notebook before typing their reports into a computer. They insisted they were more comfortable ensuring the accuracy of their numbers using this technique. Given the pressure of the winter months, Sol felt this was something she could tackle with them during the spring and summer.

Sol was intimidated by her direct supervisor, the agency's associate director, Kyle McKinley, who was a retired military commander. He had been with Tri-City for several years and worked closely with the agency's CEO and board. Kyle rarely cracked a smile, requested twice monthly reports on the metrics of both the LIHEAP and weatherization programs, and, when she performed well, simply told Sol that she was meeting his expectations. Sol worked long hours. She was proud of her work and emotionally exhausted by the sense of responsibility she felt toward the clients.

One day when Eileen was out of the office, Kyle requested that Sol immediately bring him a report on the month-to-date LIHEAP numbers. He was scheduled to have a telephone conference that afternoon with the secretary of the state human service agency about the possibility of the state providing emergency funding to support the LIHEAP program when the federal money ran out. Kyle had been keeping a careful eye on Tri-City's LIHEAP allocation and knew that it was likely that the agency would burn through its money sometime within the next few weeks.

Sol asked Mary O'Connor, the department's executive assistant, when Eileen would be back in the office. She was told that Eileen was scheduled to be gone for several hours. Sol then frantically called Eileen's cell phone, which went repeatedly to voice mail. She sent Eileen several text messages, which also went unanswered. In a panic after not being able to reach Eileen for 40 minutes, Sol asked Mary if she knew where Eileen kept her notebook. Mary shrugged and suggested that Sol look through Eileen's desk.

Conscious of the ticking clock, Sol began searching through the Eileen's desk. There were neat piles on top, although none contained the notebook. She then began searching through her desk drawers. When she opened the file drawer on the lower right-hand side, her mouth dropped open: in it was a half-gallon bottle of Vodka that was nearly empty. The mouth of the bottle was smeared with Eileen's lipstick. Suddenly, she understood why Eileen was constantly chewing mints. It all made sense.

Case Questions

1. Describe the ethical dilemmas present in this case.

2. What are the legal rules in your state for treating employees with substance abuse problems?

3. Did Sol have the legal right to search Eileen's desk?

4. What should Sol's next steps be?

5. What actions can a supervisor take, if any, to create a climate of trust between herself and her employees?

VOLUNTEERS IGNORING THE RULES: THERE'S NO PLACE LIKE HOME

Joe Bearpaw had everything going for him. He was distinctively handsome with high cheekbones and a regal nose inherited from his Cherokee ancestors, charming, and smart, having graduated near the top of his law school class. He always had a broad smile, an outstretched hand, and enough energy for two people. Before enrolling in law school, Joe had been a case manager at the Stillwater Homeless Shelter for 5 years. Once he graduated and found his footing with a commercial real estate practice, he joined the board of Stillwater.

Joe and his wife, Patty, were active volunteers at the shelter, serving meals nearly every weekend and spending time with some of the families that temporarily called Stillwater home. Joe used his bar association contacts to secure pro bono representation for Stillwater clients in need of legal assistance and twisted the arms of many colleagues to donate to the agency. He took it upon himself to raise a significant amount of money for the organization to which he added a large check from his personal funds.

Volunteering at Stillwater was an important part of Joe and Patty's lives. They both felt called to help those who were less fortunate. In fact, when Joe joined the board, he said to Tom Hartfield, the executive director, "You know I'll do anything to help Stillwater, Tom, but I don't want to become just a figurehead, fund-raiser, or paper pusher. Both Patty and I want to be engaged on an ongoing basis with the families."

The staff members of Stillwater were less enthusiastic about the couple's volunteerism. While they appreciated the time and caring the Bearpaws dedicated to the clients, the staff members felt like they couldn't set boundaries on Joe and Patty's volunteer efforts in the same way they could with other volunteers. After all, Joe carried the power of the board. The staff whispered among each other that even though Joe had done the same job in the past that rule changes since then had left him out of touch with many of the current protocols that the Stillwater higher-ups required them to follow. They feared saying anything to either Joe or Patty about these issues for fear that Tom would be upset with them for being disrespectful to a board member and important fund-raiser.

One winter, Joe and Patty found themselves in ongoing conversations with a troubled mother and her two children. The mother, Ryann, had struggled with alcohol and substance abuse and, as a result, had lost her job and apartment. The three had lived on the street for almost a year with all of their belongings stuffed into two backpacks until they managed to find their way to Stillwater through the help of a street outreach worker. Throughout it all, Brianne, Ryann's daughter, managed to stay enrolled in high school and took on the caretaker role for her younger brother, Malcom. Her relationship with a trusted cafeteria worker kept her and Malcom from starving.

Each afternoon before 5 p.m., the family lined up with others outside of Stillwater hoping the shelter could offer them a warm, safe place to spend the night. They had been coming there steadily for almost 2 months (families were allowed to stay for 90 days as long as they made progress toward work and savings goals and remained free of alcohol and drugs). Ryann told them she was clean now and used the shelter's job search services to get back on her feet. She had landed some part-time work cleaning motel rooms, had filed for Section 8 housing assistance, and was doing her best to save what little money she had for a down payment on rent for a studio apartment. Stillwater had a matching funds program and would help her with the deposit if she were able to come up with the rent during her 90-day stay at the shelter.

Brianne was 15 and full of anger at her mother. She was angry at not having a permanent place to stay, angry at not having any new clothes that hadn't already been worn by someone else, angry that she had to pack up all of her things every day and hide them in a locker at school, angry she had no privacy, angry she could never sleep past 6 a.m., and angry that she had to watch her little brother, Malcom, after school (he was 5) rather than hang out with her friends and act like a normal kid. She was embarrassed by her mother and ashamed that they lived at Stillwater. She also feared living back on the streets. She couldn't understand why Joe and Patty were so nice to her mother. She thought they treated her mother like she was a responsible adult when Brianne knew that she was just a loser drug addict.

Joe and Patty coached Ryann on how to keep a job and tried to encourage her when she was down. Ryann always thanked them profusely for their help, told them how ashamed she was that she had gotten herself and the kids into this mess, and promised that she would claw her way out of it. Even though it was outside of the rules, Joe was in regular touch with the building management company at his workplace, hoping to find a full-time cleaning job for Ryann. Patty did the same in the building where she worked. They would say to their friends, "It's one thing for an adult to mess up her life with alcohol and drugs; it's something altogether different when she's got two kids that are innocent victims. We want to do everything we can to help this woman for the sake of her children." They agreed between them that they would supplement Ryann's saving account at Stillwater if she couldn't reach the amount required for the match at the end of her 90-day stay.

One weekend, just as Joe and Patty were arriving at Stillwater, they saw Ryann, Brianne, and Malcom on the street. Ryann was sobbing; Brianne looked furious, while Malcom sucked his thumb and looked scared. "What happened?" asked Patty. Brianne responded. "They wouldn't let us in because my stupid mother was partying all afternoon with her druggie friends." "That's not true," sobbed Ryann. "I just had one little drink. I'm a grown woman. I've been working so hard these past few months to keep it all together. I just needed a little comfort, that's all. I'm sorry, baby. Mommy messed up. I promise it won't happen again." "Right," said Brianne.

Joe and Patty looked at each other. The temperature was in the low 40s and dropping. "Where will you go?" asked Joe. Ryann just shrugged through her tears. "Look," said Joe, "we want you to come to our apartment to stay for the next day or so until we can get this situation straightened out with the staff. I know they are very strict about readmitting someone who breaks the rules, and that they have a firm one-strike rule about drinking and drug use, but I'm on the board, so I think that maybe they'll make an exception in your case if I talk directly to Tom." With that, the family piled themselves and their meager belongings into Joe's car and headed for his and Patty's apartment. In the confines of the car, Joe and Patty could smell the strong odor of liquor on Ryann's breath.

Once inside the apartment, Patty showed them to the guest bedroom. It was a large, beautiful room with a queen bed and a luxurious adjacent bathroom. There was a flat-screen TV on the wall above a dresser. She apologized that the family would have to share a bed and pulled out a stack of fluffy towels. "Please feel free to settle in and make yourselves comfortable. Since we weren't expecting you, I'll talk to Joe about ordering out for Chinese food. Would you like that?" said Patty. They nodded almost in unison. "That would be very nice, Mrs. Bearpaw" said Ryann. After she closed the door, Brianne said in a whisper, "Wow, this place is like something out of a magazine. They must be rich."

Down the hallway and out of earshot of the family, Patty whispered to Joe, "Are you sure you know what you're doing? What if Tom won't take them back? Then what?" "Don't worry," he said. "I've known Tom for over a dozen years. He's a good guy, I'm on the board, and I raise a lot of money for them. I'll give him a call after dinner."

Case Questions

1. If you were Tom, what would you do when you received Joe's phone call to take the family back?

2. What policies, if any, should be in place to distinguish board members from other volunteers?

3. What policies, if any, should be in place to distinguish donor-volunteers from other volunteers?

4. What could Stillwater have done, if anything, to prevent this type of situation from occurring?

5. What volunteer management policies and codes of conduct would you recommend be adopted by nonprofit organizations?

WHEN VOLUNTEERS RUN AMOK: NEEDLING THE PRESS

Angie Fong held her head in her hands. She had no idea how something as simple as a beach cleanup could have morphed into something so wrong that it now jeopardized her long-standing relationship with City Councilman Dan Melgoza. She had worked hard to build a positive reputation for Coast First and now wasn't sure how it could recover from this debacle.

Coast First was an 8-year-old organization that was founded with the simple straightforward mission of protecting the coastline. Its work was carried out through three main areas: advocacy for clean oceans and beaches that protect the health of people and sea life, environmental education to ensure current and future generations understand the value of the ocean, and community outreach to engage people of all ages in this important work.

In its early years, Coast First was an all-volunteer organization that made its mark by successfully advocating for the state to establish a system of regularly testing the quality of ocean waters along the entire coastline in order to protect beachgoers from pollution-related illnesses. It was a simple idea born out of a rash of illnesses experienced by beachgoers (among them Angie and her family) that brought almost immediate respect and visibility to the fledgling organization. Soon after, Coast First launched a twice yearly volunteer beach cleanup that had grown over the years from 200 volunteers to almost 20,000 people across the state. Coast First's educational programs for students in Grades 1 through 3 were launched 4 years later in collaboration with the local school district. It had recently produced a well-respected environmental curriculum for Grades 6 through 8 that was being considered by many school districts throughout the state.

Grant money from the city, state, and private foundations along with organizational memberships and general donations had allowed Coast First to expand its staff over the years to encompass a small team of four that was led by Angie. These included a scientist-advocate, an attorney, a director of instruction, and an education specialist. The staff worked long hours, without complaint, for low pay and felt privileged to be working for such a noble cause.

Because it was such a lean operation, volunteers were vital to the organization's efforts. Volunteers were active in a variety of roles that included, for example, working alongside public officials to monitor water conditions, creating materials for advocacy campaigns and mobilizing the Coast First network to weigh in with their elected officials on pending legislation, serving as instructional aids in schools using the Coast First curriculum, and organizing beach cleanups throughout the state (the largest of which occurred closest to the Coast First small headquarters). The Coast First offices were always a beehive of activity; walking in one would never guess that the organization had only five paid staff.

The largest semiannual beach cleanup was headed by Leslie Hennessey, a retired police officer. Leslie was extremely organized: she orchestrated the event by assigning five volunteers to be lieutenants who each handled a separate area of the beach and a separate crew of volunteers. The lieutenants—all but one of whom had served in this volunteer capacity previously—had instructions about how to sort through the found materials (by organic and inorganic matter, of which hazardous material was a subcategory). They were provided with special t-shirts that signified they were lead volunteers, instruction sheets for training volunteers in the handling of the materials, as well as ample plastic bags and gloves, hand sanitizer, and sunscreen.

The event provided public officials with an excellent press opportunity. Dan Melzoga, the city councilman who represented the district in which the beach was located, played a prominent role in greeting the volunteers and formally kicking off the event. Dan had been a founding board member of Coast First, and it was not coincidental that he originally ran for his city council seat on an environmental platform. He made sure that Coast First received a large annual block grant and had helped the organization negotiate its education program contract with the school district where he had many friends. Dan was planning to announce his intention to run for mayor the following week and saw a natural constituency of potential voters among the Coast First volunteers. This was important since he was known for pushing through legislation that was left of center and more controversial than what was supported by the current mayor.

The day was blustery yet sunny as hundreds of volunteers fanned out across the enormous expanse of beach to begin their work. This particular cleanup took place each July 5 with volunteers stepping up to the task of reclaiming the beach from hordes of partygoers who always seemed to leave a trail of trash behind. The usual array of TV cameras came to record the event. It was a classic shot of the community in action with dots of people spread across miles of sand doing public good.

Everything was proceeding as planned until a volunteer was tapped for an interview by News 8. "Tell me," said Amy Millis, holding a microphone up to Robert Burger, a volunteer, "what brings you here today, and what kind of trash are you finding?" "I'm here," replied Robert, "because I believe that we need to keep the beaches safe for our families. I've been volunteering for this cleanup for years, but I've never seen so many hypodermic needles as what I've seen today. It's got to be because the city passed that needle exchange program. It's ruining our beach, and its endangering our kids. What if one of them got stuck with one of those needles? If the city does stupid things and won't protect us, we citizens have to protect ourselves."

With that, the story ceased to be about the work of Coast First and became focused on the needle exchange program that had been pushed through on a controversial 5–4 vote by none other than Dan Melgoza. All of the TV stations picked up the story and ran the clip on their teaser for the evening news. A reporter from *The Herald* contacted Robert for a more in-depth interview and posted the story at the top fold of the morning paper; it was a headline in the online version.

Dan called Angie in a rage. "What the hell, Angie? With all that I've done for you, you can't figure out a way to control your volunteers? Do you know who that Robert Burger is? He's a so-called citizen activist who has been trying to torpedo the needle exchange program since before it started. He just used the cleanup as an excuse to bash me in the press."

"I'm so sorry," lamented Angie. "I had no idea. Not only did he bash you; he also took away the positive momentum we needed from the event. We always attract a lot of donors after these cleanups, and now I'm afraid that no one will be paying attention to us because they'll be focused on . . . other things." "I realize that," said Dan. "And I also realize that when it comes time to advocate for funding for Coast First that

I may have to be focused on other things as well." With that, he hung up the phone.

Case Questions

1. What are the benefits and risks that nonprofit organizations encounter when they engage with volunteers?

2. What types of safeguards can nonprofits put into place to mitigate the risks you outlined?

3. When, if ever, is it necessary for a nonprofit to have a professional volunteer manager on staff?

4. What basic policies and procedures should nonprofits have in place to handle volunteers? Is it realistic for a nonprofit to prohibit volunteers from speaking to the press?

7

Risk Management

INTRODUCTION

Individuals who seek to manage and lead nonprofit organizations assume great responsibility and must be adequately prepared to protect their organizations from unforeseen harm. Lacking extrasensory perception or a crystal ball to perfectly predict the future, nonprofit leaders must work diligently to plan for and minimize potential risks to their organizations. Beyond protecting a nonprofit from potential lawsuits, good risk management practices enable nonprofits to stay focused on their services and delivery of their mission and ultimately to maintain the public's trust.

The Nonprofit Risk Management Center (2015) defines risk management as "a discipline that can help you understand the risks you face, modify your behavior accordingly, and prepare your nonprofit to thrive in an uncertain future." In nonprofit organizations, risk management most often entails having the proper policies and procedures in place to manage finances, employees, volunteers, and clients and to ensure the proper governance of the nonprofit. Additionally, nonprofits that serve vulnerable populations, such as youth, the elderly, and individuals with developmental disabilities, must actively manage unique risks associated with working with people who cannot always speak for themselves.

Who should be involved in risk management at a nonprofit, and what should they do? Melanie Herman (2011) suggests creating a risk management committee consisting of individuals with knowledge about the day-to-day risks faced by the organizations, as well as financial and legal knowledge, and volunteers who express an interest in safety or liability issues. Following this model, the committee will likely be composed of staff members (if there are paid staff in the organization), outside professionals, and board members.

The Public Counsel Law Center (n.d.) identifies three steps to active risk management in a nonprofit organization:

1. Assess Risk

The basic task of risk assessment is to identify all the actions and relationships of a nonprofit organization that possibly could go wrong. Begin by considering all of the actions that your organization must perform in order to carry out its mission. Within all of your organization's actions, there exists the possibility that an unplanned event or error may occur that could put your resources and assets in jeopardy. In other words, think of what would constitute a "really bad day."

2. Mitigate Risk

Focus on the actions that need to be taken to prevent accidents from happening and to diminish the potential of future losses. A risk mitigation strategy should include both physical precautions and administrative procedures that a nonprofit organization can take to reduce its exposure to risk.

3. Insure Against Risk

All the planning in the world will not prevent every potential risk. Therefore, nonprofits must procure insurance to transfer the organization's risk of loss to the insurance carrier. However, not all risks can be insured, and not all policies fully cover every scenario. Therefore, what to insure and how much to spend on insurance are important decisions that nonprofit managers and board members must make together.

The cases presented in this chapter explore the discipline of risk management related to the following:

1. Stolen information

2. Theft

3. Protecting vulnerable clients

4. Workplace accidents

REFERENCES

Nonprofit Risk Management Center. (2015). *What is risk?* Retrieved from http://www.nonprofitrisk.org/about/mission.shtml

Herman, M. (2011). Risk Management. In D. O. Renz (Ed.), *The Jossey-Bass handbook of nonprofit leadership and management* (2nd ed.). San Francisco, CA: Jossey-Bass.

The Public Counsel Law Center. (n.d.). *A nonprofit's guide to risk management and insurance*. Los Angeles, CA: Author. Retrieved from http://www.public counsel.org/tools/publications/files/risk_management.pdf

STOLEN INFORMATION: THE WRONG KIND OF DATA DUMP

Susan McCarty was frantic. She couldn't believe this was happening to her, and she wasn't sure what to do next—call the police, call her boss, or submit her resignation?

Susan was the director of early childhood for the Lincoln River Head Start program, a job she had held for almost 4 years. She loved the Head Start program and everything it represented. At one time, she had been a Head Start parent following a bitter divorce that left her to raise her twin toddlers alone with meager resources. Those twins were now sophomores in high school and doing well academically. Head Start had not only been a lifesaver for her at a time when she desperately needed support; it had provided her children with an excellent educational foundation.

The Lincoln River Head Start program was located in the heart of a formerly middle-class community that had become economically depressed over time as manufacturing jobs disappeared from the area. The program served the needs of 181 children and their families with a wide variety of literacy, nutrition, and social service programs. She was particularly proud of the parenting classes offered by the program as she believed they provided parents with important tools and confidence for supporting their children's education. The food and nutrition program was also extremely important for many of these families who struggled to put groceries on the table.

As director, Susan was responsible for supervising the staff, marketing the program, fiscal reporting and tracking to ensure programmatic compliance with state and federal laws, and for ensuring the curriculum and ancillary programs were innovative while meeting core Head Start standards. Among these responsibilities, she felt that her most important role was being a warm and friendly presence for parents and children in need. Mary Kelly, one of Head Start's lead teachers, often remarked, "Susan, you have a gift for sniffing out parents and kids who are in trouble. You're a magnet for them when they need something." It was true. Parents would find their way to Susan's office to confide in her about domestic violence at home, a crisis that was preventing them from being able to pay their heating bill, or a behavioral question about their children. Invariably, she was able to find a way to help them with resources that were available through her program or through the Lincoln River Family Center, the parent agency for the Head Start Program.

Her work required Susan to juggle these many different roles and tasks. Adding to the complexity, a new partnership with the school district now resulted in yet another task: Susan had to pass along the children's personal information so that they could be assigned student identifier numbers. An identifier number would stay with a student throughout their K–12 education and, in this case, would be used to track the academic success of Head Start students relative to their counterparts that did not participate in the program. Other state studies had demonstrated significant positive differences in the academic achievements of Head Start students compared to those that had not been in the program, which made Susan eager to participate in this endeavor. As applications for the program were submitted on paper, it was up to Susan and the enrollment manager to make sure that all of the data were inputted correctly.

The first time these forms were submitted to the school district, there had been an error on Social Security numbers for two children (in each case, two numbers had been transposed). The error caused an enormous scramble to correct the information in order to clear those names. From that experience, Susan decided that she needed to double-check each form that was put into the computer.

Although Susan was known for having great attention to detail, the sheer volume of work that was on her desk was overwhelming. She had recently returned from a Head Start conference in Washington, DC, that had put her even further behind. To add to the stress, two separate parents had approached her with emergency domestic violence problems that required immediate attention, and the quarterly report to the state on Head Start enrollment was due the next day. Despite a series of early mornings and late nights, she couldn't seem to get everything done.

One evening at 7 p.m., her daughter called Susan at the office. "Mom, we're starving, and there's nothing to eat in the house. This is the fourth night in a row that you've been working late. Can't you come home now?" she whined. Susan sighed on the other end of the line. "I'm sorry, sweetheart. I'll leave right now and stop off at Pino's to pick up a pizza. How does that sound?" "Great!!! Can you *pleeease* get extra pepperoni? Thanks, Mom," came the reply.

Feeling as if she had no choice, Susan threw her laptop and a stack of intake forms into her briefcase and walked out the door. She would work late at home, but at least the girls would be fed and she could spend a little quality time with them. Between the early mornings, late nights, and the Head Start conference, she hadn't seen much of them lately. She felt guilty about spending so much time away from home and missed hanging out with them.

As she walked out of the office, she called in her order to Pino's so that it would be waiting for her when she arrived at the shop. She hopped out of her car, chatted with Pino for a minute, and headed home. The odor in the car smelled delicious and made her stomach growl. She couldn't wait to share the pizza with the girls.

When Susan arrived at her house, she held the pizza with one hand as she opened the back door of the car to grab her briefcase. It was then that she noticed it was gone. She gasped as she recalled the stack of application forms that were in the bag and went into a complete panic when she realized that the computer wasn't password protected. The spreadsheet containing the information on all of the Head Start families had been left wide open.

Case Questions

1. What is at risk for the agency?

2. What policies should the agency have had in place regarding sensitive data and computers?

3. How do limited resources inform risk management decisions (or do they)?

4. What should Susan do now?

5. How should the agency respond to the theft?

6. What responsibility does agency leadership have to help promote a healthy work–life balance among its employees?

THEFT: TOO MANY COOKS IN THE KITCHEN

Dawn Alexander was one of those people everybody loved. She was active in her church, a longtime treasurer of the Rotary Club, and the bookkeeper for Maynard Meals on Wheels. Although she never married, people tended to think of Dawn as a grandmotherly figure. She was always smiling, ready for a hug, and the first to volunteer for a good cause. Every year, Dawn led the town's Christmas toy drive—kicking it off with a huge donation of stuffed animals, games, and other toys that she would purchase with her own money. She was all around Maynard doing one good deed after another and was always humble about her efforts.

When Owen Crane took over as executive director of Maynard Meals on Wheels, he was both excited and worried about the challenges that were ahead of him. Prior to joining the agency, he had been the assistant director of Waldo Senior Services, a nonprofit in a neighboring town that was funded largely through state grants. It was a job he had held for nearly 8 years. When it was announced that Rusty Daniels would be retiring as executive director of Maynard Meals, Owen jumped at chance to become an executive director himself and to lead an organization that was so important to the senior community.

Owen was 36 years old, yet he had always had an affinity for seniors and cared deeply about those who struggled to make ends meet. He knew too that he had big shoes to fill and big challenges ahead: Rusty had led Maynard Meals for almost 25 years, was beloved in the community, and known for operating a well-run compassionate organization. Owen had a lot to live up to in all of those regards, and, in addition, he would need to actively raise money from individual donors, private foundations, and the corporate community, which was something he had never done before.

During his first week at Maynard Meals, Owen had individual meetings with all of the senior staff. He was most nervous about meeting with Dawn because he was anxious to get a handle on the budget and fund-raising needs of the agency. He was immediately reassured by Dawn's warm demeanor. "I can see you're nervous, Owen; please try not to worry." Dawn explained that the $1.9 million budget fit neatly into 8 categories:

$24,000 United Way

$30,000 corporate sponsors (3 banks and LL Bean)

$47,000 private foundation grants (5 different foundations)

$915,000 government grant

$115,000 individual supporters (many small gifts and 4 people considered to be large donors)

$640,000 fee for service (meal sales)

$125,000 special events (primarily the annual dinner dance and awards ceremony)

$10,000 endowment

She said, "I worked with Rusty for 20 of his 25 years here, and I have a pretty good handle on what's what. I'm not planning on going anywhere anytime soon unless God has other plans for me that I don't know about. I'm here to help you as best I can by keeping a close eye on the revenue and expenses. Rusty can fill you in on all of the bigwigs you need to hobnob with to keep money coming in the door." Owen left the meeting feeling reassured and relieved.

Just as Dawn had mentioned, Rusty was eager to meet with Owen to give him the "inside scoop" on all of the major individual and corporate donors that had been supporting Maynard Meals during the past several years. It was clear that Rusty loved the organization and wanted to see Owen succeed. In fact, several months before he stepped down, he arranged for Ruth Rogers, a vice president at United Bank, to take over as treasurer at the next annual meeting which was a few weeks away.

Ruth had been on the board for several years and had a heartfelt connection to the organization. She had worked hard to increase the bank's annual contribution to Maynard Meals and to talk up the gala to her friends and colleagues. At her first meeting with Owen, she said, "I'm a hands-on kind of girl. I like to know the numbers inside and out before I present anything to the board for their approval. I know I haven't officially become the treasurer yet, but I'd like to dig in to see how things work around here." "I appreciate that very much," replied Owen. "I'm sure that Dawn will look forward to working with you and can provide you with whatever data you need."

As promised, Ruth took her job as incoming treasurer seriously, meeting with Dawn and requesting to look at the agency's monthly financial reports for the past year in preparation for her new duties. Sensing something was not right, she then asked Dawn if she could look at the monthly reports going back for the 2 previous years.

"I just don't understand this, Owen," she said. "It seems that our meal preparation costs have increased fairly steadily in each of the past 3 years, while the number of meals we serve has decreased. How can that be when so many people in the community need our help?"

Owen was puzzled by Ruth's findings as they didn't jive with what Rusty had told him about the organization's increasing impact nor with what he had read in Maynard Meals annual reports for previous years. Each of those reports claimed that more seniors and disabled community members had been served that year than the year before. "Let me talk to the head chef about food costs and talk to Maya Rose, who oversees client outreach and intake, about what's happening."

Owen met with the chef, Larry, who assured him that although the price of food was always rising, he had done his best to produce nutritious meals on a modest budget. "Geez, Owen, I'm not sure what you're getting at here. Three years ago it cost me $6.25 per day, and now we're up to $6.50. That doesn't seem too out of line." Owen nodded in agreement.

He then met with Maya Rose, who said, "I don't know where you got those figures from Owen. We have people come and go somewhat— after all, some of our folks do pass away—but our client numbers are growing, not shrinking. We're serving 902 people a day up from 827 people 3 years ago. You can ask Dawn; she has access to all of those records because she needs them for accounting purposes. I'm proud of our outreach, and I know the electronic client log is up to date because I'm compulsive about making sure that we have correct information for everyone we serve. It's even got little notes on each client like 'Mrs. Avery is diabetic and has a fierce dog.' We have to have info, like that in the system so that the volunteers who deliver her meals can double-check the meal type and know to watch out for Hercules, the dog, if it's their first time delivering to her. That dog can be real mean. We don't want volunteers getting hurt, and we don't want Mrs. Avery hurt by getting the wrong food delivered to her."

Before Owen reported back to Ruth on what he had learned from the staff, he spent several late nights plowing through the client logs. What he saw confused him; about 10 to 20 clients per month had their accounts on hold for several weeks at a time (meaning that they temporarily stopped having their meals delivered). Maya had explained during his first days at the organization that clients stopped meal delivery when they went into the hospital or went to visit a relative (although the latter was rare). Having 10 to 20 clients at a time have their accounts on hold didn't seem like a lot on the surface, but each of these clients was on hold for weeks at a time, which was odd. People usually didn't spend a month in the hospital, and these types of people were much too poor to afford a long vacation. Many of them paid for their meals a week at a time in cash that looked like it had been gotten from nooks and crannies behind the sofa or had been stuffed inside a mattress.

Owen then looked at the log that Chef Larry kept with the records of his food orders. Larry was as organized as Maya was, and it was easy to track his food orders going back some time. Sure enough, Larry was telling the truth about his per meal costs.

Owen called Ruth to tell her what he had found and asked her to come into the office after hours to review the records with him. They met the next day. "I just can't believe this is happening, Ruth, but I think Dawn has been stealing money from us for many years now. I dug into the records going back 7 years—I ultimately want to go back as many years as I can; for as long as she's worked here—and each year I've looked at the books, the food costs are recorded as going up while more clients are putting their meals on hold and for longer periods. Many of these clients pay in cash, which would make it easy for someone to pocket the money. It's $6.50 a day for a meal, which if you add it up, comes out to a lot. You figure about $200 per month times 15 or so clients gives you well over $30,000 a year that is missing. When you delve into the books, it looks like this whole thing started a lot smaller and then just got bigger and bigger each year. Looking at the evidence in front of her, Ruth nodded her head in solemn agreement. "I can't believe this. Our sweet little Dawn?"

Case Questions

1. What are the next steps for Owen and Ruth?

2. Assuming Dawn has been stealing money, when and in what sequence should the following people be notified about the situation? How should each be approached?

   a. Board

   b. Staff

   c. Donors

   d. Auditors

   e. Press

   f. Rusty

3. What should the agency do to prevent this type of situation from occurring in the future?

4. What are the ethical responsibilities and risks of not calling the police?

VULNERABLE POPULATIONS: ELDER HELP OR ELDER HARM?

Madeline Fenske had been coming to Mountain View Community Center since she was a little girl. In her youth, Madeline participated in a choir group and Girl Scouts that held their meetings in rooms provided by the center. When she raised her twin daughters, Sydney and Shelby, she frequented the center to attend their various club and sporting events as well. Widowed at age 62, Madeline again found herself spending many hours at Mountain View, first attending a grief support group and, later, when she was ready, enrolling in many of the enrichment courses offered at Mountain View. Along with some of her dearest friends, Madeline took courses in cooking, Tai Chi, and watercolor painting. She and her friend, Delores, especially enjoyed taking a computer course where they learned the ins and outs of Facebook. "Now I can really see what my grandkids are up to," Madeline said to Delores and giggled.

"Are you kidding me? This is just too much sharing," Delores replied.

"Oh, Delores, it's easier for you." Madeline smiled. "Your kids and their kids live right down the street . . . you see them all the time. My girls are so busy with their lives. they haven't been home in ages. They're so far away. We talk on the phone when we can, but it's not the same."

"I guess you're right." Delores smiled back. "Those girls of yours sure are superstars though, a lawyer and a banker! I know they make you proud," she told Madeline. Privately, Delores did feel a little sorry for Madeline, who had no family left in the area. She and the other ladies in their circle of friends sometimes gossiped about how Sydney and Shelby could do more to connect with their mom.

Although the computer instructor had resumed speaking, Delores leaned in and whispered in a conspiratorial tone, "Yes, but do you think the grandkids will actually *friend* you, their very own grandma?" Delores raised her eyebrows. The two old friends burst into laughter.

"They better, or no birthday money for them!" Madeline exclaimed.

For their part, Sydney and Shelby were relieved to know that their mom had a busy and fulfilling life. They were constantly amazed by the many interests she pursued at the community center. Over the years, they each in their own way had tried to convince Madeline to move closer to them, but Madeline refused to leave her own house and the community she knew and loved. They respected her wish to be on her own.

By the time Madeline turned 85, she found herself alone most of the time. Most of her friends, including Delores, had passed away. The others had moved in with their own children or moved to retirement homes. More than ever, Madeline sought companionship at Mountain View. She especially enjoyed working in the recently revived community garden.

The garden had been the brainchild of Aubrey Germane, an energetic young woman, recently graduated from a nearby liberal arts college. Aubrey had been hired as a program coordinator for Mountain View. While the pay wasn't great, she loved that she was given a lot of responsibility despite being relatively new to the organization. The minute she spied the barren plot of land adjacent to the center's main building, she knew she wanted to start a gardening program. Once she was given the go-ahead, Aubrey enlisted the help of a cadre of volunteers to build planting beds. Before long, the garden was producing enough fresh herbs and vegetables to feed a small army.

Madeline enjoyed working in the garden. Although she didn't get around easily anymore, she spent hours advising from a bench, pointing willing volunteers to all the weeds that needed pulling. She regularly shared her own knowledge of native plants with Aubrey. Before long, they two became very friendly with one another. Aubrey loved hearing Madeline's stories about growing up in Mountain View.

One day, as they were getting ready to leave the garden, Aubrey offered to give Madeline a ride home. "You shouldn't have to wait for the bus; it looks like it's about to rain," Aubrey said.

"Oh, dear, that's too far out of your way," Madeline protested.

"Not at all; it's right on my way home," Aubrey assured her.

For her part, Madeline was happy to get a ride home and equally happy to have a young person in her life. She began riding home regularly with

Aubrey. Before long, they began making a weekly stop at the grocery store so that Aubrey could help Madeline with her grocery shopping. Madeline paid Aubrey gas money for her troubles and always threw in some grocery items for her as well.

At Christmas that year, Madeline gave Aubrey a pair of pearl earrings that had been a gift to her from her late husband. When Aubrey protested, Madeline said, "Don't be silly; look at all you do for me. I know they don't pay you much at the community center, and I know you have all those student loans. You are so good to me, it's the least I can do. Besides, I can't even wear pierced earrings anymore. What good are they to me?"

When Aubrey's own friends commented on how much time she spent with Madeline, she replied, "What can I say, I'm just an old soul, I guess."

By the following spring, Aubrey noticed that Madeline seemed to be losing her memory. She became easily confused, so when they went on their weekly shopping trips, Aubrey began to make more and more of the buying decisions. Following their past practices, Aubrey threw in a few items for herself and considered the costs as an offset for her time and gas money. One day, Madeline asked Aubrey to pay some of her bills. "It's just easier; I can't get all these numbers straight. You can even do it online," she told Aubrey as she gave her the username and password for her bank account.

Toward the end of summer, across the country, Shelby received a call from her twin. "Hey, Shelbs, it's Syd. I think there is something weird going on with Mom. Have you talked to her recently?"

"Ugh, no, I haven't had a chance to call her, and I feel bad," Shelby replied. "We talked a couple of weeks ago, but we just got back from that cruise to Mexico and things have been crazy at my firm. Why, what's up?"

"You might recall that I told you a couple of years ago I talked Mom into giving me joint access to her credit cards and checking account?"

"Yea, sure, I thought it was a great idea. You are the banker after all."

"Well, I check her account from time to time, although not very often to tell you the truth. But, I did yesterday, and I noticed some weird things, so I've been doing a little digging."

"What did you find?" Syd asked.

"For starters, she's ordered a couple of things from Amazon.com and QVC, and we both know she hasn't turned on a computer herself in the last 5 years. Nothing too expensive, but the weird thing is the delivery address is not Mom's. The items have been shipped to the Mountain View Community Center care of a woman named Aubrey Germane."

"Oh, that's the girl that Mom likes so much," Syd replied.

"I know, but sadly that's what has me worried. Maybe Mom likes her *too* much," Shelby replied.

"'Why do you say that?"

"I can see on her account that beginning 3 months ago, there was a recurring $200 payment set up to come out of Mom's account, payable to a federal student loan program. I called Mom to talk to her about it, but she didn't seem to follow what I was saying. Frankly, she seemed really confused. I know we have always let Mom manage her own affairs, and goodness knows she can spend her money however she likes, but now I am worried for a whole bunch of reasons," Shelby said.

Sydney sighed. "Sounds like one of us is going to have to go out there and get to the bottom of this."

"Well, I can tell you the first thing we need to do is set up a meeting with whoever it is that runs that community center."

Case Questions

1. What are the risks to a nonprofit that deals with vulnerable populations such as the elderly?

2. What aspects of a risk management plan should be employed to help prevent a scenario like the one presented in the case?

3. What are the ethical and moral dilemmas presented in the case?

4. Pretend you are the manager of Mountain View, what will you do when you are made aware of the situation?

WORKPLACE ACCIDENTS: A ROUGH RIDE

Esmeralda Hernandez felt passionate about her work with runaway girls. Many of the girls she interacted with found had their way to Athena Youth Services as a direct result of her work on the street outreach team. The team had the difficult job of persuading girls to come off the street and into the safety of their residential program. Some used drugs, all were frightened, and many were literally branded with the name of their pimp. As a whole, they had very little faith in grown-ups, let alone people who worked for a social service agency. It was a process that often took many months of trust building and one that resulted more often than not in failure.

The girls all looked different, but their stories were fairly similar: her home was abusive and dysfunctional, a guy with swagger and money told her he was in love and showered her with flowers and gifts; the romance quickly turned to sporadic abuse and "you'll have sex with other men to prove your love to me." After that came a roller coaster of love and abuse that was used to control her. She was in a constant state of survival that required her to do what was necessary to get her basic needs met.

Despite these sad circumstances, the work was profoundly satisfying for Esmy and her colleagues. To help these girls escape their horrific lives and become who they were meant to be was amazing. She felt honored to have the opportunity to be paid to do this even though her friends and family couldn't understand how she was able to handle the emotional pressures. Esmy would say, "As hard as it is, my feelings and struggles are nothing compared to what these girls go through."

Esmy's unit at Athena offered 20 beds and a specialized alternative school that was exclusively for runaway girls (the agency also provided a wide range of other types of youth services and programming). The girls could stay for up to a year, although, for many, the beginning of their stay involved a seesaw of being in residence, going back on the street, and boomeranging back to Athena until they could trust the staff enough to make a commitment to the program and to a new life for themselves.

In addition to providing housing and school, Athena worked with other agencies to provide the girls with a wide variety of legal, medical, and dental services along with other types of support. Funding for this work came from a variety of federal and state grants, private foundations, and corporations.

The staff became like a second family to the girls, providing them with a caring environment as they transitioned into new lives. Esmy and three others provided case support. The facility was staffed 24 hours (there was a security officer at night), and a case worker was always on call. The staff were provided with cell phones paid for by Athena, and the girls were encouraged to call and text them. Although the staff worked fixed hours as nonexempt employees, it was not unusual for the girls to call them long after they were officially done for the day. Esmy's friends were used to her leaving a bar or restaurant to take a call from a girl who needed to talk. She would always come back saying, "I'm so sorry that I had to leave the table, but this girl was just *desperate* to talk, and it couldn't wait until tomorrow." It was exasperating for them, but that was the price of spending any amount of time with Esmy. She was married to her job.

One night around 10:30 p.m., Esmy got a call from Janelle, a girl who had recently entered the program. It had taken Esmy 7 months to convince Janelle to leave her pimp and come to Athena. She was barely 14 years old and tried to affect an attitude that she thought made her seem tougher and older than her baby face revealed. Although Esmy had worked with a lot of girls during the nearly 3 years she had worked at Athena, there was something about Janelle that tugged at her heart.

"Esmy," Janelle cried into the phone, "there's something real wrong with me. My pee burns real bad, and I'm really in a lot of pain. You gotta help me." Esmy reassured Janelle that she probably had some kind of infection. "You just get some rest tonight," she said. "I promise we'll make an appointment at the clinic first thing tomorrow, and I'll go with you to see the doctor."

The next morning, Esmy called Partners in Community Health to book an appointment for Janelle. She was able to get her in by 10:45 a.m. She then went to the front office to book one of the Athena vans to take Janelle to the appointment. Athena had a van pool that case workers were expected to use to transport the girls to court, medical and dental appointments, and for the rare visit with a family member. It was nice not to have to use her old Toyota to drive the girls around, and this way she didn't have to worry about paying for gas. At 10:25 when she went to pick up the van, the front desk told her they were all still out. "I have no idea why Desiree isn't back yet," the receptionist said. "She was supposed to be here 40 minutes ago, and the other van is out for the day."

Esmy walked back to Athena housing to find Janelle, who was now sobbing uncontrollably with pain and fear. Although she knew it was against the rules, Esmy decided to take Janelle to the clinic in her own car. Afterward, she remembered thinking, "I know I shouldn't be doing this, but I don't have a choice here; she's hysterical and in pain."

As they pulled out of the lot, Esmy assured Janelle that everything would be fine—the doctor would give her the medicine she needed. A few blocks later, out of the corner of her right eye, Esmy glimpsed a minivan running a red light and careening into the passenger side of her car. She looked over to see Janelle covered in blood and screaming.

Case Questions

1. How could Esmy have approached the situation differently?

2. Is she personally liable for what happened?

3. What kind of insurance would the agency typically have, and would it cover this circumstance?

4. What kind of support systems should be available, if any, to staff members, like Esmy, who are working with vulnerable clients?

5. What kinds of systems, policies, and procedures should an agency have in place to deal with these kinds of situations?

6. Was it legal for Esmy to be considered a nonexempt employee?

8

Public Relations and Marketing

INTRODUCTION

A local theater posts a flyer on the community board at the corner coffee shop to announce the opening night performance of their newest play. Mothers Against Drunk Driving (MADD) sponsors a billboard near a large university campus warning against the dangers of driving drunk on graduation night. You receive a Facebook message from a friend encouraging you to join millions of others in taking the Ice Bucket Challenge to support the ALS Association.

While distinct from one another, each of these scenarios provides an example of a variety of marketing activities undertaken by nonprofits. In 2013, the American Marketing Association (2015) approved the following definition of marketing: "Marketing is the activity, set of institutions, and processes for creating, communicating, delivering, and exchanging offerings that have value for customers, clients, partners, and society at large."

Traditional marketing theory identifies four core components that comprise any marketing strategy: price, product, placement, and promotion. These concepts hold true for both for-profit and nonprofit organizations, although the concepts are applied differently depending upon the sector. In addition to the "4Ps," effective marketing requires nonprofit leaders to create a formal marketing plan. To do so, leaders must understand their intended customers (target audience), how to segment their many customers (stakeholders), and then craft appropriate marketing strategies to produce desired outcomes from each of the segmentations. In short, nonprofit leaders must understand the constituents they wish to attract to their organization and why they want to attract them. Reconsider the initial scenarios and how they were intended to create a particular exchange between the nonprofit and the target audience. For example, the theater flyer was designed to sell tickets to the public, the MADD message was intended to change behaviors of young graduates, and the Ice Bucket Challenge was used to solicit donations. Yet, nonprofit marketing is more complex than the one-to-one exchanges described here, because, in each case, the nonprofit is also provided with the opportunity to raise awareness of its mission and promote its own brand. Nonprofits can select from a variety of marketing approaches (e.g., cause-related marketing or corporate sponsorships) and vehicles in which to carry out their marketing strategies (e.g., traditional print media, web-based strategies, or social media).

The most valuable asset a nonprofit owns is its reputation. It is the currency of good will. Therefore, in addition to marketing, nonprofits must actively maintain good public relations (PR). Managing PR entails paying close attention to the perceptions of all audiences, not just targeted audiences or your current customers. All nonprofits need communication policies and plans in place to ensure that messaging to all audiences is consistent. These plans should outline how internal and external communication are handled and by whom.

To consider issues related to nonprofit marketing, this chapter considers the following topics:

1. A change in policy with unforeseen consequences

2. Celebrity endorsements

3. Dealing with the press

4. Regaining relevance when a mission shifts over time

REFERENCES

American Marketing Association. (2015). *About AMA: Definition of marketing*. Retrieved from https://www.ama.org/AboutAMA/Pages/Definition-of-Marketing.aspx

A CHANGE IN POLICY WITH UNFORESEEN CONSEQUENCES: OUR DAILY BREAD

Our Daily Bread was a well-established ecumenical Christian organization dedicated to feeding the poor. What had started nearly 60 years ago through the vision and hard work of Peggy Donoghue, a former nun, had grown into a vast operation of food pantries, home-delivered meals, and senior lunch programs that operated in three New England states. A visitor to its administrative offices in Providence, Rhode Island, was greeted with a large smiling photo of Peggy (who had long since passed away) alongside the elegantly painted watchwords of the organization: "For I was hungry and you gave me food, I was thirsty and you gave me drink, I was a stranger and you welcomed me," Matthew 25:35. These same words were emblazoned on the organization's website and on the back of each business card.

Our Daily Bread was a darling of politicians at all levels who participated in the annual ritual of serving food to clients each Christmas and making sure a photo documented the occasion. The organization received generous financial support from city, state, and federal grants and had deep and long-standing ties to supermarket and restaurant chains. It was also popular with foundations and had a lengthy list of individual donors that provided significant funding at all levels. Our Daily Bread had a five-star rating on Charity Navigator and was known for operating with care and efficiency. Donors at all levels had deep respect for the work of the organization, which was seen as being true to its roots of service and compassion while operating with lean efficiencies.

Several months ago, Bernie Caputo, a long-standing board member and generous donor to the organization, raised the idea of changing the organizations policies to allow for hiring people who are in same-sex marriages. "I know and respect the fact that we are a deeply Christian organization," began Bernie, "but I also know that we are living in the 21st century and that same sex-marriage is legal. Although I never had the opportunity to personally meet Peggy, I feel in my heart that because she was so committed to social justice this is something she would have supported." Bernie's remarks caught Ed Flaherty, the executive director of

Our Daily Bread, by surprise. He knew that Bernie's brother was gay, but he had not had a previous discussion with him about this issue. "Bernie," he replied calmly and professionally, "as with all major decisions we consider at this organization, my recommendation would be that we refer this matter to the personnel committee of the board. Let's ask the group to work with Crystal (the organization's human resources director) and come back to the board with a recommendation.

In the intervening weeks, Crystal met several times with the personnel committee of the board. They included Jane Reinheimer, an employment lawyer; David O'Brien, the board chair who was a longtime volunteer and long-retired corporate executive; and Megan Bright, an Episcopal minister. Jane was typically straightforward. "I see my job as a board member as being someone who can provide the information we need to make an informed legal decision. The facts are that if Our Daily Bread hires anyone who is part of a legally sanctioned marriage, that we must provide employee benefits to that person and his or her family. There would clearly be some bottom-line costs involved with that; however, I do not think that that is the overarching issue for us." Megan responded. "Christian theology is evolving on the issue of same-sex marriage and is, frankly, all over the map. My church sanctions same-sex marriage, but obviously not every church does. Although Our Daily Bread isn't rooted in a single theology, we were founded by someone who was Catholic and saw her work as being part of a calling to Catholic social teachings. I do not know if we would be dishonoring Peggy's memory if we were to move in this direction, although personally I think it's the right thing for us to do." David spoke up. "I knew Peggy, and I feel certain she would have wanted us to do this. She was all about justice."

After many hours of deliberation over a period of weeks, the committee decided to recommend that the organization change its policy to allow people who are in same-sex marriages to be hired. Crystal then brought the issue to the senior management committee, a group that consisted of Ed; Sal Amato, the COO; and Susie Chin, the CFO. At the meeting, Susie asked "Shouldn't we bring Nancy into this conversation? As the director of marketing and development, she, more than anyone, has a pulse on our donor base. It seems to me that a lot of the folks who support us are conservative Catholics and conservative Christians who might not like it if we move in this direction. I know the numbers, Ed, and individual gifts make up about a quarter of our annual operating budget. We can't afford to jeopardize that support over some social statement. We need the money to feed people—that's our bottom line."

Ed responded. "I've worked with this board for 12 years, and I have a strong belief that our job as staff is to yield to their wisdom on these types of matters. Our board reflects our donor community, so if they as a group think we should do this, than I say we should. Let's see how they vote at the meeting." "I'm not sure that's the way to go," said Sal. "I mean, the board is dedicated to our work, but they don't know the ins and outs of our donor community. Personally, I feel more comfortable keeping the policy as is. There's nothing wrong with being gay; it's just that, well, I'm not sure that we want to be an organization that openly *welcomes* gays who are married. I've worked here for 20 years, and that's just not part of our tradition." Ed refused to budge from his position and repeated, "Look, the board's job is to make policy. Our job is to carry it out. We have a board committee that is making this recommendation. If the rest of the board doesn't agree, then that's that. But if they do agree, then we'll implement the policy."

Prior to the board meeting, Sal met with Nancy Donovan, the director of marketing and development, to tell her about the proposal. "You've gotta talk some sense into Ed," he said. "This is a disaster waiting to happen." Nancy agreed and immediately went to Ed to plead her case. Ed listened patiently and then reiterated his thoughts about the role of the board. "If they do vote this in Nance, I'm going to rely on you for a good PR strategy for rolling this out to the public."

The following evening, the board met to discuss the proposal. The discussion was heated and lengthy. The vote to adopt the proposal was eight to three in favor. Tim O'Malley, a longtime board member immediately announced his resignation, saying with disdain that "little children are the ones that suffer when organizations like ours, under the guise of fairness and equality, adopt policies that enshrine a false definition of marriage." He then stormed out of the room.

As she was directed, Nancy prepared a press release and drafted a letter to send to all donors informing them of the decision. Two days later, before the donor letters were mailed, an avalanche of angry mail and telephone calls began overwhelming the organization. The actions of Our Daily Bread were hotly debated on talk radio. The bishop was quoted in the press as characterizing the decision as "supporting sin and sinful behavior."

Although Ed and David tried to respond by publicly stating, "This is simply a decision about whether or not someone is eligible for employment at Our Daily Bread. This is not an endorsement of same-sex marriage," their words were drowned out by a steady drum beat of donors—large and small—who were contacting Our Daily Bread to say they would never donate another cent. Nancy and Sal pleaded with Ed and David. "We have lost 2,000 donors in 2 days!" Nancy cried. "You've put this organization in an impossible situation. This cause is taking up all of our energy and effort when all of our energy and effort *should* be going to feeding people. We can't function with this major distraction."

Faced with the enormity of the enmity and financial loss, David called an emergency meeting of the board, which voted to rescind the decision.

Case Questions

1. Now that Our Daily Bread has rescinded the decision, what should their next course of action be to address the situation with their supporters, detractors, and the broader community?

2. Do you think Ed was correct with his assessment about the role of the board as a policy-making body? What is the "right" balance between board and staff leadership?

3. Do you believe the organization made the right decision to rescind the policy? Why, or why not?

4. What, if anything, could the organization have done to prevent this backlash from the community?

5. What is the best action to take when a nonprofit finds itself the target of a negative press campaign?

CELEBRITY ENDORSEMENTS: A BiG DEAL

Alissa Hanover was bursting with excitement. She couldn't wait to tell her boss, Annie Wu, the news that the Grammy award–winning rapper, BiG $hot (aka Clarence W. Walters), had agreed to be the national spokesman for the Association for Diabetes Prevention and Research. His agent had agreed that BiG $hot would appear in a series of radio and television commercials for the organization, post a video on his website that would be linked to the association's website, and give the keynote address at its major fund-raising event, the annual spring gala.

New to her marketing director's job within the organization, Alissa had convinced the association to seek out a cutting-edge artist who could update the somewhat stodgy image of the organization and, ideally, effectively spread its message to young people who were most at risk for the disease: American Indians and African Americans. With BiG $hot they had scored on both fronts; he was an immensely popular artist who happened to be of mixed African American and Navajo heritage and had a personal connection with the disease; several of his family members had type 2 diabetes.

Securing BiG $hot was a dream come true for the organization and had resulted from Alissa developing a plan with her networked board to find just the right celebrity to represent the Association. The idea to recruit BiG $hot had come from Steven Muller, a board member who was married to a Hollywood agent, Rob Siegelman. Rob represented several major film stars and had met BiG $hot when the artist began transitioning into movies. He knew BiG $hot's agent well and was able to broker the deal for the association after several months of back-and-forth talks.

BiG $hot was sometimes mocked by his fellow rap artists for being a "Disney" rapper, because his lyrics were all about peace, love, family, and fellowship. He even had raps about his wife and children and was known for promoting family values. Although his messages were derided by some rap purists for being "too soft," his brand was wildly popular and made him a perfect fit with the association, which had sought an endorsement from a major star who had wholesome values.

The demographic for his music was young people in their early teens and 20s, which was exactly the group the association needed to reach with their messages about prevention and monitoring.

Annie, who was in her mid-50s, had, of course, heard of BiG $hot but was not familiar with his music or his message. Alissa, who was in her mid-20s, was a huge BiG $hot fan. She felt that securing his endorsement was an important achievement in her budding nonprofit marketing career. Prior to joining the association, she had worked as an associate director of marketing for the Alzheimer's Association and had jumped at the chance to prove her skills as director of marketing for a new cause she cared about so deeply (her sister had type 2 diabetes).

During the next 10 months, Alissa spent hours working with the association's special events manager, Lupe Rodriquez, on coordinating the logistics for the gala with Rob (who served as a liaison between BiG $hot and the organization) and the seven major donors who composed the gala committee, including Steven Muller. The committee was chaired by Robin Levy and Marcus Samuels. Robin was a high-profile socialite; Marcus was chairman and CEO of Edelgas, a well-known multinational corporation (he was the first African American to hold that position). The committee agreed that BiG $hot's video and commercials would be timed to appear right after the gala where, in an impassioned speech, he would announce his commitment to and endorsement of the organization. Rob had worked diligently to leak the news of BiG $hot's involvement to other celebrities and gossip columnists to increase attendance by glitterati at the event. As a result, the event had sold out 1,200 tickets at top prices.

Two days before the event, a story broke about a 15-year-old girl who claimed that she and BiG $hot had been having an affair and that she was pregnant with his baby. She purported to have proof of the affair and said she had gone public because he would not admit the baby was his. BiG $hot denied the allegations but looked shaken and grim in the newscast. He responded with his wife, looking teary-eyed, standing beside him, and gripping his hand tightly. Alissa and Lupe flew into a panic. Annie said grimly, "We must call an emergency meeting of the gala committee to decide what to do."

That same evening, the committee convened. Annie opened the meeting by saying, "You all know why we asked you to come this evening.

We need to make a decision about how to proceed with the gala and, specifically, whether we should disinvite BiG $hot given the recent press coverage. If we decide to go in that direction, we must come up with a substitute keynote speaker ASAP."

Rob responded. "Annie, I think you need to take a deep breath and calm down. This thing will blow over. Who knows anything about this girl? She's probably just some shyster who is trying to take BiG $hot's money. If we disinvite him we, will be dissing him and the enormous commitment he has made to this organization. The package of ads and videos that he has committed to us—and, let me add, has already produced and is prepared to release in 3 days—is worth hundreds of thousands of dollars to say nothing of updating the stale image of this organization. We need to make sure we don't blow this opportunity. I've personally put in hundreds of hours of time to make this happen. If you cancel his appearance, Steven and I will back away from our involvement with the association."

"Now wait a minute, Rob," said Robin. "Threats aren't going to help solve anything. We value all of the work that you've done over these many months and greatly value Steven as a board member. It's just that . . . would it be right for us to have BiG $hot keynote at our gala right *now* given all of the bad publicity that is swirling around him? My concern is that having him at the gala will jeopardize the image of the association."

Annie chimed in. "Personally, I don't think it's a risk we should take."

"I'm surprised at you, Annie," said Marcus. "As a person of color you should be sensitive to the fact that Black men, and in particular, successful Black men, are frequently the subject of slander and other types of unwarranted character attacks. All Black men in America face an onslaught of false judgment every day. As a case in point, my driver told me he was stopped by a cop last Tuesday as he was heading to pick me up because he made a right turn on red. The officer told him that he hadn't come to a full stop before he made the turn. It was purely a case of a Black man driving a fancy car that triggered the officer's actions.

The situation is even more acute for those of us who have achieved success. BiG $hot has made an enormous commitment of time, energy, resources, and good will toward our cause. Just because he's been *accused* of fathering this child doesn't mean that he is indeed the father.

This is simply an accusation at this point. If we alienate him by disinviting him to the event, we will be throwing away all that he has done on our behalf. We are also likely to alienate the coterie of music and film stars he has attracted to our cause. I say we stand firm with BiG $hot."

Nodding his head at Marcus, Steven added, "I have one more point to say on this matter: If one of our American presidents, Bill Clinton, was able to admit that he had an affair while in the White House, I can't see why this allegation against BiG $hot, even if it is true, will adversely impact the association. Men have affairs all the time; it shouldn't be a deal breaker for us. He is hugely popular, and his popularity will carry the day."

"But the girl is only 15," Lupe blurted out.

Alissa's eyes darted back and forth to each face as the conversation became more heated. Landing BiG $hot as a spokesman for the association seemed like such a sure thing. Now she wasn't so sure.

Case Questions

1. Do you think the association should disinvite BiG $hot to speak at the gala and cancel their agreement with him to be a spokesman for the organization? Why, or why not?

2. What could the organization have done, if anything, to protect itself this from this type of situation?

3. If the association decides to terminate its relationship with BiG $hot, how should it proceed? What are the next steps that need to be accomplished within the next 48 hours?

4. What kinds of constituencies, both individual and organizations, would the organization alienate if the association severed its relationship with BiG $hot?

5. Should race be a factor in making this decision?

DEALING WITH THE PRESS: A BOARD NOT ON POINTE

Abigail Burke felt her telephone vibrate in her pocket as she was walking off the airplane from a 3-week European vacation. She juggled her carry-on bags to grab the phone, thinking that it could be a call from her only son who was away at college. "Hello," she said.

"Hello," came the reply. "Is this Mrs. Abigail Burke?" the caller inquired. Abby did not recognize the voice. "This is she. May I ask who is calling please?" "Um, yes, Mrs. Burke, this is Jason Anders with the *Tri-City Tribune*. Sorry for calling out of the blue, but I was wondering if I could ask you a couple of questions related to a breaking story I'm covering about the impending closure of City Ballet?"

Abigail couldn't process what the caller was saying. "I'm sorry," she said. "Could you say that again? I didn't understand you." The reporter repeated his introduction and asked her once again to comment on the announcement that after 30 years in business, the City Ballet would close at the end of its current season.

After hearing the question a second time, Abby's head cleared quickly. "I'm afraid I can't provide any information about such a thing. I am not aware of any plan of that kind."

"Well, can you tell me what was voted on at last night's board of directors meeting? We are hearing that the board officially voted to disband the company at the end of May."

"I actually can't comment," Abby said. "I just flew back to town this very moment. I've been away in Europe for 3 weeks. Have you spoken to the board president, Bill McClelland? Or, the company director, Abram Bessonov? Although I am most sure that your information is incorrect, one of them could surely answer your questions."

"Well, frankly, Mrs. Burke, I started with Mr. McClelland and Mr. Bessonov, but neither has returned my calls as of yet. Your generous support of the company over the years is well known, and your name is on their list of board members on the company's website. Would you like to comment?"

Against her better judgment, Abby continued speaking with the reporter. "To the best of my knowledge, there is no way this company is closing. Sure, fund-raising is a challenge, but we are solvent."

"What about Mr. Bessonov? I hear he was planning to retire soon." Abby responded. "Yes, I believe that is true, but that doesn't mean we are closing; after all, Abram is really the only reason we even have a company. This is his creation; he would never want Tri-City to lose its ballet."

Anders asked, "Can you respond to reports that the board just signed a very lucrative contract with Mr. Bessonov? For about $450,000 a year, according to what I've heard." Although she had not been privy to the details of the actual contract, Abby did her best to respond. She told Anders, "I am sure that sounds like a lot of money to most people, but I believe someone did a salary survey to make sure we are in line with other ballet companies of our size."

"Well it sure seems like a lot of money for a company that is going to have to close its doors," Anders replied. "That remains to be seen," Abby reminded him.

Anders peppered Abby with a couple of follow-up questions. Finally she said, "That's all I can really tell you. I'm tired; I'm literally just walking off a plane, so if you will excuse me, I think you should talk to someone in the office tomorrow morning," she told him.

After hanging up, Abby was in shock. Before returning the phone to her handbag, she looked at the screen and noticed several unread text messages from her close friend and fellow ballet board member, Dana Denardi. The final message read, "Call me as soon as you pick this up! You won't believe what happened at the board last night. We are in BIG trouble." Considering the urgency conveyed in the messages and the unexpected call from the reporter, despite the late hour, Abby dialed her friend's number. Dana picked up on the first ring. "Oh, I am so glad you called!" Dana exclaimed. "I have been trying to reach you all night."

"I'm sorry," Abby said. "I had my phone off for the plane ride and then didn't look at the screen when I turned it back on. The minute I walked off the plane, I was called by a reporter who said the ballet is going to close, and then I saw all your texts. What is going on, Dana?"

Dana explained that the board meeting was attended by 25 of the board's 47 members. Attendance at board meetings had been notoriously poor for some time, and much of the work of the board was handled by the executive committee. She told Abby that Bill McClelland opened the meeting with a report from the executive committee. Bill explained that the executive committee had been struggling for some time to come up with a sustainable strategy to bridge the company's annual $1 million budget gap. "He told us they decided it was unrealistic to continue operating under these conditions, that it is simply too hard to raise that kind of money in Tri-City every year," Dana explained. "He went on to intimate that ballet may be a dying art form."

"What happened then?" Abby asked

"Basically, the exec committee made their case and then put it to us for a vote," Dana explained. She told Abby, "The vote actually carried 26 to 1. It was so nerve wracking, I was the only no vote, Abby. I think if you and others had been there, it might have been different, but it's hard to know."

"That fast? That's unbelievable? What did Abram do?" Abby said, incredulous. "Well that's the strangest part," Dana said. "Closing was apparently his idea, which in some ways is not surprising since he's planning to retire next year anyway. I think he got the executive committee behind him, and next thing you know, we have this vote before us. They made a pretty compelling case. Abram said that it would be better to go out with dignity than to face certain bankruptcy."

"How is that possible? We've had a balanced budget for as long as I can remember, and now we're bankrupt? How does that happen?" Abby asked. "I know," Dana said. "I was sort of speechless."

"Can they even do that? Vote to close the organization, I mean?" Abby asked. "I have no idea, but there was a quorum of the board," Dana answered. "I wonder if anyone in Tri-City will even care," Dana mused.

The next morning when Abby opened her iPad to check the *Tribune* online, she had the answer. The paper featured the closure of the ballet as a front-page story. Unfortunately, throughout the article, the board was painted as a group of out-of-touch country clubbers who bought their board positions (board members were required to donate $20,000 a year to gain a seat on the board) as a way to secure social status in the community. To Abby's dismay, she had several quotes attributed to her throughout the article that seemingly reinforced this characterization. She smacked her hand against her head. "Why did I ever talk to that reporter?" she admonished herself while she read the rest of the article.

The article provided details of Bessenov's employment contract, noting that he was the second-highest paid company director for a ballet of its size. The story also included quotes from City Ballet staff and performers who were outraged that they were not consulted about the decision to close. An anonymous staff member noted that it was convenient that the executive director was the only person who worked in the company with a contract that allowed for long-term severance. The staff member was quoted as saying, "There was no financial incentive for him (Bessonov) to keep it going. If you read his contract, he stands to make more money by closing us down. He'll get a big payout, and the rest of us will be out on the street. A different unnamed source said, "There are so many things we could do to scale back costs, but I think they (the board and Bessonov) want the big traditional ballet and all its associated expenses or nothing at all. There is a lot of personal ego at stake here."

The story also featured Tim Mickell, speaking on behalf of the local performers' union. He said, "The union was never approached about this. We could have worked with management and the board on cost-cutting ideas, but we were never given the chance." There were similar comments from community leaders who were concerned about the potential economic impact associated with closing the company since it also had long-term contracts with the local symphony and its performances brought valuable visitor dollars to local restaurants and hotels.

What was by far the worst aspect of the story, however, were the comments left by readers on the paper's website and on other social media outlets that were quickly piling up and spreading to other social media outlets revealing a deep divide in public opinion.

> Luvmydog: There is a saying "When the going gets tough, the tough get going." Mr. Abram Bressonov, along with the acquiescence of all but one board member, has apparently interpreted "get going" as "throwing in the towel" and leaving, showing that he is decidedly not tough.

Artslover333: Its obvious the board and management never intended to continue as a budget for next season was never put in place. The only thing they got settled was a fat employment contract for Mr. Bressonov. Unfortunately, this is about greed on the part of the executive director.

MisterK: Let City Ballet close before it hemorrhages next season; honoring its contracts—the performing arts will suffer from even lower sustainable business donors if dance companies default on their obligations.

Case Questions

1. What are the critical management decisions presented in the case? Who is responsible for making those decisions in this non-profit? At what points in the process could different decisions have been made?

2. As a board member, what should and shouldn't Abigail have done?

3. Considering the ongoing problems with absenteeism at board meetings, do you think the board of this nonprofit is constructed properly? Aside from establishing a policy, what are some ways to combat absenteeism on a board?

4. What do you think about the way information was shared with the key stakeholders in the case? Could information have been managed differently? If so, how?

5. Assume you are a public relations specialist. Outline a communications plan for City Ballet to manage the public announcement of its closure. Who should speak to the press on behalf of a nonprofit organization?

DEVISING MARKETING STRATEGIES: REGAINING RELEVANCE

Six board members and four executive staff members gathered around a conference table at the monthly meeting of the marketing committee for CHS. The organization had originally been called Crippled Children's Home Society but had changed its name in the 1970s to be merely the initials CHS when the word *crippled* began to be recognized as an offensive term. When the name changed, the logo was kept the same. It depicted a child in a wheelchair.

"You ready to make the report, Dan?" asked Adrienne, the committee chair.

"Sure," replied Dan. "But I'm afraid the news isn't promising."

"Well, we know we have challenges so let's hear it and go from there," Adrienne replied.

Six months prior, Dan, who was the chief development officer for CHS, had been charged with hiring a marketing and branding consulting firm to conduct an assessment of CHS. A once vibrant and highly recognized nonprofit, CHS had a national office headquartered in Washington, D.C., and affiliated chapters in each of the 50 United States. Larger states commonly had multiple affiliates in different counties. Founded in the 1940s, the core mission of CHS had originally been focused on assisting young people, primarily those who had been orphaned and those who had physical disabilities. At that time, it was common to see "CHS Homes for Crippled Children" in major cities across the United States. In alignment with its mission, CHS was a proactive partner in testing and, later, dispensing the polio vaccine.

One way CHS raised awareness and funds was by giving elementary school children across the United States a bright purple box with a slot cut in the top to collect loose change and small donations from their parents and neighbors. This annual event cemented CHS into the minds of children growing up in the 1950s and 1960s, so much so that, when reflecting on their youth, most baby boomers easily and fondly recalled the brightly colored boxes from their youth. This recognition of, and attachment to, CHS created a broad base of support for the organization that lasted for decades. At one point in the mid 1970s, CHS was arguably one of the top 10 most recognized nonprofits in the world, and its brand was considered a household name on par with Coca-Cola or McDonald's.

As the organization evolved, its priorities and strategies changed with the times. CHS no longer housed children in orphanages, and they had long since stopped referring to children with disabilities as *crippled* or *handicapped*. Changing rules at public schools brought an end to the annual fund drive, and the widely recognized purple boxes disappeared. Affiliated chapters were encouraged to develop regional priorities and to develop programs to meet the needs of their local communities. As a result, by the turn of the century, the services provided by CHS varied greatly from one region to another, from providing accessible transportation to educational services to low-cost vaccinations. While affiliates managed their own programming, the national office maintained responsibility for the marketing and the majority of fund-raising. Each year, the CHS deployed a national direct mail campaign and held a prime-time telethon that raised over $20 million dollars.

Despite its longevity and success, as of the end of its most recent fiscal year, CHS had experienced declining revenues for 4 straight years at both its national office and in many of its affiliate chapters. Although CHS had been able to rely on its strong national brand identity to attract generations of donors, the marketing committee intuitively suspected that the organization was somehow losing its relevancy.

Dan cleared his throat and began to make his report. "As you can see from the executive summary, the consulting firm conducted a fair amount of focus groups as well as phone and online surveys covering every region where we have a chapter. Basically, their findings confirm our suspicions; we are trying to reach too many people, and our brand image doesn't resonate with people the same as it did in the past. According to this report, younger people don't associate our logo with a specific cause. Hard to believe, but the CHS name doesn't mean *anything* to some people anymore. Furthermore, they found that our messaging is inconsistent, lacks inspiration, and means different things to different people."

"Oh, is that all?" Adrienne said with more than a hint of sarcasm in her voice.

"Unfortunately not," Dan continued. "Some of our regions have gotten quite good at developing messages about specific programs, but the consultants feel like this is preventing us from crafting and promoting a consistent national message for the organization as a whole. We do so many different things, it's causing confusion in the mind of the public."

Marianne, the director of membership who was charged with affiliate relations and general coordination said, "Well, what do they think we should do, try to reign them all in and get them to follow our lead? That will never fly; the chapters have too much autonomy. It's not our culture, not in our DNA, if you will." There were nods of consensus around the table.

"Do they make any specific recommendations?" Adrienne asked.

"They have a couple of broad suggestions for us to consider initially and then, based on what we are amenable to, they can develop more detailed plans," Dan replied. "You might want to brace yourselves, because some of these ideas might seem a little radical." Dan saw that all the members of the committee leaned forward in their chairs.

"First of all, and this is likely the most controversial of their ideas, they recommend we consider a name change." Dan leaned back in his chair and crossed his arms in front of his face to ward of the onslaught he knew was coming.

"What?" several committee members said in unison. "Impossible! Not going to happen," were some of the other responses hurled Dan's way.

Adrienne frowned slightly. "That's a tough one to swallow. How do you change a name and a logo that has been around for almost 80 years?" she asked.

"I think that's the point they want us to consider; people don't know us anymore. We are kind of like a dinosaur out there. They think we need to make ourselves more relevant to today's donors," Dan replied.

"Well, do they have any other ideas for how to go about that?" Marianne asked.

"They think we need to break with tradition, get away from mass direct mail marketing and the telethon, and really create some directed messaging for specific audiences," Dan said.

"Why would we give up our biggest fund-raisers?" asked Marianne. "I hate to be negative, but I feel like these people don't understand us or what we are about."

"I don't think they want us to give them up entirely, just consider rethinking our marketing approach. We need to work out ways to connect more personally with donors," Dan suggested. "Based on the data and comments we have from the market research, I would say I have to agree. Our current approach causes us to think about donors as numbers or widgets, not as individuals. We just aren't connecting with people in a way that inspires them or engenders the trust and dedication that CHS enjoyed with our parent's generation."

Case Questions

1. Assess the case using the 4Ps of marketing. What are the elements of price, product, placement, and promotion that need to be considered?

2. What are the key components of a marketing plan that the committee needs to consider? Develop specific strategies for CHS to pursue to market themselves to younger donors.

3. Should CHS consider changing its name? Why, or why not?

4. Are there specific marketing approaches you would consider? Justify your answer.

9

Generating Revenue

INTRODUCTION

When asked where nonprofits get their money, most individuals will say "from donations." However, research on the sector shows that three quarters of nonprofit revenue is actually derived from fees for service. Fees for service are generated when, for example, someone buys a ticket to museum, pays a fee to join Girl Scouts, or writes a check for college tuition at a private university. Government also funds fees for services (and separately makes grants to fund nonprofit programs). For instance, government fee for service subsidizes health care through Medicare and Medicaid payments and child care through Head Start. Figure 9.1 shows the primary ways that nonprofits generate revenue. However, as Figure 9.2 shows, these proportions change depending on the kind and type of nonprofit. As the figures indicate, generating revenue entails both philanthropic fund-raising and earned income strategies at least to some degree. Some, but not all, nonprofits will also generate revenue from investments and endowment funds.

Figure 9.1.   Sources of Nonprofit Revenue

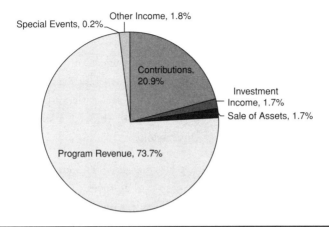

SOURCE: The Urban Institute, NCCS Core File (Public Charities, circa 2012). National Center for Charitable Statistics, nccsweb.urban.org.

Figure 9.2.   Sources of Nonprofit Revenue by Major Subsector

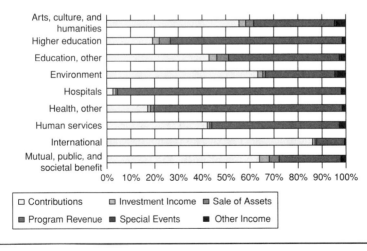

SOURCE: The Urban Institute, NCCS Core File (Public Charities, circa 2012) National Center for Charitable Statistics, nccsweb.urban.org.

Philanthropic fund-raising is the act of soliciting funds from individuals, foundations, and corporations. Successful fund-raising strategies address the unique needs and motivations of each of these entities. For example, an individual may be moved to make a donation to a nonprofit to which he or she is connected in some way, as in the case of a cancer survivor making a donation to the American Cancer Society. A corporate donor, on the other hand, may make donations to causes that are aligned with his or her business objectives. Foundations may have specific giving guidelines set forth in their own missions.

The process of fund-raising is well studied, and careful planning and thought should be given to each step of the process. There are legal and ethical elements of fund-raising that leaders must attend to as well. For instance, nonprofits should be able to discern the intent of the gift and make sure that it is used for those expressed purposes. Establishing formal processes for accepting gifts and using donated funds helps to ensure integrity and transparency in the fund-raising process. Additionally, the amount of money spent on fund-raising should be monitored to ensure that fund-raising activities are reasonably efficient.

In an effort to develop sustainable sources of revenue, nonprofit leaders are increasingly looking to develop or enhance their ability to earn income. Although nonprofits are constantly developing new and creative sources of revenue, earned income is derived, generally, through partnerships with corporations and business ventures. Similar to philanthropic fund-raising, generating earned income requires careful planning. Selecting appropriate partners and crafting well-researched business plans are critical to success. Ultimately, nonprofit leaders must effectively evaluate each opportunity and understand its impact on the organization, its stakeholders, and overall mission. The cases presented in this chapter explore the complexity of revenue generation related to the following issues:

1. Donor management

2. Endowments

3. Fund-raising costs

DONOR MANAGEMENT: THE BIG GIFT

Tina Argosian couldn't believe what she had gotten herself into. The Little Theater that Could (TLtC)—the youth theater company she founded 7 years ago—found itself in a situation that she couldn't have imagined several months ago.

Tina began her career in Chicago where, for many years, she performed as an actor at several well-known community theaters. She moved from Chicago after she married Jeff, leaving her career behind to start a family. Watching her kids grow gave Tina the idea of starting a theater company with a mission to foster creativity, self-esteem, and social confidence in youth between 5 and 18 years old through the performing arts. TLtC offered a variety of classes in acting and play production that were age appropriate. It hosted four sold-out productions per year attended by the family and friends of the student actors as well as members of the public.

Tina loved her work. She worked long hours but was thrilled to be doing something that incorporated her life's greatest passions—her children and theater. She also enjoyed being in the limelight as the head of a small but popular theater company. She was often sought after for her advice on community issues and quoted in the local paper. Jeff was proud of his wife and awed by her dedication to TLtC.

TLtC rented office, workshop, and performance space at a performing arts center that housed several other community theater companies—one that primarily produced new works and was called the 22nd Century Theater and another that focused exclusively on Shakespeare. The directors of the companies worked together on a big annual fund-raiser to support the maintenance of the shared space and occasionally collaborated on programming (recently two of Tina's actors had starring roles in Romeo and Juliet). The theater directors respected one another and got together informally on a monthly basis to talk shop and share ideas. Occasionally, there was some competition for donors and board members, but the missions of their companies were distinct enough to avoid most conflicts. For the first few years of its founding, Tina's company was the smallest of the three, but it grew quickly to be comparable in size to the others.

Six months ago, Marjory Shapiro, who was new to town, approached Tina with an idea. She wanted to sponsor a program where young people would write original works that would be performed at TLtC. As she explained to Tina, "Irving and I have decided that if TLtC would be willing to do this, we would provide you with an $80,000 gift for the program. To our way of thinking, that would cover your expenses for hiring a staff person to manage the project and to produce a play that was written by one of the young playwrights. How does that sound?" Tina was so excited to hear this proposal that it was all she could do to keep herself from jumping in the air and screaming for joy. She told Marjory that she was thrilled with the idea of giving kids an opportunity to develop works of their own and would share the idea with her staff and board.

Moments after the meeting, Tina called Richard Cohen, TLtC's board chair and an attorney for a high-tech company. Richard said, "Wow, Tina, that's pretty amazing. I love that idea. Who is this woman? That's a lot of money. From a mission-related perspective, I think it's right in line with what we're all about, but procedurally we should have a meeting to discuss it so that we can make sure that the board agrees we should go in this direction." After speaking with Richard, Tina ran into the office of LTtC artistic direc-tor, June Peters, to share the news with her. "OMG," said June. "I don't know how you do it, Tina. You're just a magnet for good luck. That kind of programming would really put us on the map and be a great complement to the programs we already run. The kids would love it."

At the board meeting, everyone agreed the idea was a natural fit with TLtC's mission. They were all amazed at their good fortune. Tina put together a committee, staffed by herself and June, that did research on how other theaters operated similar young playwrights programs. They presented their program plan to the board, and it was voted on enthusiastically. Marjory was impressed with the planning work and sent along a check for $40,000 telling Tina that the second part of the gift would be made once the play was selected.

June met with Ricky Edwards, the coordinator of the theater arts program at Monroe high school, to let him know about the competition. At the meeting, he said to June, "I'm not at all surprised that Marjory and Irv gave you that gift. I've had dinner at their house several times since they gave us the money to remodel our theater. It was such a wreck before they rescued us. Now we have new lighting, a new curtain, a new sound booth, a new pulley system—the whole works. Our setup at Monroe is now equal to any major theater in the country. In fact, just today the guys are putting up the new marquee that says 'The Irving and Marjory Shapiro Theatre.' They're great people and great theater lovers, and I'm sure there will be a lot more money for LTtC down the road if this project goes well. I'd love to serve on the play selection committee and will certainly encourage my students to submit work to the competition."

June reported the news back to Tina, who went to work recruiting others members of the committee. They were Richard Cohen; Sarah Calloway, a founding LTtC board member and high-level donor to the organization; and Xavier Figueroa, artistic director of the 22nd Century Theater, which would coproduce the play. June and Tina would serve on the committee as well.

On the closing date for applications, the committee received 42 one-act plays that had been written by local high school and college students (the cutoff age for submitting an entry was 19 years of age). They screened all of the plays against the criteria they had established (including, for example, each play could have no more than five characters, all of whom had to be between the ages of 5 and 18 years old, and the work had to be an original story). Thirty plays met their criteria and were read by the group over a series of weeks to determine which would be selected as finalists.

On the last Sunday in January, the group met around the dining room table at Tina's house to select the winner. Each committee member was instructed to come to the meeting with his or her top three choices. The group would then see how many of those choices they had in common in order to choose a winner. After a spirited discussion, the committee winnowed the field to three choices: Eva Goldstein, Marissa Rodriquez, and James Floyd. Both Eva and James were students at Monroe. James was active in LTtC and had been involved in acting in plays there since the seventh grade. Of the works, Eva's was the most sophisticated and compelling. All agreed she rose to the top as the winner of the competition. Just as the discussion appeared to come to a close, Ricky said "Well, I'm sure her grandparents will be happy about that." "Who are her grandparents?" asked Tina. To which he replied, "Marjory and Irv Shapiro. Didn't you know that?"

Everyone other than Ricky was stunned. Richard was the first to speak. "In that case, I'm not sure we can select her play. It will look like a conflict of interest to people outside of this process. There's no way that the public will be convinced that Eva won it on merit alone. Everyone will think the Shapiro's funded this project to get Eva's play produced."

June spoke up next. "That just doesn't seem fair. She won the competition fair and square. Also, what if Marjory and Irv decide to withhold the second part of their gift if they find out somehow that Eva won, and we didn't produce her play? We might not only jeopardize this gift from them but future gifts as well."

"I have a similar concern to June's," said Xavier. "Our fates here are intertwined since this is planned as a joint production between Little Theater and 22nd Century. If we don't perform Eva's play, future money from the Shapiro's for 22nd Century will be at risk, too. My finances aren't as strong as yours. That's a chance I just can't take. Besides, she won."

Sarah spoke up with some anger in her voice. "As a major donor to Little Theater, I'm troubled by all of this. My children have been in plays you've produced for years. Should I think they got leading roles only because I've been a major donor? Are the children and grandchildren of major donors treated differently from everyone else?"

Tina put her head in her hands. The gift from the Shapiros seemed like such a blessing, and now it was turning into a morass. Each of the concerns being raised was valid, yet she wasn't sure what to do to bring everyone together.

Case Questions

1. What are the underlying reasons for the problem?

2. What next steps would you take to address the situation?

3. How would you propose resolving the conflict within the committee?

4. How would you propose moving forward regarding interacting with the donor?

5. Would you do anything special regarding other major donors?

6. Would you do anything special regarding the wording on your website or with a news story about the event?

7. What are the ethical, legal, organizational, and financial considerations that this situation raises?

8. What types of rules should be developed to ensure fairness and transparency when donors' children are involved? Who should determine those policies?

ENDOWMENTS: TO SPEND NOW OR SAVE FOR A RAINY DAY

Journey Center, a drop-in center for teens aged 13 to18 years old had been operating in the predominately low-income community of Kingston for almost 10 years. The organization was established by members of a church in the neighboring upscale town of Middleton as a separate 501(c)(3) nonprofit with the mission of giving local kids a safe place after school to spend their free time and receive homework assistance, if needed. The majority of funding for the center came through the support of church parishioners in the form of cash donations and fund-raisers held at the church on behalf of Journey Center. The center's founding board was made up of Kingston community members, some of whom were also parishioners.

Journey Center operated out of a rented storefront two blocks away from the local high school. When they first opened the doors, word spread about the center, and before long it was viewed as the "cool" place to hang out. On average, 20 students used the facility every week-day when school was in session. The center was closed on the weekends and during the summer. Brightly painted rooms were filled with a hodgepodge of donated bean bag chairs, board games, and a worn pool table. There were chairs and tables scattered about where students could complete their schoolwork.

The program was run by a part-time executive director, Jorge Partida. Jorge enjoyed the lively chaos that the teens brought to the center and prided himself on knowing all of their names. Jorge carefully monitored every penny of the center's annual $300,000 budget. He employed several part-time staff who, along with volunteers, helped deliver tutoring programs and monitored the teens' activities.

For their part, church members were also very proud of the center they had helped to build. One spring, parishioners and staff were working on the annual giving campaign for the church when Barb Sandke, a longtime parishioner and major donor to the church and the center said, "You know, I've been thinking . . ."

"Oh, that's never good," kidded Mark, her husband.

Everyone smiled. Mark and Barb were a retired couple that did virtually everything together, and most of their spare time was spent on volunteer activities at the church. As a team, they had been quite successful in the real estate market, and in retirement they were more than happy to share their wealth as generous donors to many local causes. Barb swatted Mark's arm and continued. "I'm thinking, we've had such good luck with building our endowment fund here at the church, we should get one going for Journey Center. What if this year we did a special appeal for that along with our regular campaign?" In general, the folks around the table seemed in favor of the idea.

"How much do you think we should shoot for?" asked Father James, the church's long-standing rector.

"I'm thinking maybe $250,000 with the idea that we will build it to $1 million over time," Barb responded. "Then, they can withdraw a certain amount based on the investment returns from the million-dollar corpus every year. It could eventually be enough to cover a large part of the director's salary every year. That should really help them. What do you all think? Having our church endowment has certainly helped us these past few years," she said. "I know it won't cover much right now, but it's enough to give the center a nice financial cushion that they can rely on in the future," Barb added.

"And it's a good way to ensure they stay in business for the long haul," added Mark.

After further discussion, the group decided to add the appeal to their regular fund drive. Parishioners responded favorably to the campaign, and many made gifts to the Journey Center fund in addition to making their annual pledge to the church. Behind the scenes, Mark and Barb also marshalled the resources of several well-heeled church friends, getting each to commit gifts of $10,000. "Nobody is going to want to come to dinner anymore, Mark." Barb laughed. "They know you're going to hit them up for the center."

By the end of the campaign, the church had raised $270,000 to establish an endowment fund at Journey Center. Father James happily presented the check to Journey's board chair, Steve Crawford. "You know, we will keep at this on our end until we reach the million-dollar goal," he assured the entire Journey Center board. And indeed, over the next 2 years, the church added another $85,000 to the fund.

As the Journey Center neared its 13th anniversary, the center's board met for a strategic planning retreat. They began with a report from their executive director. Jorge informed the board that attendance at the center had dropped off sharply. "The kids aren't hanging out with us like they used to," he explained. "They all head to the local coffee shop for the free WiFi. That's what's got their attention now," he reported. "I'd like to propose that we make some investments in infrastructure to get these kids back and to perhaps attract even more. We need to set up some computers, maybe even a mini computer lab. We have to make Journey Center relevant again, and then we can really meet our mission"

The board launched into a lengthy discussion about the idea. Several board members suggested looking for donated equipment. "I just don't think that gets us anywhere," Jorge countered. "I think we need to do it right, get the kids' attention by making the place really nice. We could use some of the endowment money; it's just sitting there doing nothing for us right now."

Sue Shirey, a Journey Center board member and parishioner at the church, raised an objection. "I'm not sure how people at the church will feel about this. When we raised the money, I think everyone thought it was going to be set aside until it reached $1 million, then we would use the annual interest to cover our costs here."

"At the rate we are going with that, we'll all be long gone when we hit $1 million. These kids need our help today. If it's our mission to serve these kids, we need to help them now, not wait till it's too late," Jorge stated. Several board members nodded in agreement. "I would only be comfortable with this if we devise a plan to pay back the fund as soon as possible," said Sue.

"I was thinking that if we use the money now and start attracting more kids, we could build a better case for support and leverage it to raise more money in the future. Then, hopefully, we could pay back the fund," Jorge said. "Think of it more like an investment than a withdrawal."

"OK, I'm convinced," said Casey Ralphs, the board treasurer. "I motion we pull an initial $100,000 from the fund to cover the costs of what Jorge has proposed here," he said. "Then we can reevaluate our position in 6 months." Hearing no objections, the motion passed.

In short order, Jorge's plan was successfully implemented, and the Journey Center was once again a lively teen gathering place. In fact, with the computers, staff at the center began a more in-depth tutoring program. Board members were pleased with the success, and at the 6-month review, they voted to take another $50,000 from the endowment fund to start a music program.

Despite the initial success of the plan, Sue remained uncomfortable with the idea that they were spending down the endowment with no real plan in place for paying it back. She raised the issue with some parishioners who she knew had donated large sums of money to the original campaign, and it did not take long for the word to get back to Mark and Barb.

"I'm dumbfounded," Barb said. "That is *not* what I had in mind when I said we would build an endowment for them. They missed the whole point."

"Not to mention that some of our friends aren't really happy with us right now for twisting their arms to support this." Mark continued. "And, I have no idea if their plans are even sustainable. For all I know, they could be out of business tomorrow, and what would we have to show for it? I don't know why they didn't ask us first."

"It's going to make it seriously difficult to get support for them in the future. People feel duped," Barb added.

The following week, Jorge received a letter signed by 40 "concerned" parishioners admonishing the Journey Center to be more transparent in their financial matters and calling upon them to leave the remaining endowment principal untouched as originally planned and to provide the church with a written plan for repayment of the funds.

Case Questions

1. Should endowments be untouchable, or should they be used as rainy-day funds? Why, or why not?

2. What aspects of donor intent are raised in the case?

3. To whom is the Journey Center board accountable? How should board members prioritize their accountability to the various stakeholders in the case?

4. What policies and procedures should be instituted when an endowment fund is created?

5. Could the center have done anything to mitigate the negative response to spending down the endowment?

ACCOUNTING FOR FUND-RAISING COSTS: HELPING THOSE MOST IN GREED

Years after returning from fighting in Vietnam, Reggie Harley was haunted by memories of the war. It was a secret he carried with him every day. Not even his wife knew that years later he still woke in the middle of the night terrorized by what he had seen decades earlier.

Reggie knew that he had been extraordinarily lucky. He not only returned from Vietnam physically unscathed; he had also been able to blend fairly quickly and easily back into civilian life. His former employer, Liberty Mutual Insurance, had welcomed him back into a managerial position; his wife, Judy, loved him and was enormously relieved to have him back; and his boy was too young to really know that he had been gone. He settled back into the rhythm of suburban life, had two more kids, and continued to rise through the ranks of the company. Given all of that, it came as a great surprise to Judy when 1 week before his retirement, Reggie announced that he planned to start a nonprofit called In Service to Veterans (ISV). He told her he was torn up inside at seeing the lack of support for veterans who had returned from more recent wars in Iraq and Afghanistan, many of whom because of advances in medical technology, had returned with serious wounds and myriad life challenges. He wanted to do something to help these people and saw that he now had the time to do so.

Reggie had never been part of a nonprofit organization before starting ISV; however, he was a supremely confident person. He called a friend of his who was an attorney, who wrote up the incorporation paperwork. He then reached out to two work colleagues, who he knew had connections to military service. Ron Lynch had been a Navy pilot, also in Vietnam, and Sid Burns had served in Desert Storm. They agreed to become the board of directors alongside Reggie who would serve as the unpaid president and CEO of the organization. Reggie's son, Reggie, Jr. (who was known as "G") volunteered to put together the website for them. He was not an expert web master, but he knew enough to create a website that looked professional.

The men met to craft their mission, which was simply to serve individual veterans and their families with resources, referrals, and dignity. They purposely included the word *individual* because they wanted each veteran and his or her family to receive services that were tailored to their particular situation. The idea was to provide personalized assistance, such as helping veterans navigate the Veterans' Administration (VA) system to secure the benefits to which they were entitled, providing funding to retrofit the homes of vets who needed assistive help and purchasing equipment for them such as wheelchairs and scooters, and helping families who were in financial hardship. Each of the guys agreed to chip in $5,000 initially to provide seed funding for supplies and direct services. In addition, Reggie secured a $20,000 gift from The Liberty Mutual foundation. They were determined to keep the organization lean; Reggie would operate out of a spare bedroom in his house, and he would meet veterans in need either at their homes or, failing that, at a coffee shop.

Soon after the organization was established, Ron called the *Gazette,* which agreed to run a story on the organization. It was front-page news featuring a photo of Reggie with the headline "Retired Liberty Mutual Exec Gives Back to Vets." The article lead to an immediate flood of calls from veterans and their families that made Reggie wonder if he knew what he had gotten himself into. "It's incredible," he told Ron and Sid. "People are calling, writing letters, and sending e-mails describing desperate situations. Sometimes I find myself on the phone with one person for well over an hour. I'm going to do my best to help these people, God love them, but making decisions about who to help with how much money and how much of my time isn't going to be easy."

As the weeks went on, Judy worried about Reggie. The work was just consuming him—he wasn't sleeping well, and she just knew that his blood pressure was sky high. She tried to joke that this wasn't how most people approached retirement, but beneath the joke, she was genuinely concerned for his health. It was obvious that he had become completely immersed in other people's problems, and that he was despairing that he didn't have enough money or time to help everyone who had a legitimate need. Every waking hour he was glued to his phone and computer; he was spending hour upon hour answering inquiries, trying to cut through the bureaucracy of the VA, and making little progress. Just as she was about to talk to him about rethinking this project, he came bounding into the living room, "You're not going to believe this, Jude. I just got the most amazing call from a guy who is going to be the answer to our prayers."

Reggie went on to explain that he had spoken with a man named Dennis Kowalski, CEO of a firm called MODO Fund-Raising that specialized in charity solicitations. Kowalski said he had read the story about Reggie in the *Gazette* and thought he could help. "I imagine that you're feeling pretty overwhelmed with requests by this point and aren't sure how on God's green earth you're going to be able to meet all of the demands that are coming your way. My firm is a commercial fund-raising outfit. What we do is work with organizations like yours to take the burden of fund-raising off your back. In fact, many of our client organizations are focused on helping veterans. The clients we serve are located all across the country, and, in fact, that's what makes our outfit so well-known and successful. For example, if you were intending to solicit funds from folks who live out of state, you would have to apply for fund-raising permits in 40 out of 50 states. We take care of all of that so that you can concentrate on the work you need to get done. I'm based in Virginia and will be up in your area next week if you'd like to get together." As he listened to Dennis, a wave of relief flooded over Reggie. He immediately set a date to meet with Dennis the following week.

Reggie arranged for Sid and Ron to be at the meeting to hear Dennis's business proposal. The arrangement he laid out would be as follows: MODO would develop the messaging for all appeals for ISV, including telephone, direct mail, Internet, and other communications (occasionally they produced television commercial for clients if MODO believed the message was selling well with the public). ISV would approve the wording that would be used to raise funds to be sure that it accurately represented the mission and work of the organization. In exchange, MODO would retain 80 cents on every dollar raised.

"Eighty cents seems like a steep fee," said Sid, furrowing his brow. "I know that it seems like quite a bit," replied Dennis. "But the truth of the matter is that none of you guys has the marketing expertise that our team does. We will be able to generate millions of dollars on your behalf, and you pretty much won't need to lift a finger. Wading through the paperwork of 40 state attorney general offices alone is quite a feat, never mind crafting messages that will appeal to the public. As I told

Reggie on the phone, our job is to do the heavy lifting on raising the money so that you guys can focus on getting things done. As I mentioned earlier, I'm also happy to provide a long list of veteran organizations that have used our services so that you can speak directly to them about our success rate. I promise you that if you sign on with us you won't be sorry."

After he left, the three men discussed the proposal. Reggie argued that they should sign the contract. "Look, you guys, we are never going to succeed if we don't have the cash to help people, and we don't have staff, other than me, who can sort through the mountain of requests we're getting and work with people on their issues. I can tell you firsthand that the need is tremendous, and that I can't keep up with the workload even at the small scale we have things at right now. I know MODO would take a big cut off the top, but there's no way that we'd ever come into that kind of cash without them. I also take a lot of comfort knowing that they have seven other prominent veterans' charities as clients. All of us can't be stupid." The others agreed that signing on with MODO was the best way to move forward.

A check and statement from MODO arrived 6 months after the contract was signed. Reggie and the others were amazed. MODO had sent them $200,000! They now had real money that they could use to hire two additional staff people with some left over to help the veterans and their families (Reggie agreed, with prodding from Judy, that he would also take a paycheck). Ron announced that he had found affordable office space that Reggie and the new staff could use that was offered by a close friend who was a Vietnam veteran. They celebrated with high fives and slaps on the back. At the end of the year, a second check arrived from MODO for $427,000. The group was elated.

As time went on, ISV continued to provide funding and referrals to veterans and their families. The two new staffers, Cindi and Andy, worked closely with Reggie to sift through the calls, letters, and e-mails to systematically decide which veterans and their families they were able to assist. They worked with a communications firm to professionalize their website and polish all of the nonprofits collateral materials, bought comfortable office furniture, and established an area of the office that was set aside for client meetings. They all loved their work and felt a strong sense of purpose and dedication. The board continued to meet and was diligent about keeping track of the funds and filing all of their required paperwork. They were proud of what they had been able to accomplish in such a short period of time. They had books filled with heartfelt thank you notes and all had been the recipient of hugs and tears of gratitude for the work of the organization.

Reggie was excited when he was called by a reporter from the *Gazette* who was writing a profile on the organization and wanted to interview him for a story that afternoon. A few minutes into the conversation though, he was startled by the question he was asked: "Mr. Harley, if your organization is doing such a great job, why does it have an 'F' rating from Charity Watch? It appears from your 990 that ISV is only spending 10% of its funds on support for veterans with the other 10% going to administrative expenses and 80% for fund-raising." Reggie's smile disappeared. He began to explain that operating with 20% of what MODO raised was a blessing for ISV, but the reporter just shook his head in disgust.

Case Questions

1. Did Reggie and the other board members do anything wrong when they entered into a contract with MODO?

2. Is it ever reasonable for nonprofit organizations to spend 80% of their revenue on fund-raising expenses?

3. What criteria do Charity Watch, Charity Navigator, and other watchdog organizations use to evaluate the effectiveness of nonprofits? Do you believe these standards are fair and/or accurate?

4. What are the pros and cons of working with a commercial fund-raising firm?

10

Financial Management

INTRODUCTION

It seems fairly obvious to say that leaders entrusted with the fiscal oversight and leadership of a nonprofit organization should have a basic understanding of nonprofit finance. Equally understandable is the fact that unmanaged or unstable finances are a threat to the success of any organization. What is less obvious to some is the extent to which it is imperative to integrate financial strategy with organizational mission and desired outcomes. Any manager would be happy to say, "We have enough money to pay our bills today." However, we would suggest that it is equally, if not more, important for those tasked with setting the strategic direction of the organization to also ask, "Are all the resources of the organization being deployed in a way that helps us to achieve our strategic objectives?" While the first statement demonstrates the basics of good accounting, the second question reflects a more holistic financial leadership approach needed to successfully operate and govern a nonprofit.

Transparency, especially financial transparency, is an important organizational practice for nonprofits. Many think that being transparent simply means making information available to the public. However, nonprofit finance expert Bob Beatty suggests that true transparency is more than a paper blizzard of information. To be transparent, Beatty suggests, requires a sophisticated understanding of goals, success drivers, and progress in an organization and an ability to clearly communicate about the substance of each. To achieve transparency under this definition requires nonprofit leaders to commit to a deeper understanding of the organization's program, fund-raising, and administrative activities (Beatty & Deitrick, 2014). Although financial management is unquestionably important, finance often intimidates even the most savvy nonprofit executives and board members. In an attempt to make financial management accessible to lay people, financial ratios are often used to define financial success or efficiency in a nonprofit.

The following are some common financial ratios used in nonprofit finance:

- Profitability—Does revenue exceed expense?
- Liquidity—How is our cash position compared to organizational need?
- Long-term solvency—What are our net assets?

In addition to ratios, staff189 and board members primarily use the following four reports to monitor the finances of a nonprofit:

- Statement of Financial Position (Balance Sheet)—Describes the capital structure of an organization
- Statement of Activity—Describes the operating structure
- Cash Flow—Describes sources and uses of cash
- Statement of Functional Expense—Details how expenses are allocated to one of three categories: (1) program, (2) fund-raising, and (3) management.

While ratios and financial statements are helpful to understanding aspects of an organization's financial standing and future outlook, they are by definition backward-looking, and, considered on their own or without context, do not provide a comprehensive financial picture of the organization.

Good governance practices, budgeting, and thorough financial policies all contribute to sound financial leadership at a nonprofit. When reporting and communicating about financial matters it is helpful to consider the following questions:

- Who needs what kinds of information and when? For example, board members will require different types of financial data than will be needed by a program manager.
- What kinds of financial controls need to be in place to ensure accountability?
- Who is responsible for creating and implementing budgets? What stakeholders need to be involved in the budgeting process? What criteria should be considered in the developing of a budget?

This chapter explores the financial leadership issues such as the following:

1. Budgeting
2. Misallocation of grant money
3. Transparency

REFERENCES

Beatty, B., & Deitrick, L. (2014, December 5). *Both sides now: How great financial management can connect stakeholders with your mission.* Presentation to the Association of Fundraising Professionals, San Diego, CA.

DECISION MAKING: THE SPOILS OF A BUDGET SURPLUS

Amy Jefferson was enormously relieved. After a long meeting with Tim Schultz, her new finance and operations director, she knew for certain that Jersey County Protects (JCP) would have a budget surplus for the first time in 5 years. "Yep, we're going to be $207,000 in the black going into the new fiscal year" said Tim. "The county contract is back up to full funding, the United Way increased its support by $35,000, the Society of Angels raised its gift to $5,500, and the Jersey County Community Foundation increased its grant by $65,000 and also identified that new donor for us. Profits from our thrift store are pretty much what they were the year before even though they are nowhere near what they were 5 years ago. Still, we can use that money, money from the new donor, and money from our annual dinner to create a nice little cushion for our $1.1 million annual operating budget."

Amy was surprised to feel tears welling up in her eyes. It was the first time in years that she felt assured the agency could meet its mission of protecting victims of domestic violence in their rural county without the having to do it with another round of layoffs. In the 15 years she had served as executive director of JCP, one third of it had been spent struggling to balance the budget without drastically reducing services to people who were in desperate need of help. Sure there had been a series of staff and program cuts over the years, but JCP had gotten through the worst of it, just like the people they served.

During the first few years of the bad economy, when the county, United Way, and the community foundation all reduced their support for the agency, Amy, along with the previous finance director, Camila Torres, made the difficult decision to recommend that the board vote to fully fund their operations using the agency's reserves. They made that recommendation without hesitation, knowing that people's lives depended on JCP. Amy will never forget the meeting when Camila presented those bleak financial statements to the board and together they made an impassioned plea for a vote to use the reserves to fund programs. As John Hughes, a local minister and longtime board member, said at the time, "This is a rainy-day fund, and by God it's pouring out there. Domestic violence has already gotten worse in this bad economy, and we have a moral obligation to do everything in our power to help those folks who need us." The board voted swiftly and unanimously to spend down JCP's safety net. There was enough money to make up for 2 years of cuts, after which time the board and staff were confident the economy would begin to recover.

Two years later, the reserves were gone, and JCP was faced with more difficult decisions as the county announced further cuts to social service programs. The community foundation, itself reeling from the financial crisis, told Amy that it, too, would have to reduce its annual grant to JCP by $75,000.

Amy volunteered to take a 15% pay cut. Camila reduced her hours. She eventually left the agency for a better-paying job but joined the board as a way of expressing her commitment to the work of JCP. Silvia Ruiz, the director of programs and herself a former victim of domestic violence, told Amy that as it was she was barely making ends meet raising two kids as a single mother and couldn't afford to take a pay cut. There was no choice left other than to reduce and eliminate programs.

The first programs to go were the anger management therapy groups JCP ran at the local high school and community college, along with a similar but separate program offered at the county jail. Deputy Sheriff Michael O'Rourke, a board member of JCP, said, "It's a darn shame. I know for sure those therapy groups have had a tremendous impact on those guys who were an incident away from exploding in anger. Being able to talk about it and to learn how to handle their issues has made a big difference in our community—you can just see it in the statistics on violent crime in Jersey County." O'Rourke appealed to the Rotary Club to fund the program, but it was unable to help. The board reluctantly agreed to eliminate the program and to lay off Marne Brooks, the social worker responsible for directing it. Marne also had case worker responsibilities at JCP, which had to be filled by other staff.

Also on the chopping block were the paid staff members for JCP's thrift store. Even though the store produced a steady source of revenue for JCP, the board felt strongly that it could be staffed by volunteers. Reverend Hughes convinced the group that several women from the Society of Angels would be willing to step in to run it. Although Amy had serious doubts that the Society of Angels, mostly elderly church volunteers, would have the expertise to run an effective retail operation (and one that was an important revenue generator for JCP), she was outvoted by the board. As a result, Jody Smith, the thrift store director, was laid off.

As the situation worsened, more social service staff had to be eliminated. Two full time social workers were laid off in the fourth year of the cuts. The remaining four case managers worked 60-hour weeks in heroic efforts to meet the steady demand for services.

Finally, the day they had all been hoping for had arrived. Their revenue stream, which was based on firm numbers, was showing a $207,000 increase over the previous year. The question before the JCP staff and board was, what to do with the money?

Silvia approached Amy with an impassioned plea for a pay raise for herself and the four case managers. No one had gotten a raise in 5 years, and everyone was feeling the pinch. Silvia felt strongly, too, that she and the others should be rewarded for their extra effort during these past 3 years. She also told Amy that reinstating the two eliminated staff positions would go a long way toward helping alleviate burnout among the staff and to JCP being able to more effectively serve its client population. Silvia argued that even though JCP had been able to serve the same number of women and children each year for the past 5 years, the quality of the services provided to those families had decreased due to a lack of staff. For instance, there was no longer a special counseling group for the children, which Silvia felt was critically important for helping the kids address the trauma they were facing and, in particular, to make sure the boys were broken of the cycle of violence to women.

Tim felt strongly that a new rainy-day fund should be established. As a longtime nonprofit financial manager who worked for several organizations, he believed that responsible organizations should have 6 months of operating reserves in the bank. He argued that $207,000 wasn't even equal to 2 months of reserves and that the entire amount should be placed in a high-yield investment account.

Camila had other ideas. She approached Amy to talk about the need to restore the position of a paid manager of the JCP thrift store. She argued that revenue from the thrift store had been in steady decline since Jody had been laid off as store manager. In fact, the store was looking a little shabby and disorganized these days and had, on average, made $60,000 less each year since Jody was gone. She knew the members of the Society of Angels were dedicated volunteers and appreciated their efforts but felt that a professional could increase the revenue with internet marketing and other merchandizing strategies. She also thought that Silvia and the case managers needed a small raise to boost their morale.

Sheriff O'Rourke met with Amy to talk about restoring the anger management therapy programs. He argued that the impact of not having those programs was evident in the increase in domestic violence in Jersey County. Since the programs had ended, the rate of domestic violence had soared 22%.

Amy's head was spinning as she considered what to do with the money. What seemed to be something wonderful was actually a huge dilemma. All of the suggestions were different, yet each person had valid reasons for why they thought the funds should be allocated in a certain way. All of the ideas presented had merit, but the fact was there was not enough money to meet all of the requests.

Case Questions

1. Silvia, Tim, Camila, and Sheriff O'Rourke all made proposal to Amy for how to allocate the surplus funds. In what ways do these various proposals advance the mission of the organization? What decision-making criteria would you use to prioritize the proposals?

2. Which proposals are most likely to have the greatest impact on clients?

3. What are the advantages to each proposal? What are the disadvantages each proposal?

4. What impact is each proposal likely to have on the effort contributed by the board and staff?

5. What solution or set of solutions will generate the most support from the board, staff, and community?

6. Where does the ultimate decision-making authority for allocating this funding rest?

MISALLOCATION OF GRANT MONEY: WHEN THE FIGURES DO NOT COMPUTE

Darren Herrod was proud to have landed at job at Technology for You (TfY), a nonprofit founded in 2005 for the purpose of making technology available and accessible to underserved populations by providing equipment, training, and support. This was his first job out of college, and he was excited to work for a nonprofit doing exactly what he loved most: teaching people how to use technology to improve their lives. Darren had interned at TfY during his final spring semester of college in the hope that a permanent position would open up by the time he graduated. The job perfectly combined his college major and minor: computer science and education.

TfY offered three core programs. The first was its *Trash to Treasure* program that accepted old computers that they refurbished and sold at cost to other nonprofit organizations and low-income people. That program included free technical support and low-cost computer repair services to any person or organization purchasing equipment from TfY. This program was largely self-supporting through the fees collected from those who purchased the equipment. The free technical support arm for anyone who purchased equipment was managed largely by volunteers that worked the hotline. *Trash to Treasure* was the first program started by TfY back when the organization was run entirely by volunteers.

Senior Tech, TfY's second core program, provided people 60 and older with free technical assistance on what to look for when purchasing a computer or cell phone as well as workshops on how to use that technology effectively. Workshops included topics such as understanding your keyboard, Web browsing, social media, Internet security, sending e-mail and photos, text messaging, and so on. This program was funded by the County Senior Service Grants Program and was the earliest staffed effort launched by TfY.

The third program was *Career-IT!*, an information technology (IT) training, certification, and job placement program that served military veterans, as well as unemployed and underemployed individuals, in the general population. Those two efforts were respectively funded by the U.S. Department of Veteran Affairs (VA) and by the U.S. Department of Labor (DOL). TfY had been operating those programs for 7 and 5 years, respectively, and had an excellent track record with both programs, placing 80% to 85% of all students in good-quality entry-level jobs as help desk technicians or IT support technicians. These programs had signaled important growth in TfY's revenue and operations, requiring the organization to move to a larger space to accommodate a steady stream of students. Darren was hired as a full-time lead instructor for these programs, replacing a staff member who left to work in the private sector.

During his internship, Darren had honed his skills as a teacher and had been trained on the record-keeping requirements pertaining to each of the enrolled trainees so that TfY could accurately report its results to the VA and DOL. Each agency had a separate contract and reporting require-ments even though TfY classes contained a mix of both types of stu-dents. Darren loved seeing his pupils transformed from the first week of class to the last. They went from knowing next to nothing about comput-ers and feeling insecure about whether or not they could master all they needed to know when they entered the program, to graduating with certifications in CompTIA A+, Network+, and Security. Students' body language often went from shy or hunched at the beginning of the pro-gram to confident and smiling as they graduated with their certifica-tions. The program was truly transformational.

To accommodate the steady stream of students, Darren delivered the program alongside longtime TfY senior instructor, Tao Wong (who referred to himself as Ted). Ted was a Gulf War veteran who felt passion-ately about serving his fellow vets. Darren had enormous respect for Ted as a teacher and as a human being. He felt that Ted's teaching style was direct yet kind. He prodded when he needed to, provided encourage-ment at just the right moments, and engendered a sense of trust and caring among all of the students. Ted was one of the reasons why Darren was so excited to be working at TfY; he saw Ted as a gifted teacher who would be an excellent mentor and supervisor.

Eleven months into his job, Ted told Darren that TfY had landed a new grant that would allow the organization to train disabled adults for entry-level computer tech jobs. The grant was funded through a generous grant from the Nancy M. Smithfield Foundation, a family foundation that was dedicated to improving the lives of people with physical and intellectual disabilities. TfY would promote the program in collaboration with the County Office of Persons with Disabilities whose office would also be a conduit for student referrals. Darren was excited about this new challenge and proud that TfY had chosen to expand its work with this population. The program would be called *Abil-IT.*

Six weeks later, the first clients began enrolling in the *Abil-IT* program. The program was designed such that these students, regardless of their disability type, would be incorporated into TfY's *Career-IT* program. Although the new students were interviewed and screened for aptitude, Darren had concerns (that he kept to himself) about how that model would work, whether it would be effective, and whether he personally had the skills to teach all of these different types of students in a single setting. However, he was open-minded about trying it out as he had deep personal beliefs about helping disadvantaged people live independent and productive lives.

During the first week of the new class session, Darren's worst fears were confirmed. He felt unprepared to assist students with such a wide array of disabilities (some physical, others intellectual), requiring specialized attention that he was unaccustomed to handling. Darren was further discouraged that he could not dedicate the time and care he was accustomed to providing to the *Career-IT!* students as he had done with past classes. He was surprised, too, at how large the class had become. Previously, he had taught 15 to 20 students per session; now he and Ted were being asked to instruct 30 students, including those in the *Abil-IT* program. Although he had minored in education in college, nothing had prepared him for the challenges of working with these special populations. In addition, he found that each student disability required individualized instruction that made the TfY model of cohort-based instruction ineffective.

Several times during the first 2 weeks of class, Larry Bowling, TfY's executive director, stopped by to observe. He made a point of telling Darren that he was doing a great job teaching these blended classes. "I know it's not easy, Darren, but you're making it look like it is. You do such an amazing job connecting with the students." Darren was flattered by the attention; however, he was puzzled by the compliment. He didn't feel as if he had command of the classroom and was concerned about meeting the benchmarks laid out in the VA and DOL contracts, let alone those that were part of this new grant.

By the fourth week of the new session, it was apparent to Darren that this new program wasn't working as planned. His traditional student population wasn't progressing nearly as quickly as they should through the curriculum (most were still trying to master the lessons they would usually have learned in week 2), and the *Abil-IT* students were even further behind the *Career-IT!* students. This was happening despite the fact that Darren found himself working much longer hours to provide more individual help to students. His girlfriend complained that he was more in love with his work than he was with her because she barely saw him before 9 p.m. on weeknights. He felt like a failure as a teacher, although he wasn't sure that it was entirely his fault. Shyly, he approached Ted to discuss the situation.

"I know it's tough," said Ted, "and maybe you and I can make a few tweaks to the schedule to separate out some of the more promising students from the rest of the group so that we can at least help a few of them. After all, we have to keep our numbers up for the VA and DOL contracts no matter what, and to be completely honest, we have crossed the line in double-counting heads on more than one occasion, checking boxes for both programs when a longtime unemployed vet is hired, for example. But here's the deal: the rent for the office went up this year at the same time that the county grant went down. On top of that, TfY has been losing money on the *Trash for Treasure* program for the past couple of years because we don't have enough volunteers to help refurbish the equipment or answer the technical assistance hotline so we have to pay people to do that. That's hurt us, especially since that's what we're known for out in the community. When we were a new organization, everyone wanted to be part of us. Now that we've been around awhile, volunteers are scarce, and the county has moved on to funding other things. Larry told me that this grant money is making the difference between being able to support our operations and having us go out of business."

Darren nodded in response to Ted. He knew that nonprofit work was hard, but he never imagined something like this would happen.

Case Questions

1. If what Ted says is correct, is TfY's use of the Smithfield funds illegal, unethical, or both?

2. What are the consequences, legal and ethical, of comingling government money with private foundation funds?

3. What are the legal and ethical consequences of double-counting clients for separate government contracts?

4. What recourse does Darren have? What should be his response or next steps?

5. What could Larry have done, if anything, to avoid this situation?

6. Do you think situations like this are common in nonprofit organizations?

7. What practices and strategies can nonprofits use to avoid this type of situation?

TRANSPARENCY: THE RISK OF SILENCE

The Historical Society of Evansville was abuzz with excitement. They had just learned that their town had been selected to host a film festival and commemoration ceremony celebrating the history of silent films. This made perfect sense since several of the first silent films ever produced were filmed in and around Evansville. Additionally, the city's historic main street and train station made a perfect backdrop for the event since they had each retained much of their original character from the times the films were made.

The Historical Society was led by a part-time executive director, Charlotte Simms, a native of Evansville. When she received word of the selection, Charlotte called together a meeting of the board and its key volunteers. "This is very exciting for us," Charlotte told the assembled group. "It's a huge opportunity for Evansville. I'm tickled!"

"What will this mean for us?" asked Jack Su, a newer member of the board. "What kinds of resources are we going to have to commit to the effort?"

"Well, as I understand it, the event production group, called What's Up Productions, manages all of the festival activities," Charlotte answered. "They ask that we help them get the city permits needed, host the opening night party, and provide volunteers over the 3 days of the festival. When they do these things, they usually look for a local nonprofit to partner with so we can collect any tax deductible donations associated with the event. Or we can even look for grants."

According to the letter from the event company, it was expected that the festival could draw close to 15,000 people to town for the weekend, including some current movie stars and film producers. The idea of celebrities coming to Evansville heightened the excitement of many in the room.

"An event like this can really boost tourism, which all the shopkeepers on Main Street can tell you has been dropping off these past 2 years," Jack noted.

"You may recall, when they came here for the site visit they talked a lot about the economic impact of the event in terms of generating local tax revenue," Charlotte reminded the group.

"All the more reason for us to promote the heck out of this," interjected Jenna Rogers, board chair for the society and a professional event planner by trade. "I think there are several things we could do to add to the celebration," she said. "Just think, we could have a very elegant party right in the middle of Main Street. We could bring in spotlights, really decorate around the old-time Hollywood theme," she said. Before long, Jenna had the majority of the group enthusiastically throwing out ideas for ways they could promote Evansville, and the ideas kept coming. "We could host a director's guild cocktail party and maybe even a red carpet type of awards ceremony," someone chimed in.

"This seems like it could require us to lay out a lot of cash," Jack pointed out.

"Oh, don't be a party pooper Jack," Jenna chided. "We'll use a lot of my company connections and we'll make it great. We may have to think of this more like a friend raiser than an actual fund-raiser, but it's going to be so important for Evansville. I'm going to hit up the city council for some support," Jenna said.

"Let's make sure we at least break even," Jack asserted.

True to her word, the very next day Jenna made her way into the office of a local realtor named Carl Peters. Peters was one of five local council people elected to govern the city of Evansville. He and Jenna had attended the same high school and had been family friends for years. Peters loved the ideas Jenna was throwing out. "Do you think we could get some city funding to underwrite some of this?" she asked him.

"I don't think that will be a problem. We have funds set aside to use to support nonprofits. Usually you have to make a grant request, but in this case, I think I can make the request on your behalf. Then it will have to be approved by the entire council. We could get it done in the next few weeks."

"Perfect!" Jenna replied.

At the next meeting of the city council, the councilmembers, at Peter's behest, voted unanimously to make two grants for $25,000 each to the Historical Society. The first grant was funded through the special fund mentioned by Peters, and the second was made from the city's general fund. As they left the meeting, Peters leaned over and whispered to Jenna, "Go forth and plan a big party. Make us proud."

When all was said and done, the festival was deemed by most to be a big success. "I admit I went a little over the top, but it was everything we could have hoped for," Jenna said in the debrief meeting following the event, "glittery, opulent, and fun!"

However, the next week, enthusiasm for the event was dampened when a letter to the editor of the local paper was published calling into question the Historical Society's use of public funds for the purpose of, as the writer put it, "throwing a party, when there are people with more important needs going unserved in our community." The issue resonated with others, and more letters to the editor followed. Soon a local blogger took up the issue demanding that the Historical Society provide a full public accounting for every penny spent. Council member Peters received the following note:

> Dear Mr. Peters and members of the City Council:
>
> Since both of you saw it fitting and necessary to give $50,000 in taxpayer money to throw a party, I am formally requesting a line item statement of all expenditures that said money was used for, along with receipts, a statement of how much money is left over, and an explanation of what happens to it.
>
> I assume that you had the foresight to request that such records be kept for auditing purposes. Taxpayers and citizens are entitled by law to know where every dime of their money goes. If such an accounting cannot be produced, then I would request a full audit of the Historical Society's books.
>
> Thank you.
>
> Jay Roberts

Mr. Peter's reply was posted on the blog:

Dear Mr. Roberts,

As you know, the Historical Society is an established and respected nonprofit doing good work in our community. I see no reason to ask for an accounting of these funds from such a trustworthy organization. Anyone who can't see the benefits of the film festival is shortsighted and isn't looking at the common good.

Mr. Roberts posted this response to his blog:

Councilmember Peters and the board of directors of the Historical Society of Evansville,

Ms. Jenna Rogers, president of the board of the Historical Society and a professional event planner, was easily granted $50,000 from two city funds for entertainment purposes related to the Evansville Film Festival, which occurred this past week. In the wake of this event, it has proven quite difficult to find out what taxpayer money was used specifically for. How do we know that her company did not benefit financially from this transaction? It's about transparency, not whether we like or trust someone. Please provide a public accounting of these funds.

Jenna was hurt and incensed by the negative comments and ongoing public scrutiny. She asked Charlotte for a meeting.

"While I really think most people don't care, some persistent members of the public are demanding answers," Charlotte reported. "I suggest we open up the books and provide a full accounting of how you spent that city money, Jenna."

"I am not giving them the satisfaction of an answer," Jenna said. "By law, we only have to provide them with audited financial statements not line item expenditures. I don't need those jerks adding up every penny I spent on glitter and red carpet. They'll have a heyday with that information and make me look like a fool. They don't see the bigger picture of how this was good for the community. And, as for making money personally? Ha! If anything, this event cost my company big in terms of all the favors I had to call in."

"Put them off and hopefully this will just go away," Jenna concluded. "And get that blogger Jay Roberts off my back!"

Case Questions

1. What kinds of information are nonprofits required to legally provide to the public when public funding is granted?

2. What kinds of information should nonprofits provide to the public (e.g., beyond what may be legally required)? Is following the letter of the law enough?

3. What level of transparency is or isn't required for large-scale events that impact an entire community?

4. How might a situation like this impact future giving to the Historical Society?

5. Was there a conflict of interest with having Jenna plan the event?

6. Special events such as galas, golf tournaments, and large races can be costly to put on. What are some ways that nonprofits can evaluate the effectiveness and efficiency of raising money through events?

11

Advocacy and Lobbying

INTRODUCTION

Many nonprofit organizations are confused by what is meant by the terms *advocacy* and *lobbying*. According to Pat Libby, *advocacy*, indicates that an organization is engaged in influencing public opinion and public policy (Libby, 2012). Lobbying, which is legally defined by the Internal Revenue Services (IRS), entails directly expressing views to elected officials and others involved in the policy-making process to affect or create legislation. There are nuances pertaining to definitions of grassroots and direct lobbying which nonprofit leaders should learn.

The National Council of Nonprofits (2015) provides detailed proof of the many ways "the U.S. Constitution, Congress, and the IRS have protected the rights of nonprofits to engage in advocacy and legislative lobbying." Yet, many nonprofit leaders and board members mistakenly believe that 501(c)(3) organizations are prohibited from lobbying, some foundations mistakenly believe that they cannot make grants to support lobbying, while other organizations believe that having tax exempt status greatly limits their ability to lobby. Nonprofit leaders are also often misinformed about the legal rights their staff members have to lobby (even on their own time). In addition, nonprofits are intimidated by the legislative process and feel unequipped to lobby (see Libby, 2012, for an easy guide to participating in the legislative process). The simple fact is that public charities that are not private foundations may choose to elect the 501(h) designation that allows an organization to expend up to 20% of the first $500,000 of its core expenses on lobbying.

Confusion about lobbying leads nonprofits to be much less engaged in this important work than is warranted by their missions and the very work they do on a daily basis. For example, a social service organization may be involved in helping low-income people access government services but choose to not be involved in lobbying for legislation that could improve the types of services available to these people. This illustration is backed up by numerous studies that have shown, on average, merely 2% to 4% of nonprofits leaders at 501(c)(3) organizations are engaged in lobbying (Bass, Aarons, Guinane, & Carter, 2007; Salamon, Geller, & Lorentz, 2009; Berry, 2003).

The cases in this chapter explore nonprofit advocacy and lobbying issues including the following:

1. Whether an organization should take a position or not

2. Public policy versus the bottom line

3. Staff advocacy

REFERENCES

Bass, G., Aarons, D., Guinane K., & Carter, M. (2007). Seen but not heard. Washington, DC: The Aspen Institute

Berry, J. (2003, November 27). Nonprofit groups shouldn't be afraid to lobby. *The Chronicle of Philanthropy*. Retrieved from https://philanthropy.com/article/Nonprofit-Groups-Shouldnt-Be/164771

Libby, P. (2012). *The lobbying strategy handbook*. Thousand Oaks, CA: Sage.

National Council of Nonprofits. (2015). *Everyday advocacy*. Retrieved from https://www.councilofnonprofits.org/everyday-advocacy

Salamon, L., Geller, S., & Lorentz S. (2009, November 19-21). *Nonprofit America: A force for Democracy?* Paper presented at the 2009 Conference of the Association for Research on Nonprofit Organizations and Voluntary Action, Cleveland, OH.

MEETING YOUR MISSION: TO TAKE A PUBLIC POSITION OR NOT?

Jeanne Wolfe had been the executive director of Kids First (K1) for 8 years. K1 was a local education foundation that raised money to support public education in the Mapleton school district. Although the district was small with just two elementary schools, a middle school, and a high school, Mapleton schools were known for providing high-quality education. The community of Mapleton was proud of its schools and the reputation of the schools helped support a prosperous real estate market. In her role, Jeanne was tasked with raising money to bridge the gap between dwindling government funds and what was needed to maintain the high level of programming Mapleton residents demanded from their schools.

K1 was originally founded by a group of caring community leaders and alumni from the Mapleton schools who were concerned about the long-term impact of changing funding formulas for public schools that had been passed by the state legislature. Peter Litrentra, the founder of K1, had the foresight to realize the negative impact the new laws could have on small school districts in the future. "It may not happen for some time," Pete warned. "But we need to act now to ensure we have a way to make up for reduced funding down the line." With that idea, K1 was born.

The bylaws of K1 outlined the purpose of the nonprofit organization, which was to ensure that every child in the district received an outstanding education. To root itself in the community and to differentiate itself from traditional parent groups like the PTA, the nominating committee of the board adopted a policy that the board of directors must include at least four local business owners. This helped ensure a broad diversity of perspectives would be present in the governing of the organization. That strategy served K1 well in its early years as business owners sponsored many K1 fund-raisers and activities. After 5 years, K1 hired Jeanne as its first ever full-time employee. After her first year, Jeanne hired a part-time bookkeeper and a part-time special events coordinator. K1 quickly became a favorite charity of almost everyone in town. Jeanne often told her staff, "Our reputation is everything to us. As long as I never read a negative letter to the editor about K1 in the *Weekly Journal*, I know we are on track."

In the early years of her job at K1, Jeanne was focused on raising money for what she called the "extras." When a classroom wanted to take a special field trip or the art teacher needed new supplies, the money from K1 bridged the gap. Monies raised by K1 were also given out in the form of innovation grants to teachers who wanted to try new things in their classrooms. The bulk of K1's money was raised through two special events: a golf tournament and a very large black-tie dinner. When all was said and done, K1 was reliably returning $350,000 a year to Mapleton schools.

In her third year on the job, Jeanne received a request to meet with Dr. Richard Alvarez, the Superintendent of Mapleton schools. As she entered his office, Jeanne noted that the normally good-natured Alvarez looked troubled.

"Jeanne," Alvarez began, "I wanted to make you aware that we have just received a revised budget from the state that does not look good. We are going to have to make some midyear cuts that are going to be quite painful. And next year looks even worse. We are talking about cuts to core programs and we are going to really need K1 to help us offset these cuts."

"How much are we talking about?" Jeanne asked.

"Somewhere in the $500,000 range now and upward of $2 million next year" Alvarez replied. "We can absorb some of it by asking a couple of teachers to take early retirement, but if we don't find a way to guarantee the rest by next fall we will be increasing class sizes and cutting every-thing but the most basic programs. To get us through these first mid-year cuts, the school board is hoping you could help us with a special appeal for now."

"Sure," Jeanne said. "We could do a targeted 'save our schools' appeal. It would be a stretch for us, but I think the community would respond favorably."

Alvarez looked somewhat relieved. Next he told Jeanne, "I also wanted to let you know that we will be moving forward with a parcel tax initiative in the fall to help guarantee future funding. Essentially it amounts to asking folks to pay $125 more per household into a special property tax fund that stays right here in our community. As you know, they have been very successful with these up north."

Knowing the conservative nature of Mapleton residents, Jeanne said, "I think that a parcel tax might be hard to pass here, don't you? Just think about the new library bond that went down in flames in the last election"

"Well, if these folks want to protect their schools and their property values, they will have to jump on board. There is no way we are going to make it otherwise. You all really help us, so I mean no offense when I say this, Jeanne, but no amount of bake sales or special fund-raising is going to be able to fill the gaps we are looking at in the coming years. To tap the really big money we are going to have to go for the parcel tax. I am hoping that K1 will endorse the project and really help us get out the vote."

Jeanne nodded. "Trust me, I'm with you, Dr. Alvarez. Just the idea of trying to raise that kind of money in this small community makes me dizzy. I'll take your ideas to my board at our monthly meeting next Wednesday and let you know their thoughts."

Prior to the board meeting, Jeanne gathered data and wrote up a short brief for the board to review in advance of the meeting. She outlined the historical data showing a constant decline in school funding over the past decade and the stable but insufficient amounts offset by K1. Based on information provided by the district, she showed how a tax increase of $125 per household could yield the school district an additional $2 million in annual guaranteed revenue. Seeing this as a viable and worthy option, she recommended that K1 endorse the passage of the parcel tax. She e-mailed the information with the monthly board packet.

Within an hour of sending the packets, she received a call from K1's vice president, Frank O'Neil, a local realtor and major contributor to K1. "Jeanne, what is this you are sending out to board members? Are you crazy? Do you know how much we pay in taxes already, and now you want us to pay more? What gives you the right to tell the board we should do this?" he hollered into the phone.

Unaccustomed to being spoken to this way by her board members, Jeanne was silent for a moment. She weighed her options in her head. Frank was known around town as someone you did not want as your enemy and had a reputation for giving money with strings attached. Secretly, Jeanne had mixed feelings when the nominating committee selected Frank as a candidate. However, he had been on the board for about a year, and things had thus far been smooth.

"Excuse me, Frank," Jeanne said. "I can hear that you are angry—"
"You bet I am," he interrupted her.

Jeanne began again. "If we could step back for a minute and discuss this calmly I would appreciate it."

"There is nothing to discuss," Frank countered in a somewhat calmer voice. "K1 is a neutral organization. We are a nonprofit and have no business getting into politics. And if we did get involved, especially in something like this, we stand to lose a lot of donors . . . people like me," Frank asserted.

They spoke for a few minutes more, and Jeanne did her best to get Frank to understand that she was providing the board with her professional opinion based on her knowledge of the organization, its mission, and future trends in education funding. "If having the best schools and providing the best education possible is truly our mission, then, in my opinion, a parcel tax is the only way we can get there," she told Frank. "I'd say it's almost incumbent on this organization to support this initiative."

"I don't see it that way at all, and I for one will fight this tooth and nail with the rest of the board. If they vote for, this I will quit!" Frank exclaimed before disconnecting the call. Jeanne slumped down in her chair, wondering how she was going to contain Frank, have a productive board meeting, and avoid a potentially ugly fight in her tight-knit community.

Case Questions

1. Jeanne told Frank that since the parcel tax was directly linked to the desired outcomes of K1's mission it was "incumbent" upon the organization to advocate for the tax. To what extent do you believe this is true?

2. Do you think the K1 board should vote to support the parcel tax? Why, or why not?

3. What are the aspects of the case that must be considered?

4. If the board decides to engage in lobbying, what is K1 legally allowed to do in this situation?

5. Should the board decide to support the tax, what are some strategies that the organization could consider to make the process successful and keep its favorable reputation in the community?

PUBLIC POLICY VERSUS THE BOTTOM LINE: LIVING WAGE RAGE

Betty Singer knew she had one of the biggest fights of her career looming. She just didn't know whether the fight would be with her own board or with the city.

The organization she directed and founded, Still Waters, had been providing mental health and social services "to those in need without regard to their ability to pay" for more than a quarter century. The vast majority of the agency's clients were working poor, low-income, or homeless. Still Waters also had a contract with the school district to provide auxiliary support to 15 elementary and high schools that did not have an on-site social worker. Betty had established the agency with a passion for providing mental health services to the most disadvantaged people in society and had developed Still Waters into a national model.

Betty was compassionate, direct, and a no-frills kind of person who operated Still Waters as a reflection of herself. Her management philosophy was to stretch every dollar as far as possible in order to do the most good for people who needed the organization's services. Still Waters was housed in a modest office building with donated furniture and office equipment (an ongoing staff joke was that even the donuts at staff meetings were day-old). Betty was the type of person who would give someone the coat off her back if she knew they needed it. She surrounded herself with people who thought like she did, putting others before their own needs. People worked there because it was a calling.

Over the years, Still Waters had grown to serve more than 35,000 clients a year with a staff of only 32 full-time employees. Betty, her associate director, staff therapists, and school counselors had graduate degrees in social work or marriage and family therapy (MFT); however, most of the street outreach staff (responsible for working with the city's homeless population under a special contract) held bachelor's degrees in social work or human services as did her human service specialists (responsible for connecting clients with public benefits). In addition, the organization was assisted by many social work and MFT interns. These interns vied for the few permanent jobs that became available at Still Waters because working there was seen as a badge of honor for those who wanted to make a difference in the lives of low-income people.

Betty was proud of the work done by all of her staff but perhaps proudest of the street outreach staff who worked tirelessly to counsel homeless families and individuals in order to give them access to shelter and other support services that enabled them to get off the streets. The mayor and city council had publicly commended Still Waters for their superb work in this area, and the organization was featured in the newspaper annually when the homeless count was conducted.

Then one day, Adam Burrell, a new city council member, proposed instituting a requirement that all organizations under contract to the city pay their employees working on that contract a living wage of $14.00 per hour. In announcing his proposal to the press, Burrell said, "One in six residents of the city currently lives below the poverty line. Although we cannot mandate a requirement that all businesses pay a living wage, we can ensure that those organizations doing business with the city pay their workers enough to live decent lives. Income inequality begins at home, and I say it's time to help the good people of this city take home the pay they deserve and have earned."

Betty was stunned by the announcement. If she paid her eight street outreach staff $14 per hour (they were currently making $12 per hour), then what would be the reaction of all of the other staff at Still Waters? She had five human service specialists with equivalent credentials earning $12 per hour and three support staff earning $11 per hour. The street outreach staff and human service specialists were viewed within the organizations as equals; the new city ordinance, if passed, would disrupt that harmony among staff.

Betty's school counselors, all of whom had graduate degrees, were earning $32,000 per year and would certainly believe they deserved raises if the lowest paid staff were suddenly earning more than $29,000 per year. And then there were the therapists who would need raises as well. The total cost to Still Waters of the living wage ordinance (assuming it passed) could potentially be as follows:

Staff	Average $ Increase Each
8 outreach staff	$4,160
5 human service specialists	$4,160
3 support staff	$6,420
6 therapists	$3,000
7 school counselors	$3,000
CFO and associate director	$3,000
Total dollar amount	**$85,060**

As was typical of Betty, she did not factor in a raise for herself. Reeling from this news, she picked up the phone to call her friend and colleague, Reverend Darryl Powers, director of the United Methodist social service agency. Over a hastily arranged lunch, they talked about the city councilor's proposal. Darryl told Betty, "Adam was kind enough to call me to talk about this before he made the public announcement. He wanted to make sure that our agency would get behind the proposal because he's worried that many nonprofits will oppose it or apply for an exemption from it, and he knows the business community will certainly come out against it. After we met, I prayed about it for several days. The conclusion I reached, after much discernment, is that we must increase the pay for our lowest paid workers. Adam is right: We cannot ask these people who work for us to serve the most needy while being needy themselves. I don't know where on God's green earth we will get the money to fill the gap, but morally speaking, it is something that we must do." Moved by his words, Betty knew that she needed to discuss the matter with her board.

Ten days later at the regularly scheduled board meeting, Betty raised the issue. She had spoken to her chair, Lexi Allan, who had agreed to put the item near the top of the agenda after the committee and financial reports. Betty explained the council member's proposal, handed out a simple sheet projecting the cost of implementing a living wage throughout Still Waters, and ended by saying, "It is the right thing to do for our staff members who dedicate their lives to others."

After her presentation concluded, the room was silent for a brief moment. Then Arturo Rivera spoke up. "Your points are well taken, Betty, but the reality is that we cannot afford to do what you are proposing. I have been on this board for 7 years, 4 of them as treasurer, and I can tell you that not once during that time did we end the year without a deficit. Every year we have to call in all kinds of special favors to close a budget gap, and I remember more than one occasion during the past 7 years where we had to ask staff to hold off cashing their checks until we received a late reimbursement check from the city. Your ideas are noble—they always are—but what you propose is impossible."

"I'm not so sure about that," said Quynh Lam. "We can make a decision to pay some people more and to lay off others. There's a trade-off that may need to be made. Perhaps we simply need to agree to serve fewer clients in order to pay the staff we have a decent livable wage." Betty looked horrified.

"As the newest member of this board, I'd like to add my 2 cents," said Jerry Westerly, getting red in the face. "With all due respect to Betty and to all of you, this is a preposterous proposal by the city. It will not only wreak havoc with Still Waters and every other human service agency around but with all of us who are trying to eke out a living. You all know that I'm in the construction business. There's no way I can afford to pay all of my guys who are working on city contracts $14 an hour! It will bankrupt me, and if I go bankrupt then none of those guys will get any salary, then what? I say that Still Waters should take a position to actively oppose this legislation. If it passes, you'll just have more people coming to Still Waters for help because they'll feel stressed out about being laid off."

"I have to agree with Jerry," said Arturo. "I don't like the city driving this living wage agenda. I'm also on the board of the senior community center, and we've had a discussion about actively opposing the legislation. Not only is it bad for our bottom line as a social service agency; we also risk alienating some of our most important donors if we don't oppose this thing. And let me remind you, some of those donors are the same people who have saved our bacon year after year when we've struggled to balance the books. If we want to institute a living wage policy at Still Waters, that's for us to decide, not for the city to dictate to us."

Case Questions

1. What are the ethical tensions presented in this case?

2. What process should the board use to decide whether to formally endorse or oppose the city's living wage proposal?

3. If you were on the board, how would you vote on the following proposals, and why?

   a. A proposal to pay all staff a living wage, which would result in some layoffs

   b. A proposal to endorse the proposed living wage ordinance

   c. A proposal to oppose the living wage proposal

CASE 11.3

STAFF ADVOCACY: ACTIVISM THAT BLURS BOUNDARIES

Anyone who knew Azadeh Ahmadi knew these two truths about her: she was proud to be American and passionately devoted to her work at Interfaith Mosaic, a social service organization where she worked as a case manager in the department of Refugee Resettlement and Immigration Services (RRIS). The daughter of refugees from Iran, she understood from her parents what it meant to flee their homeland in the dark of night under threat of persecution for her father's political activism. They had given up everything to come to the United States, and she felt deeply thankful to live in a country where freedom had no limits. She proudly wore an American flag lapel pin and took great delight in gifting one to each of her clients.

Interfaith's RRIS department, consisting of seven staff and numerous volunteers, was responsible for a broad array of services that included providing newcomers with furnished apartments, acculturation assistance and English as a second language (ESL) classes; job training and placement assistance; and assistance with all matter of legal and document assistance (e.g., green card applications, assistance in replacing missing immigration documents, help applying for work authorizations and refugee travel documents, petitions for family members, legal assistance for asylum seekers, etc.). Interfaith received funding to provide these services through a federal contract from the Department of Health and Human Services, Office of Refugee Resettlement and through private donations and grants.

Azadeh's work was focused on greeting new families and getting them settled into their new homes and life in America. Hers was the first face they saw when they stepped off the plane, and she was dedicated to ensuring their arrival was as welcoming as possible. She made sure every apartment was spotless and as well appointed as possible with donated items that created a special touch, for instance, she made sure there were age-appropriate toys for the children and that each new home contained a small care package of food that was culturally familiar to the dazed arrivals. Although her relationship with these individuals and families technically ended once they were settled, she often followed up with them for many months afterward to ensure they were adjusting as well as could be expected to their new country. She was keenly aware of the fraught circumstances that led these people to immigrate to the United States and wanted to reassure them that they would be welcomed in their new land.

Christina Burch, director of Interfaith's RRIS department, appreciated Azadeh's attention to the care of these newcomers, although she thought that Azadeh went overboard when it came to procuring and providing all of the extra specialty items for the families. Christina viewed Azadeh as being energetic and passionate about her work, although a little naïve.

The longer Azadeh worked at Interfaith Mosaic, the more she began to believe she needed to get involved in immigrant rights issues. It just didn't make sense to her that immigrants needed to wait so long to get work permits and permanent residency status. She was upset, too, by the stories of friends who were born in the United States to parents who came to the country illegally and lived in fear of their parents being deported because of a broken taillight that might reveal their illegal status. She became an active volunteer with the American Civil Liberties Union (ACLU). From there, it was a small leap to organizing some of Interfaith's former and current clients to attend meetings she arranged for the group with members of Congress and their legislative aids (these meetings were held in the representatives' home districts as the group did not have money to travel). She helped organize marches, letter-writing campaigns, and press coverage of the issue. She talked about immigrant rights constantly to her coworkers and encouraged them to join these efforts. After a few months, a reporter from *The Globe* did a Sunday feature story on Azadeh that highlighted her family background and her activism on immigration issues.

After the story appeared, Christina was alarmed. She quickly arranged a meeting with Dan Montgomery, the executive director of Interfaith Mosaic. "Dan," she said. "I really think Azadeh is getting out of hand. While we have to applaud her commitment to social justice, I don't think we want the agency to be caught up in a politically divisive issue. Of course, we have an obligation to help, but we are a 501(c)(3)! We don't want to jeopardize our legal status, and we certainly don't want to jeopardize our funding for this program." Dan agreed that Azadeh's actions were bringing unwanted visibility to Interfaith. "Please talk to her, Christina; this has got to stop."

Christina set up a meeting with Azadeh for that afternoon, conveying the concerns she and Dan had for her work on immigration issues. Azadeh was stunned to hear Christina's words. "I don't understand," she said. "I do this work on my own time after hours, on lunch breaks, and I've even taken vacation days when I've had to go to long meetings about immigration reform. I believe I have a moral obligation to get involved in these issues, and I believe Interfaith does as well. How can we serve these people without fighting for their rights?"

Case Questions

1. In what ways is it legally permissible for nonprofit organizations to lobby?

2. What rights do employees have (if any) to legally work on advocacy issues that are not endorsed by their organizations?

3. What are the legal, ethical, and moral quagmires for Dan and Christina?

4. What role, if any, should the board play in determining the advocacy agenda for a nonprofit organization?

12

Technology

INTRODUCTION

Nonprofits are increasingly turning to technology to, among other things, evolve their business practices, reach broader audiences, track outcomes, and improve the efficiency of service delivery. However, integrating technology is challenging for nonprofit leaders who are often focused on meeting very pressing needs and challenged with maintaining low overhead costs. Despite the innumerable benefits that technology can bring to nonprofits, many nonprofits remain underinvested in this area. A study by the Johns Hopkins Listening Post Project found that nearly one third of nonprofit organizations did not have enough computers to meet their needs and one third described their use of information technologies for program/service delivery as "limited" (Geller, Abramson, & deLeon, 2010).

Managers in the nonprofit sector will likely confront internal challenges when integrating technology into their organizations. For example, the use of social media and the Internet as a marketing and fund-raising resource is rapidly evolving. According to Blackbaud, in 2014, approximately 6.7% of overall fund-raising, excluding grants, was raised online, an increase of 8.9% over the previous year (MacLaughlin, 2014). However, Jones (2015) has found that most nonprofits lack appropriate human resource policies to cover employee use of social media. Additionally, while technology provides many useful tools for tracking outcomes, program staff may lack the training needed to fully use such technology effectively. In other instances, introducing technology may have unintended consequences that actually decrease effectiveness. The Affordable Care Act, for example, which provided access to health insurance to many uninsured Americans, introduced mandated computer reporting that is actually slowing down the rate at which community health clinics are able to serve patients.

Deciding when and how to integrate technology into a nonprofit organization can be a daunting task as well as deciding who within the organization should be primarily responsible for overseeing hardware, software, and social media. If technology is ignored, or if the wrong technology is purchased or used, then a nonprofit runs the risk of losing its competitive edge (and even damaging its reputation and frustrating its employees and constituents). If technology is adopted too quickly, resources may be wasted on systems that don't serve their intended purposes. In successful organizations, technology serves the people. If people have to serve the technology, the organization's mission will suffer. Nonprofit technology consultant Anna Crotty (2014) suggests that technology should advance the organization's mission, suit the human beings involved, and allow time and money to be used wisely. She proposes that nonprofit leaders should engage in strategic technology planning to answer the following questions:

- Which organizational challenges can be solved with technology?
- Which vendors and consultants should the organization use to get the solutions it needs?
- How will the humans in the organization adopt the new technology and thrive with it?

This chapter gives nonprofit leaders a chance to consider the following issues:

1. Internal systems

2. Integrating new technology

3. Social media

REFERENCES

Crotty, A. (2014, June 1). *Leveraging technology for nonprofit success.* Lecture presented at State of Nonprofits and Philanthropy, San Diego, CA.

Geller, S., Abramson, A., & de Leon, E. (2010). The nonprofit technology gap—Myth or reality? [Communique no. 20]. *The Johns Hopkins Listening Post Project.*

Jones, J. (2015). Developing social media policies: A team learning approach. In Asencio, H., & Sun, R. (Eds.), *Cases on strategic social media utilization in the nonprofit sector* (pp. 210-236). Hershey, PA: IGI Global.

MacLaughlin, S. (2014). Charitable giving report: How nonprofit fundraising performed in 2014. *Blackbaud.* Retrieved from https://www.blackbaudhq.com/corpmar/cgr/how-nonprofit-fundraising-performed-in-2014.pdf

INTERNAL SYSTEMS: AT THE BREAKING POINT

"Great shot!" Peggy Templeman exclaimed as she high-fived Ila Pecus, the quietest member of Breakpoint's fourth-grade tennis team.

"Thanks, Coach Peggy," Ila smiled shyly. Ila had just delivered the winning serve in a hotly contested match of doubles, and all the kids were cheering and patting her on the back. Peggy gave them a few minutes to fuss over Ila, enjoying what she considered to be a real growth moment for the child who, until recently, barely spoke to any of her peers.

After a few more minutes of reverie, Peggy said, "OK, kids, get changed, grab a snack, and then it's time to hit the books."

Despite some grumbles, the kids began grabbing their backpacks and heading for the clubhouse. Peggy followed them inside and retreated to her office at the back of the building. Coach Peggy was the program director for Breakpoint, a nonprofit tennis association whose mission was to teach life skills and provide educational support to at-risk youth in Port Angelo, a sprawling city with a large urban population.

When it first launched, Breakpoint was located in a run-down community tennis center owned by the city of Port Angelo. The city provided the facilities to the nonprofit for free and made an annual grant to support a modest remodel and maintenance and to purchase equipment for the participants who attended schools in the neighborhoods surrounding the Breakpoint facilities. Breakpoint staff employed a nationally recognized mentoring approach to tennis instruction, one that emphasized teamwork, goal setting, nutrition, and fitness, both on and off the court. To incentivize participation, kids earned Breakpoint Bucks when they achieved specific goals. When they accumulated enough Breakpoint Bucks, students could then spend them in the center's pro shop to purchase snacks, tennis equipment, and gift cards to local businesses.

Since she was required to provide the city with basic attendance and demographic information for program participants as part of their grant agreement, Peggy recognized early on the importance of good record keeping. Through some connections in the world of tennis, Peggy was able to secure access to a database software package that was commonly used by tennis clubs throughout the country, usually in their proshops. Since Breakpoint was a nonprofit, they were allowed to "rent" the software for $1 per year. This pleased the Breakpoint board of directors to no end, as they were extremely sensitive about trying to ensure that as much of the budget as possible was used to directly provide services to the kids they served.

Initially, Peggy was responsible for all the data entry into the system. She was able to enter and monitor simple contact information for the children, as well as some information about what they were doing at Breakpoint. Additionally, because the system was originally designed to track pro shop purchases, it was useful for tracking points that kids earned through the Breakpoint Bucks reward system.

For the most part, Breakpoint staff members were pleased with the ease of the system. When they engaged in different activities at Breakpoint, kids were required to swipe a participant ID card that had a barcode on the back. This process enabled staff to easily track things like attendance, time spent on the tennis courts, and tutoring sessions attended. However, the system couldn't track more complex demographic information like grade level, ethnicity, family income, or improvements made at school. To overcome some of the system's limitations, staff members became adept at making up their own ways to track such information, usually recording it in handwritten logs or on computer spreadsheets.

As Breakpoint grew and attracted more foundation grant money and support from individual donors, Peggy had an increasingly difficult time accessing the information she needed as the head of the program. For example, a foundation program officer called one day and asked her how many active members came from families below a certain income level. Peggy spent the better part of that afternoon pulling reports from their system to list out active members and then looking up their income levels on paper registration forms. Furthermore, she became frustrated with the fact that it was not easy to determine that certain children were siblings with others. Internally, the system was very good at tracking individual activities but not at all helpful with knitting them together into a story that made sense to people outside of Breakpoint.

One day, Peggy's frustration with the system boiled over. "Ugh!" she groaned in exasperation.

"What's wrong, coach? You mad at the computer again?" asked George, a senior staff member who had overheard Peggy's comment from the hallway.

"This thing won't tell me what I need to know!" she grumbled as she threw her pen at the computer screen. "I just want to be able to show that kids who are in the program are getting better grades than they were before they enrolled."

"Well, we track that stuff, so we know it's true," George replied encouragingly. "What's the big deal?"

"*You* know it, George—Peggy pointed her finger at him—"and I know it, but it sure would be great if this computer could know it without me having to spend so much time trying to match things up by hand."

"I don't get it," George said. "We have spent the last 3 years keeping track of really detailed data on every single thing that has been done by almost every kid that has been in the program—every game played, every class attended."

Peggy responded. "But that's only output data, which, if you think about it, are really similar to the customer purchase data this thing was meant to collect. But, what it doesn't do is sort the data or relate them to other data, so I have no way to access the information that people are asking for. I can't tell what parts of the program are having an impact on different kinds of students. Worse, I can't track their progress over time, so it takes me forever to answer some of the simplest questions from donors and our board members. I know this software is essentially free, but I am going to have to look into buying a new system."

"On one hand, you get what you pay for," George noted. "But on the other hand, I hope we don't go for something too expensive or complicated. Right now the kids swipe their badges so we capture that information easily. But, you gotta know, the staff will probably balk at anything more onerous that takes away from instruction time. I just don't see them going for that."

"Yes, but we are growing, George. We are adding a new site on the north side of town. People want to know about our outcomes. We have to show that our participants are improving their grades and meeting their other education and fitness goals. We have to be able to categorize them by age and ethnicity, that sort of thing. I can't just keep telling people to trust us that the program works. I need the data to prove it. The frustrating thing is we actually have most of the data we need to make a really compelling case, it just happens to be in ten different places, and you need a degree in computer science to bring it all together. The bottom line is we've outgrown this system, and we need something new."

George looked skeptical.

For the next few months, Peggy reviewed database management systems and identified a partner that could implement a system designed to provide the information that Breakpoint needed to run the program day to day, improve its effectiveness, and provide compelling information to funders. It looked like the answer to all of her problems, and she received board approval to contract with the company to purchase the software and consulting services needed to get the system up and running and the staff properly trained. While Peggy was very excited, the rest of the staff members weren't convinced that a new system was needed. They were used to the old system, which they viewed as simple and easy to use.

Although the installation of the system was relatively simple, getting the staff on board with using the system regularly and correctly proved difficult. She asked George to help her understand what was going on with the staff. "I just don't think they see the value and how it helps them. They don't need the same information that you and the board do, so I think they are sort of boycotting. I know they wish we were using the old system."

"That's absurd," Peggy replied. "This system should make everyone's lives easier. I am so frustrated! Because they aren't using the system, I now actually have less data than I had to begin with."

Case Questions

1. What are some factors that a leader needs to consider when adopting new technology?

2. What role does organizational culture play in supporting or rejecting a change like the one presented in the case?

3. How can Peggy ensure that the system is in fact the right one for the entire organization?

INTEGRATING TECHNOLOGY: REFORMING THE SYSTEM

Ken and Cheri Walters were partners in marriage and in work. When they were first married, they were employed as pastors in large urban church. As part of their ministry duties, the Walters were assigned to work in a local prison teaching inmates to read and helping them to earn high school diplomas. Ken and Cheri gravitated toward the work and found it very rewarding. They recruited a host of volunteers, including retired teachers and judges to help deliver services. Although not formally trained as teachers, the Walters developed a strong appreciation for the power of education. They kept in touch with many of their "graduates," as they referred to them, even after they were no longer incarcerated.

Despite their success, it did not take long for the Ken and Cheri to notice that earning a high school diploma was not enough to ensure that formerly incarcerated people successfully integrated back into everyday life. It saddened them when they realized that it often did not take long for some of their grads to return to the prison system.

"What we do here is not enough to ensure that they will be successful on the outside," Ken observed.

"True," Cheri responded. "I thought that giving people a high school degree would boost their chance for future success, but in hindsight, that seems kind of naive. It's obvious we need to do more, or our work will be for meaningless."

With the help of some of their key volunteers and members of their church, the Walters formed Bridges, a nonprofit designed to provide integrated services for inmates that included job training, career counseling, and mental health and substance abuse services. Participants in the Bridges program were also assigned to a life coach who provided one-on-one mentoring during the transition process and for 6 months after they had been released. Life coaches focused on job placement and helped inmates set personal and professional goals and, when needed, connected their Bridges clients with additional support services.

The Walters designed Bridges to leverage support from existing programs, and the organization primarily served an important coordinating function. This model allowed Bridges to offer a holistic approach at a very low cost; in fact, the organization had an annual operating budget of only $250,000. Although the program was small, serving about 40 inmates in its first 3 years, data about graduates of the Bridges program were positive. The local paper ran a story featuring the stories of successful inmate transition and lives reformed. The story caught the attention of Ralph Kelly a well-known philanthropist who had made his fortune in business. He contacted Ken and Cheri and asked them for a meeting at a local restaurant.

"I've got to say I am mightily impressed with what you have been able to accomplish," Ralph told the Walters. "Your work touches me personally, because my nephew has been in prison on drug charges for some time now. I know he is due to be released next summer, and I am worried that without the kind of help you are offering, he likely won't make it."

"Unfortunately, the odds are not in his favor," Cheri said. "However, with a reasonable education, substance abuse treatment, and a marketable skill, research shows that people have a better chance of staying out of prison, which is a win–win for everyone," she added.

The meeting continued with the Walters, explaining the details of their program and sharing some success stories. At the conclusion of the meeting, Ralph informed the Walters that he wanted to support a major expansion of the Bridges program to include working at two additional prisons in different parts of the state. He informed Ken and Cheri that his foundation would be making a $500,000 dollar grant to the organization. The Walters were stunned.

"What's the catch?" asked Ken.

"There's no catch, but I'd like you to be able to significantly increase the number of people you serve." Ralph paused to sip his coffee. "Oh, and there are some reporting requirements for the grant that you will have to meet." He explained, "It is my hope that you can re-create your success. If we can prove that what you do works, you will likely be able to secure even greater funding from government sources."

"What do think that will entail, exactly?" Cheri asked.

"Well, you will need to keep good records about the program participants and track them for some time after they exit the program. The key is to show evidence of what you already know to be true, that they are less likely to return to prison than those who do not participate in Bridges."

Later, after Ralph had departed, the Walters discussed their good fortune.

"Are we ready for this kind of growth, Ken? Cheri asked.

"What do you mean?" Ken replied.

"Taking this kind of gift will mean big changes for our little nonprofit. It's challenging enough to do this work in one prison relying on a bunch of different partners to get the work done. Just thinking about how we will coordinate our work at three different sites is enough to make my head spin. Not to mention the tracking we will have to do to report back to Mr. Kelly. How are we going to keep in touch with every single person after they get out? It's no small task to do that now with the ones we know personally."

"I hear your concerns, but I imagine there has to be a technological solution that can support this expansion."

"Technology? Ha-ha!" Cherie chuckled. "You mean something bigger than my Excel spreadsheet? Aside from using our cell phones, you and I are not very tech savvy, Ken. I don't even know where we would begin."

Ken responded. "You know as well as I do that we have underinvested in technology for some time now—"

"Underinvested? More like total avoidance," Cheri interrupted.

Ken smiled. "Everything we do works, but it's so old school and certainly won't serve us well if we expand in the ways we and Ralph are envisioning. The real problem is that the way I have things calculated in my head, the grant is just enough to cover our services and added staff without much room for expensive technology and the trained staff to use it effectively."

"Do you think we can follow up with Ralph about that?" Cheri asked.

Case Questions

1. How should Ken and Cheri approach integrating technology into their nonprofit? What are the hard and soft costs that they need to consider?

2. What sorts of managerial issues will they confront when they add new technology?

3. Which organizational challenges can be solved with technology?

4. How should they approach the topic with Ralph?

SOCIAL MEDIA: A FUND-RAISING CURE OR A POTENT VIRUS?

Bridget Flores, chief development officer for Community Solutions Corps (CSC), a thriving social service and community health focused nonprofit, was brimming with excitement. CSC had over 100 employees and served homeless families and at-risk youth. CSC was well known for its strong one-on-one mentoring model of service delivery intended to provide continuous care and stability for individuals whose lives were often in chaos. Youth especially responded favorably under this model, building trusting relationships and close bonds with program staff, sometimes for the first times in their lives.

Bridget smiled broadly as she entered the weekly program staff meeting for the youth division of CSC. "Well folks, we have finally come into the 21st century," she announced. "I am happy to report that, at long last, we have taken our new website live, and we will launch it tomorrow in conjunction with our annual fund-raising campaign."

Bridget turned on her laptop and projected the website homepage on the screen. The staff responded with a round of applause.

"This is such an improvement," Liam Nelson, CSC youth programming director said, complimenting Bridget. "Finally, a site that makes us look like the professional organization we are," he continued. The rest of the staff members nodded in agreement as Bridget walked them through the site and explained its functionality.

"And here is the part I am most excited about," she said. "The site is completely compatible with social media so we can really build our profile and enhance our fund-raising efforts."

"That's really cool," said Maddie, a newly graduated social worker who had started with CSC as an intern the previous year.

"I'm glad you think so," Bridget replied, "because we are going to need all of you to help us launch this thing with a bang." She went on to explain that the annual fund drive had a virtual component that included social media. She asked all of the program staff to make sure they "liked" and shared the campaign announcement on their personal Facebook pages.

"Currently, CSC has about 200 Facebook friends, and we want to get that number up . . . way up," she told the group. "We think this will be an effective way to attract donors. It will go a long way toward making CSC real for people, so when you the share the page be sure to write a little blurb about your personal experience at the organization. Keeping it real makes it meaningful."

"Also, to make it fun for you, we are going to have a little contest. Tell your friends if they make their donations through the website there is a place where they can mention your name. The employee that gets the most referrals will win a $500 gift card, so be creative and get the word out. Tweet it, Instagram, Facebook, whatever . . . let's take this thing viral"

"Awesome," Maddie said, obviously reflecting the sentiment of her coworkers, who all appeared excited to promote the campaign.

Over the next week, Bridget closely monitored the website and social media associated with the campaign. Within one day of launching, the CSC Facebook and Twitter feeds exploded with employees sharing stories and pictures that made the work of CSC come alive in ways that they had never been able to achieve in previous campaigns. At the same time, donations increased, and the number of new donors was quickly rising. As the week progressed, Bridget gave the staff contest updates, letting them know each day the name of the employee who was in the lead to win the $500 gift card. This spawned friendly competition between departments and employees. Because of the close relationship between staff and clients, it wasn't long before some of the youth took notice and joined in the social media frenzy themselves. A sense of excitement grew throughout CSC as the campaign surpassed its original goals in short order.

In the second week of the campaign, Bridget received a call from Lydia Brantley, a long-standing member of the board and major donor to CSC. "Hello, Lydia," Bridget answered the phone cheerfully. "How can I be of service to my favorite board member today?"

"Good morning, Bridget," Lydia said warmly. "I am calling to congratulate you on the terrific success of the campaign. We got a board update last night. Very impressive."

"Oh, thanks so much," Bridget replied. "All that work on the website really paid off, that's for sure, and our employees and volunteers are really getting the word out on social media. We have over 1,000 people following CSC now."

"Well, that's partly why I'm calling today," Lydia said. "I don't mean to put a damper on everyone's enthusiasm, but I have some concerns." Lydia explained that she had been looking at all of the stories appearing on the Facebook page. "The stories are great, very moving," she told Bridget. "However, I'm worried about the privacy of our clients. Did they agree to have their stories and pictures shared?

"Nothing formal was signed or anything," Bridget replied. "But we did ask that employees only use the first names or pseudonyms when they shared stories.

"I'm sure you did, but that doesn't keep other people from tagging their real names to photos and such. It's virtually impossible to keep that from happening. People can even track the location of the picture. Although everything seems to be positive in nature, it worries me that we aren't in control of our message anymore, and we might be putting our clients at risk."

Beginning to feeling a little nervous herself, Bridget attempted to assure Lydia. "I don't think anything bad will come of it. I will double check our page and delete anything that could put us at risk."

"That would probably help, but the cat is really out of the bag since these things have already been shared over and over in cyberspace. And that raises another issue," Lydia added. "When I was looking at Facebook, I saw some really creative posts by a young woman named Maddie Donaldson."

"Yes, she is one of our social workers," said Bridget. "Very popular with our teen clients."

"I know. I met her briefly when I was volunteering last month," Lydia commented. "I was impressed by her ability to relate to the kids we were working with."

"So, what's the problem then?" asked Bridget.

"When I saw her comments and stories, I clicked on her name, and that took me to Maddie's personal Facebook page, which was not private. I know she is a good worker and all, but there were lots of pictures of her out drinking with friends and at least two posts about marijuana use. Frankly, I don't care what Maddie does on her own time, but anyone can see this. I am not sure it is consistent with the messages we are trying to convey to our teen clients."

"Obviously, I did not foresee that being a problem, Lydia. I am really sorry. How frustrating. We are making such headway with our campaign," she added. "I will raise the issue with our executive team today in our afternoon meeting."

Lydia thanked Bridget and hung up. Bridget swiveled in her chair and opened the CSC webpage.

Case Questions

1. What are some of the potential legal issues raised in the case?

2. What policies and procedures should nonprofits have in place for social media?

3. Given the issues raised in the case, what are some strategies that nonprofit leaders could employ to effectively use social media?

4. Should Maddie be reprimanded?

5. If you are Bridget, how do you lead this discussion with the executive team?

13

Grant Making

INTRODUCTION

One defining feature of the nonprofit sector is its structural reliance on philanthropy. In the United States, organized philanthropy is primarily carried out by foundations that are tax exempt nonprofits. The Foundation Center (2014), the nation's premier source for data about foundations and grant making identifies over 86,000 foundations in the United States. There are three major categories of private foundations, each with its own grant-making practices and purposes. Family foundations, for example, are the largest category of foundations in the United States with assets derived from one or more members of a family. Governance of family foundations and their grant-making practices are usually carried out by family members or by trustees appointed by the family. Some family foundations have paid staff. Corporate foundations are established with funds designated by for-profit corporations to carry out philanthropic grant making, usually aligned in some way with the business and community interests of the corporation. In contrast, private independent foundations and their grant-making activities are not usually tied to a specific family or corporation (although they may start as family foundations). Regardless of type, private foundations are tax-exempt organizations that must pursue a charitable mission and follow laws about disbursement of funds. Private foundations may be established to exist for a specified period, or they may be designed to carry on in perpetuity.

Community foundations are public charities that engage in grant-making practices similar to private foundations. Whereas private foundations derive their assets from a single source, the assets of community foundations are pooled from multiple sources or individuals. Grant making by community foundations is usually meant to benefit a particular geographic area or community.

Regardless of type, foundations are the vehicles for philanthropic grant making. Nonprofits may access philanthropic dollars by making a grant request to a foundation. The act of grant making is informed by the goals and objectives of the grant maker (funder). Some foundations do not accept unsolicited grant proposals, and some have very strict requirements for grant making. Therefore, to write a successful grant, it is paramount that the applicant organization understand and comply with the specific guidelines set forth by the foundation.

Like nonprofit organizations, managing foundations and the act of grant making is an intricate process that is often shaped by personal motivation. While it seems like it should be easier and more desirable to be the grant maker than the grant seeker, this is not always the case. For example, there can be a perceived or very real imbalance in power between grant makers and grant seekers, and lines of accountability can be blurry. This chapter explores different aspects of grant making and includes cases about the following issues:

1. Deciding when to hire staff

2. Donor advised funds

3. Foundation-initiated collaboration

4. When a foundation accomplishes its mission

REFERENCE

The Foundation Center. (2014). Foundation stats: Aggregate fiscal data of foundations in the U.S., 2012. Retrieved from http://data.foundationcenter.org/#/foundations/all/nationwide/total/list/2012

DECIDING WHEN TO HIRE STAFF: FAMILY FEUD

Marion Sisson was the matriarch of the Sisson family. She and her husband, Harvey, had worked side by side for 60 years to build a luxury raincoat and accessory business that had altogether become nearly as famous as Burberry. The business was now run by their children, Barry and David and son-in-law, Aaron (their daughter Sarah's husband who had joined the business when he married into the family 30 years ago), along with several grandchildren who were being groomed to take over the company.

Until her death at age 87, Marion, who had been widowed for 5 years, had been a shrewd businesswoman, a loving mother, and a doting grandmother to her nine grandchildren and great-grandmother to three little ones. In her obituary, *The New York Times* reported on her deep love and devotion to her husband and family, her belief in practical fashion that was beautiful, and her dedication to the Jewish concept of *Tikkun Olam*—a Hebrew phrase meaning "to repair the world," which she and Harvey manifested through charitable gifts to a wide variety of organizations and causes. She was quoted as saying, "My husband and I both came from families that had nothing but dreams. Our success in business has allowed us to help others who have not been as fortunate and to give in ways that make the world a better place."

At the time of Marion's death, the Sisson Family Foundation was valued at $76 million. While she and Harvey had been responsible for endowing the foundation with the bulk of its assets, they had always insisted that their children contribute to it as well. Barry, David, and Sarah each had a seat on the board of the foundation; however, they merely rubber-stamped the decisions made by their mother. It wasn't that they were disinterested; rather, they had implicit trust in Marion's judgment of which organizations would be good recipients of the funds distributed by the foundation. They used to joke that they didn't worry about organizations soliciting them for large gifts as everyone in the nonprofit world knew that Marion held the purse strings of the foundation. After she died, they realized that they needed to pay much more attention to the foundation and began looking at it in earnest for the first time.

It was David who discovered that the corpus of the foundation was not being invested wisely. Marion and Harvey had entrusted the management of the foundation's money to an old friend who was now quite elderly. Even in his youth, Sumner Goldman had never had a stellar investment career (it was typical that Marion and Harvey gave business opportunities to people they thought needed a break). Looking over the portfolio, David realized that the foundation had the potential to grow substantially if its funds were handled by a more competent professional. After meeting with Sumner to gently extricate the funds, he handed them over to an investment professional who was experienced with managing funds for foundations. Within 5 years, the corpus grew to more than $120 million including additional contributions from him and his siblings. Pleased with his success, David convened a meeting of the board to discuss a giving strategy for the foundation.

"At this point, we have a fairly sizable corpus that, at 5%, has us looking at approximately $6 million in annual distributions since we aren't paying much at all for admin beyond our investment fees. For the past 5 years we've pretty much been increasing our grants to the organizations that mom supported all those years, but I think it's time for us to take a closer look at the charities we give to and how we're going about giving away money. I think we need to get a better understanding of how our money is being spent by these organizations. Maybe we need to consider giving money to more or different organizations? None of us is getting any younger either. I think it's time we put the kids on the board so that they can get involved in this, and that we should hire a professional to oversee the work of the foundation."

"Whoa! Slow down a minute, David," said Barry. "We've always done things this way. Mom was adamant about not having any overhead associated with our giving because she and Dad wanted to be sure that the money was going to causes and not to fees for professional managers; she hated that idea."

"I know she did," replied David. "But the fact of the matter is that she wasn't giving away as much money as we have now, and toward the end of her life, she was pretty much dedicating herself to giving money away—she wasn't *really* running the business at that point. For us, it's just the opposite: We're still fully engaged in Sisson Enterprises and barely taking a look at this stuff except to write our own checks to increase the foundation's kitty."

"Well, I'm not running the business," said Sarah, "but to be honest, I'm not really interested in taking on this project at my stage in life. It's not that I don't think charity is important—of course I do; that's how we were raised—it's just that I'd rather Aaron and I write a check to the foundation and have someone else make the decisions about where the money would be best spent. I just don't know enough about all of these organizations to have confidence in my judgment about who should get what, never mind how much more complicated it could get if we started to look at the possibility of funding new organizations. What if we asked one of the kids to take it on as a paid position?"

"Who would that be?" asked Barry. "My kids are in the business, and I don't think any of them would want to leave to take this on, your Ruth is an artist, and Rachel and Leah are stay-at-home moms. That leaves the possibility that Michael or Daniel could do it, and I have no idea whether either one would be interested. But they could handle it if they wanted to, and I'd be supportive of that."

"What makes you think they could handle this, Barry?" replied David. "Philanthropy, done right, is too complicated for people who aren't trained to do it. That's why I think we should hire a professional."

"What do you mean?" said Barry. "How complicated can it be to give away money? The kids are smart; they could figure it out."

Case Questions

1. What policies and procedures do you believe Marion could have put in place while she was alive to ensure the healthy functioning of the foundation after she was gone?

2. What is the role of a professional foundation manager?

3. Do you believe that a large family foundation can be managed on an all-volunteer basis? If not, why not? What dollar amount, if any, is too large for a family to handle without professional assistance?

4. What can foundations do to ensure their gifts are being expended properly?

DONOR ADVISED FUNDS: DO DONORS KNOW BEST?

The Pacific Coast Community Foundation (PCCF) had been formed in 1985 to charitably serve the local community. The foundation was started by a group of wealthy families that each contributed $1 million of seed money. Of that initial investment, 25% of the money was used to hire a small staff, to set up an office for the foundation, and to cover the foundation's operating costs for the first year. The remainder of the money was put into an endowment account to be used for discretionary grant making in the community. Any nonprofit organization working on projects deemed by the board of directors to be important to the health and well-being of the community could apply for a grant.

The board of directors was composed of 10 voting members that each served 4-year rotating terms. The original board members, who were members of the founding families, eventually were termed out and replaced by other philanthropists and community leaders. To prevent conflicts of interest, PCCF had a policy that prevented potential grantees from sitting on the board. Consequently, there were never any leaders from the nonprofit sector asked to sit on the board, as all nonprofits were eligible to apply for grants from the foundation.

During the late 1980s and the early 1990s, the foundation raised funds by taking donations and by establishing donor advised funds (DAFs) for individuals that did not wish to hassle with starting their own foundation. Leu Mengarelli, a former bank executive, had been hired in 1998 to head the foundation. Under Leu's guidance, the foundation grew in leaps and bounds; during the boom years of the early 2000s, she increased the foundation's portfolio of DAFs. When she was congratulated by people for her success, she often said, "People put their charitable money here because they know we have a proven track record of investing their funds wisely, which is to say, we make big bucks for our clients."

Before long, DAFs became the primary source of income for the foundation. Donors appreciated the tax advantages offered through a DAF as well as having a say over how the funds were spent. Nonprofit leaders in the community had mixed feelings about the direction that PCCF was taking as the foundation had fewer discretionary grant dollars to give out every year. The amount of money that the foundation was able to distribute for competitive proposals had diminished to less than 2% of the foundation's yearly distributions. Instead, donors were earmarking their funds to their favorite causes. The foundation went from having a model where professional program officers sorted through competitive proposals and made funding recommendations to the board, to one where there were no longer program officers on staff but rather fund managers who managed the portfolios of the individual DAFs and administered the distributions. Seth Meyer, the head of the local nonprofit membership association, convened a meeting between several prominent nonprofit leaders and PCCF's chief executive officer (CEO).

Seth opened the meeting by providing an overview of their concerns. "We want you to know that the nonprofit community has a great appreciation for the community foundation. We have been strong partners for nearly 3 decades. However, we feel like we are losing some of that original spirit of partnership that was once a big part of the foundation." Seth went on to describe how difficult it had become to access grant dollars from the foundation.

Leu acknowledged his concerns. "I know the direction of the foundation has changed a bit, but you have to understand that we have a mission to adhere to just like any nonprofit, and that has not changed one bit. We exist to increase the pool of philanthropic dollars to benefit our community."

"Well, we are here to tell you we aren't seeing as much of those dollars flowing to the nonprofits that are on the front lines solving community problems every day. We've reviewed your annual report, and it seems like a lot of the money is going to animal groups, symphonies and ballets, and people's alma maters and not toward addressing real community needs," Seth said. "I mean, I like kittens and puppies as much as the next guy, but don't your donors understand what's important to the community?"

"Now, Seth, I think that's sort of an exaggeration on your part. If you look at that report you will see that our donors have allocated funds to over 1,000 nonprofits last year," Leu responded.

"That's our point exactly. What happens here is determined by individuals. There is no collective approach, no strategic direction. When they give you the money, they are technically giving up control, but instead, it's sort of a wink and a nudge arrangement where you let them call all of the shots for how it gets distributed. That means we are at the whim of the donor. All we can do is hope that they care about the homeless problem we have downtown more than saving the seals," Seth said in frustration. "You're no different than a bank . . . And worse yet, since there is no representation from the nonprofit community on your board, we feel like the board is shielded from really hearing our concerns and isn't fully informed about the very real problems they should be addressing in our community . . . which is the whole reason this place was established to begin with!"

Leu looked at the group before her. "I don't really know what to tell you," she said defensively. Our job here at the foundation is to serve our donors, to grow their portfolios, and to increase the philanthropic pie, and that's what we are doing. We try to let them know what's going on in the community, but in the end, it's really their decision where they choose to invest their charitable dollars."

Seth and his group looked extremely frustrated.

Case Questions

1. What is your assessment of donor advised funds? What are the pros and cons?

2. From the donor perspective and the nonprofit management perspective, describe what is gained or lost for each group under the donor advised funding model.

3. What are some ways that community foundations bridge the needs of the community to the philanthropic dollars they steward?

4. What are the advantages and disadvantages of more government oversight or regulation of DAFs? Do you believe government should increase regulation over DAFs? Why, or why not?

5. What are the long-term consequences of increased donor control that nonprofit leaders should consider?

FOUNDATION-INITIATED COLLABORATION: FOSTERING FRUSTRATION

Dominique Wells loved her job as a program officer for the Bedford Hale Foundation (BHF). She had come to the foundation after working for many years in corporate philanthropy where her grants were more closely tied to the mission of her former employer. She relished the opportunities she had at Bedford to provide nonprofits with funding that was much more suited to their needs and the people they served. The portfolio she oversaw focused on programs to strengthen youth and families, which included grants to more than 65 organizations each year. Dominique prided herself on having open communication with her grantees and a solid working knowledge of the work they were doing in the community. She was well respected among her colleagues at the foundation.

Several years into Dominique's job at the foundation, Silvia Enriquez was hired as the new president/CEO of BHF. Prior to this position, Silvia had been a vice president at the Eichler Foundation. She was known for expansive thinking and for her ability to create change. She was determined to put her stamp on BHF and, specifically, to increase its impact in the community. Three months after she arrived, she convened a meeting of BHF's four program officers to discuss her vision for the foundation (it had already been enthusiastically approved by the board). She explained it this way: "Each of you has an extensive portfolio of grantees that is grouped respectively under the categories of health, the environment, youth and families, and civil society. Many of the organizations that are in your portfolio are operating in silos. What I would like you to do is envision how your grantees could forge innovative and successful collaborations that cross and blur boundaries. I want you to color outside the lines to conceive pioneering multiagency partnerships and to then assemble folks who will explore these new frontiers of dynamic cooperation. The goal is that your collective action initiatives will result in new paradigms that are exponentially impactful. We will provide our grantees with the resources to explore these opportunities in anticipation of the outcomes they will yield."

Dominique was electrified by Silvia's remarks. Her head was spinning when she left the meeting as she began to think about the grantees in her portfolio and how she might bring several together for this new BHF initiative.

A few days later, Dominque had the answer: For her collective action initiative, she would propose a collaboration among three of her grantees: Vicki Barton, executive director of Fostering Love (an organization working with foster youth); Mary McDonald, executive director, Whole Family Adoptions; and Anthony Jeffords, president and CEO, New Friends Senior Center. She asked her executive assistant to convene a meeting of the three CEOs to explain the project.

When Vicki, Mary, and Anthony were called to meet with Dominique, each felt unsure about the purpose of the meeting; however, none shared this confusion with Dominique or each other. BHF had been a consistent and therefore important funder to each organization for several years; all thought their working relationship with Dominique was strong. The three CEOs knew each other only casually (they ran into each other at events around town) and had limited knowledge of each other's work. When Dominique described the project, she reassured them that the collective action grant, $10,000 per organization, would be provided in addition to their annual operating grant (approximately $50,000 per agency). As she described it, the funds would allow them approximately 9 months to get know one another and to develop what she envisioned would be a dramatic new paradigm for a family continuum embracing foster children, adoptive families, and seniors who would serve as proxy grandparents. This money was to give the directors time to think, explore, and ultimately present a new proposal to the foundation. The full cycle would take a year from conception to funding.

Toward the end of the meeting, Vicki cautiously asked, "Once this new effort is launched, will it replace the funding that BHF has been providing to our three organizations?" Dominique nodded in assent, a big smile on her face. "It doesn't necessarily mean that we will award less money to your organizations," she added. "It means that we are moving the foundation to a new mode of operating, one that emphasizes collective impact and collaboration rather than supporting the efforts of singular organizations."

The three filed out with words of thanks and quickly grouped on the sidewalk outside the building. Anthony spoke first. "It's obvious that BHF is shifting the way it gives. If we don't hop on the bus, we're going to be left standing by the side of the road without a ride. We don't have a choice but to see what we can work out between our three organizations." Mary replied, "I agree, Anthony, and I'm also excited about what might come out of this joint brainstorming. It could be pretty neat." They agreed to set up a regular meeting time every Thursday morning from 8 to 10 a.m. starting the following week. The idea was to rotate the meeting location so they could become familiar with each other's organizations. Mary volunteered to host the first meeting.

At 8:20 on the morning of their first scheduled meeting, Anthony and Mary chatted politely while they waited for Vicki to arrive. They were just about to call her office when Mary's executive assistant walked in to tell her that Vicki had called to say that she was running late and would be there by 8:45. "Maybe she thought we set the meeting for 8:30," said Mary cheerfully. "I don't know how that would be possible," said Anthony. "I spoke to her administrative assistant and personally confirmed the date and time twice." While they were waiting, Mary introduced Anthony to the two case workers who were on her staff and explained the focus of the organization: "Our work is principally with mothers who for whatever reason don't feel they can keep their children. They find us through the church, the county, advertising, community clinics and other health providers, the school system, and social service agencies. We offer both closed and open adoptions, with an open adoption being one where the birth mother can interact with the adoptive family on an ongoing basis and can play a role in choosing the family that will adopt her child. Since our focus is on newborns, we also work with children from other countries and facilitate adoptions in many places around the world, primarily through a network of Catholic organizations. Those adoptions take longer, but our clients are all looking for babies. The work is labor intensive and involves extensive counseling of birth mothers and screening and counseling of prospective adoptive parents. We also handle extensive legal issues and do a lot of community outreach and education. We are proud of our record of placing 25 children per year with families. I know it doesn't sound like a lot, but it is for our small staff and the degree of work that is involved in each situation."

"This is a whole new world for me, Mary. I'm impressed with what you do and with the love and care you so clearly dedicate to this important work," said Anthony. "I'm not sure though just how we would begin to get our seniors involved in the adoption process. What we do is provide recreation and other kinds of support for seniors including lunch and transportation, health screening, social activities, and counseling. This doesn't seem like an easy fit to me, but we can brainstorm more after you see our facility. We serve 300 seniors a week in a variety of ways. Most of our seniors are frail and low-income."

When Vicki arrived, she was breathless and apologized for being late. After settling in and hearing Mary's explanation of Whole Family's work, Vicki began to describe the work of Fostering Love. "Our goal is to reunite children with their families, if at all possible. We work with 200 foster children per year, of which roughly 12 end up being available for adoption. Most of those children are at least 8 years old or older. Our first step with those kids is to look for a relative. Of that group, approximately half or more don't have anyone to step in so they stay in foster care. I suppose we could explore having some of your seniors act as foster grandparents, and maybe, Mary, you could help those kids get adopted."

The more they talked, the more they realized the challenges of working together. Most of the seniors didn't have cars or weren't able to drive. Anthony was concerned about the ongoing role of the grandparents if the children were permanently adopted. Mary was worried about helping to adopt older kids as she had never done that before.

As the months went on, a pattern developed among the members of the group. Vicki was late to every meeting, and she was always disorganized. She frequently forgot important details of their earlier discussions and was easily distracted during their conversations. She often had to leave meetings early to "put out a fire" at her organization. Invariably, she would say something like, "I apologize for this, you guys. It's just that Fostering Love runs on a shoestring. I don't have enough staff to cover everything that needs to be done, and this work with the two of you is just heaping more work on top of what I can't get done already. I feel bad, but I have to take care of the stuff that needs to get done now."

When Mary attempted to set up a time to meet with Vicki or her staff to initiate a discussion about how they might work together, the meeting was invariably canceled at the last minute. Mary couldn't get a solid understanding of how Fostering Love operated. Despite those enormous obstacles, Mary was perennially upbeat and didn't seem to mind Vicki's behavior (at least, she didn't demonstrate feelings of frustration to Anthony). She would often say to him, "I've learned to be a very patient person as one has to be to deal with the adoption process."

Anthony was a consummate professional at the beginning of the process but grew irritated with both Vicki and Mary several months into the project. He had no patience for Vicki's behavior, and while he appreciated Mary's kind demeanor, he found her saccharine sweetness to be tiresome. He wanted to work with professionals who knew how to accomplish a goal and felt that he had already exhausted $10,000 of his time with no return for the effort. Six months had already passed, and the group had nothing to show for its efforts. He decided to send a staff person to attend the meetings in his place and to report back to him on the progress (if any) that was being made. He selected a young staffer who was smart and ambitious, although she had relatively little experience as a manager. He wasn't sure what his next steps should be with Dominique and BHF and decided he would wait to see how things played out for a few more months.

Case Questions

1. How would you describe the essential criteria of a successful collaborative effort?

2. Based on your understanding, how did Silvia and Dominique's design for the collective action initiative meet your criteria? How could their effort have been structured differently to maximize success?

3. How would you describe the most significant issues facing the three grantees? How could Dominique have helped to overcome those issues? How might the three directors have addressed the issues themselves to create a more successful collaboration?

4. Is it always a good idea to have a collaboration? Why, or why not?

5. Given that 6 months have passed, what do you think the three directors should do now?

WHEN A FOUNDATION ACCOMPLISHES ITS MISSION: THE Q FOUNDATION

Brad Jenkins grinned from ear to ear. He never imagined that he would be able to marry his partner in Idaho, the conservative state where he had been born and raised (and tormented endlessly throughout elementary and high school for being different). Nor could he believe that same-sex marriage was now legal across the country. It was incredible.

When Brad was hired in 2008 to lead the Q Foundation (the Q was short for "queer"), he believed same sex marriage in Idaho was an aspirational goal that might be possible in the far distant future if he and others did all they could to bring about change. Marriage equality was something that he and his partner, Joel, and their friends could only envision happening after decades of work and *major* shifts in how people like his parent's friends, grandparents, and other run-of-the-mill folks thought about people like them. It had happened so much faster than anyone ever would have imagined at the start of this effort.

Prior to becoming the founding CEO of the Q, Brad had been employed as the marketing director of a successful Silicon Valley tech firm. The circumstances of his hiring at the Q were like something out of a movie. He and Joel had been at a summer party in 2008 with a bunch of techies when the conversation turned to Proposition 8, California's ballot measure to establish a constitutional amendment banning same-sex marriage. The proposal's backers had submitted more than a million signatures to the state that May, qualifying the measure to appear on the ballot; in June, the state had certified the initiative was eligible to be voted on. At the party, a small group from his company was sipping Napa Valley Cabernet and debating about whether Prop 8 had a chance of passing. Bill Andrews, the CEO of the company (who was also gay), said, "We're screwed if this thing passes on the left coast. It will be the death-knell for gay marriage in most of this country for the foreseeable future, never mind in Hicksville, Idaho, where you guys are from."

"Hey, I resemble that," joked Brad. "But all kidding aside; I think that if someone has a good sense of public relations and business to dedicate to this fight, then just maybe we have a chance at marriage equality in Idaho." To Brad's surprise, Bill responded. "You're on, buddy. I will bankroll a foundation in Idaho that is dedicated to the cause if you agree that you'll run it." After they left the party, Brad asked Joel if he thought Bill's offer was serious, and they agreed that it was. "You know, Joel, "he said solemnly, "I think I really could make a difference."

A few weeks later, they packed their bags and moved back to Boise to set up the Q with Bill as chairman of the board, Bill's best friend Cliff (an architect and gay activist) as secretary and treasurer, and Brad as a director and the CEO. Joel quickly found employment as a tax attorney at a prominent Boise law firm.

Bill's agreement was that rather than park his funds in an endowment, he would provide $1.2 million to the Q on an annual basis, of which $300,000 could be used for operating expenses. Brad understood that Bill wanted to run a lean operation and managed to do so by leading the operations with a highly competent executive assistant.

Although the Q focused its efforts on funding gay marriage efforts in Idaho, it also supported similar work in surrounding states. Brad was part of a collaborative effort with many other foundations and national organizations that were dedicated to advancing the cause of same sex marriage. He was proud of the fact that, according to Funders for LGBTQ Issues, foundation support for the community had soared from nearly $48.8 million in 2004 to slightly more than $129 million in 2013, and, of that 2013 amount, $11 million was dedicated to marriage equality (Funders for LGBTQ Issues, 2013). He knew that the dominoes had fallen across the country in no small part because of the influx of foundation dollars to support the cause.

In the weeks after the Supreme Court's ruling and his own wedding, Brad began to think about next steps for the Q Foundation. He spoke to Bill on the phone, saying, "Now that we've reached the finish line, I'm really not sure what's next for the Q or whether there should be a next chapter in the life of our foundation. You've been incredibly generous. It seems time for the board to have a deep conversation about where we go from here." Bill agreed, saying, "Let's all get together for a few days next month at my house to dedicate some serious time to talking this through."

Prior to the retreat, Brad spoke with several directors of other foundations that had been actively funding marriage equality efforts. Some of these foundations were exclusively LGBTQ-focused while others, much larger in scope and resources, funded an array of causes of which marriage equality was just one. His conversations with these leaders raised as many questions as they answered, for each organization had a different strategy for how it planned to work in the future. He also took long walks to think about whether it would be personally selfish of him to lobby for an expanded mission and vision for the Q. After all, it was a full-time job he loved.

In preparation for the retreat, Brad compiled the following set of questions (which you should consider) to guide the discussion with the other board members:

Case Questions

1. Should the foundation sunset now that its mission has been accomplished?

2. If the foundation does not sunset, should it

   - dedicate itself to a next issue or set of LGBTQ civic equality issues that have a "bright line" legal goal(s) (for instance, nondiscrimination protection issues in employment, housing, public accommodations; parenting issues [e.g., the ability to get both parents names on the birth certificate]; laws relating to the safety and well-being of youth such as antibullying laws and laws that ban gay conversation therapy; elevated punishment for hate-crimes protection);

   - broaden its focus to one or more LGBTQ "lived experience" issues, that is, quality-of-life and well-being issues (These could include, for example, access to health-care [i.e., is the care that is being provided culturally competent, is there an emphasis on prevention behaviors and wellness?], bullying and assault prevention to change a climate within a school; homelessness among youth; the medical treatment and social acceptance of transgender people; the treatment LBGTQ people of color, immigrants and elders);

   - continue to focus on Idaho; or

   - become an operating foundation, specifically by operating programs to provide support services to same-sex married couples to help ensure strong marriages (e.g., child-care subsidies, financial management classes, etc.)?

3. Should the foundation seek to change its financial structure such that it is not wholly dependent upon Bill's generosity? If so, what are the legal and practical implications of such a change? How would the governance structure need to change?

REFERENCE

Funders for LGBTQ Issues. (2013). 2013 tracking report: Lesbian, gay, bisexual, transgender, and queer grantmaking by U.S. foundations. Retrieved from https://www.lgbtfunders.org/files/2013_Tracking_Report.pdf

14

International Nonprofits

INTRODUCTION

We live and work in an increasingly globalized society that, among other things, has spurred tremendous growth in the worldwide nonprofit sector. Technology and improved communications systems have made this growth possible, bringing to light issues such as poverty, disease, human rights, and environmental preservation and connecting donors to these and other issues often times far from their own backyards.

The concepts presented in this case book have been designed to explore traditional Western nonprofit management concepts. And indeed, many around the world look to America's nonprofit sector as a model for nonprofit governance, management, and service delivery in their own countries. Yet, the word *nonprofit* is not widely used or conceptualized in the same way across the globe. A growing body of literature about the international nonprofit sector contains numerous terms to define and describe the international nonprofit sector and its activities. Outside of the United States, nonprofits are typically referred to as nongovernmental organizations (NGOs), civil society organizations, or voluntary associations. Salamon and Anheier apply a more comprehensive term, *international nongovernmental organizations* (INGOs), to identify the many widely recognized nonprofits that "make significant operating expenditures across national borders and do not identify themselves as domestic actors" (Helmut & Themudo, 2011).

Beyond terminology, there are dimensions of managing an organization in an international context that are not fully accounted for in typical Western nonprofit management models. For example, successful day-to-day management of an NGO and the ability to craft long-term strategies for developing and deploying resources requires a deep understanding of the larger environment in which the organization works. In particular, managers must be knowledgeable about the different legal, cultural, and political systems that must be navigated. Leading and managing nonprofits with a presence in more than one country, as in the case of INGOs, presents additional layers of complexity. For example, a country director in Kenya must align on-the-ground practices with directives often issued from home offices located across oceans and continents. Furthermore, NGO and INGO leaders are responsible for finding ways to connect with and engage remote donors and, at the same time, properly manage donor expectations to ensure ethical and culturally competent delivery of services to those being served.

This chapter presents cases that allow students to explore the following challenges of nonprofit management in an international setting:

1. Cross culture clash

2. NGO Accountability

3. Grassroots out-of-country efforts to help overseas people

4. The difficulty in securing donations for overhead expenses

REFERENCE

Helmut, A., & Themudo, N. (2011). The internationalization of the nonprofit sector. In D. O. Renz (Ed.), *The Jossey-Bass handbook of nonprofit leadership and management* (2nd ed.). San Francisco, CA: Jossey-Bass.

CROSS-CULTURAL CLASH: AN UNHEALTHY DYNAMIC

Andy and Judy McMillan were thrilled to pack up their Minnesota home, divest themselves of the bulk of their worldly possessions, and head south for a new life in Guatemala. The couple, who had recently retired as primary care physicians, had met decades earlier in medical school, married before they graduated, and raised three children who were now grown with families of their own. They had visited Guatemala the previous year where they found themselves surprisingly and profoundly moved by the beauty of its land and the kindness of its people. During that visit and after a series of late-night conversations with a group of expats they met in Antigua, the McMillans decided they were ready to trade in their white coats and stethoscopes for a quiet life in the beautiful country they had discovered.

It did not take long for Andy and Judy to feel at home in Guatemala. They were immediately welcomed by the large expat community (composed mostly of Americans and Canadians) as well as their Guatemalan neighbors. They loved exploring all corners of their new country and hosting their children, grandchildren, and friends for visits. Through a combination of intensive classes and daily interactions with Guatemalans, their rudimentary Spanish improved significantly. The more they traveled throughout the country, the more deeply attached the McMillans became to Guatemala.

One morning as they were sitting in their garden drinking coffee, Judy said, "I just love living here. It's so wonderful. And I also feel like after a year of an extended vacation that I want to do something meaningful to help this country. We have plenty of good years left, Andy, and I want to use them to build a health clinic here." Andy's eyes lit up. "Honey," he replied, "you must have been reading my mind! I've been feeling the exact same way. Let's do it!"

And with that, the McMillans began to explore a location for their new clinic, eventually settling on a rural community that was located about a 45-minute drive from their home. The run-down area held little more than a bodega where drinks, vegetables, and fruit were sold; a Catholic church;

a dry goods store; a shoe repair shop; a tire repair shop; an inexpensive clothing store; and a bus station. The McMillans thought the bus station would enable people to come to the clinic more easily from surrounding communities, which were dotted with subsistence farms. They found a plot of land located next to the bodega, began sketching out a drawing of the facility, found a local builder who could do the construction, and put together lists of what supplies they would need to operate the clinic.

After doing this background work, the McMillans flew to Minnesota to meet with friends from their old Rotary Club, associates from the hospital where they had worked, and a group from their former church to discuss their plans and the funding that would be required to put the clinic in place. By the time they flew back to Guatemala, they had raised a sufficient amount of money to build the clinic, stock it with medical supplies, and hire a nurse.

Within 7 months, the Clinica de Salud de Nuestro Valle was open for business, offering free and low-cost care for a nominal fee (for the very few patients who might be able to pay something). Although its focus was on family medicine, Judy and Andy sought to promote wellness in the form of vaccinations, disease control (for example, diabetes was rampant in the area), and family planning. Aurelia Morena, the nurse they had hired directly out of a nursing program in Guatemala City, was instructed to offer all patients who came to the clinic help in these areas regardless of whether that was the purpose of their visit. Aurelia was happy to have a job right out of school, but she had no connection to this part of the country and did not speak the local language.

During the first days and weeks the clinic was open, business was slow. Indeed, most of the early patients who came to the clinic were farm workers who had injured themselves with what was, more often than not, rusted equipment. Once they were provided stitches, antibiotics, and bandages, they headed immediately back into the fields. As word spread, the second wave of patients, elderly clients, came in search of remedies for common complaints such as a severe upset stomach (often caused by parasites), toothache (a dentist was scheduled to visit once a month), vertigo, or migraines. Finally, young mothers with babies strapped to their chests, gripping toddlers and other young ones by their hands, found their way to the clinic. Andy and Judy were particularly happy to serve that population as they believed that was where they could have the greatest impact.

Judy and Andy thought they could promote family planning by engaging a mother in a conversation about birth control while they treated her children (parasites were the most common problem). However, the women were shy and suspicious about why Judy or Aurelia would bring up the subject with them (and they were mortified when the topic was raised by Andy). Aurelia tried to explain that the topic of sexual relations was seen by rural people as a very private matter that *might* be able to be broached with them several months from now once the clinic had longer standing relationships with these patients. The fact that none of them spoke the local dialect made things worse (she didn't tell the McMillans that their English-accented Spanish wasn't helping matters either). She advised Andy to confine his discussions about birth control to his interactions with male patients, although she suspected that few would listen to him.

Aurelia was able to make some inroads with a few women who had especially large families. Yet even then she primarily dispensed condoms and was unsure if they would be used. Andy and Judy argued for inserting more birth control skin patches and IUDs; however, Aurelia believed that would be a much harder sell.

Aurelia, Judy, and Andy were even more concerned about the women who came to the clinic displaying clear signs of having a sexually transmitted disease but who were confused about how or why they could have these symptoms. When Aurelia and Judy attempted to explain the cause (most often, an unfaithful husband), the women stared in disbelief and often left the clinic without taking the medicine that was vital to their recovery. They would return when the pain worsened (or not if the symptoms disappeared for a time), which led the medical staff to worry about a more severe infection. In addition, because these women had low levels of literacy, the staff worried that when they did convince them to take the medicine, they doubted the patients would be able to follow the treatment directions (and there was also a question about access to clean water for taking the pills).

Complicating matters, 3 months after it opened, the clinic received a visit from Father Florido, the parish priest who ministered to the community twice a month (he was responsible for serving a network of rural churches). Father Florido entered the clinic and asked to meet with Andy. Although he initially seemed cordial, it soon became apparent that he was incensed that the clinic was promoting and dispensing birth control. "Who gave you the right to come into this community and do this?" he demanded. "This is not what God intended. You must stop this at once. You came to this community pretending to do good, but you are instead spreading evil." With that he walked out the door.

As Andy and Judy drove back to their home that evening, they felt emotionally drained. It had been almost a year since they conceived of the idea of the clinic, and it already seemed to be failing. It was becoming increasingly difficult to keep a positive spin on their work to the friends, colleagues, and community members that had funded the work, and, moreover, they were already running out of money (the construction had gone over budget, which they suspected was a result of them being seen as wealthy gringos who could afford to pay double the usual cost). "We've tried to do so much for this community, and it doesn't seem to be working," sobbed Judy. "I just don't know what we've done wrong."

Case Questions

1. What, if any, are the principle differences in operating a nonprofit in North America versus a developing country?

2. Do you believe the McMillans' clinic will be successful in the long run? Why, or why not?

3. What additional research could Andy and Judy have done in the planning stage that would have created a greater chance of the clinic succeeding?

4. What are your thoughts on the funding model for the clinic?

5. What is meant by the term *cultural competency*, and how does it apply to this case?

NGO ACCOUNTABILITY: TOO MUCH OF A GOOD THING?

"We have a real problem brewing here," reported Adisa Turay, the indigenous country director for the Liberian unit of Women and Children First (WCF), a well-known international nonprofit headquartered in Washington, D.C. WCF had many chapters around the world and focused much of its attention on public health and economic development.

Adisa, who worked out of a small rented office in Liberia, was taking part in a quarterly Skype meeting with Terri Wray, the director for all WCF activities in Africa. Also on the call was Nancy Roberts from the home office. The purpose of the call was to discuss the opening of the first ever WCF Academy for Girls in Liberia. Although WCF had been doing maternal and child health care for many years all over Africa, the academy was its first formalized attempt at providing direct education services as a larger economic development strategy.

"What's going on?" Terri inquired. "It was my understanding that we were finally getting the kinds of funds that we need to get some traction around getting girls off the streets and into school."

"Well, the increased funding is actually part of the problem," Adisa informed the group. "With Liberia currently facing a huge problem of youth employment, teenage pregnancy, and idle youths causing problems in communities, working in our space has suddenly become popular and proven to be an eye-catching and marketable item to big international donors."

She went on to tell her team that the amount of money from the United Nations and other foundations directed to youth development causes had led to a proliferation of new NGOs on the ground. "It's like they are coming out of the woodwork. New groups pop up every day, and it's causing big problems because there is no accountability. Some cease to exist after getting a grant and implementing a single project. So, to the outside world the numbers look huge, but here on the ground, it's another story all together. Reporting requirements are

minimal at best. Photos and attendance sheets are all some foundations are asking for."

"I guess in some ways we should be happy that people are finally taking
a serious interest in your little corner of the world," Nancy said.

"Normally I would agree, but I think we are going to see more harm
than good come out of this, and it's causing me all kinds of problems
with locals here on the ground. For example, one group started a
program last month, promised all kinds of good things, even paid the
girls to come and sign the attendance sheets. A week later, they were
gone, and the girls were no better off. Now I'm going to have an even
harder time convincing them to come to our new school when it opens.
Plus the local media is starting to write about it, so it won't be long
before the headlines reach our donors and stir up more distrust," Adisa
explained. "In fact, Terry, why don't you tell Nancy about the article I for-
warded to you this morning?"

"I'll do you one better, let me read you the part of the story." Terri
reached over and picked up a sheet of paper. She proceeded to read
excerpts of several interviews, some with girls as young as seven, who
had been working as prostitutes. The girls had been promised skills
training and schooling but had nothing to show for it. One girl was
quoted as saying, "They told us to join them, they say we should stop
going to the street saying they will provide skill training for us, but since
the beginning of the program we have not seen anything."

"Great." Nancy sighed. "All this right on the heels of that big report
about misuse of Ebola funds. It's hard to separate ourselves from all the
bad apples out there. Where is the UN on this?"

"They're actually right in the middle of it. They're sending some funding
to the usual folks, us included, but they are also funding all these fly-by-
night organizations, too, relying on them to implement on the ground
but not expecting much proof that what they are paying for is being
received, let alone making a difference. A few have trotted out some
Western celebrities for photo ops so things look good back home, but,
seriously, there is no communication and no accountability back to the
UN, the big foundations, or individual donors. In the end, the girls are
the ones that lose."

Case Questions

1. What are some challenges that nonprofit leaders face when they engage internationally?

2. What sorts of issues hinder accountability for NGOs working in developing nations? What are some ways that accountability can be promoted in NGOs?

3. How can WCF or other reputable nonprofits engender trust with the local people they seek to serve?

4. What strategies could be used for better coordinating in-country activities?

THE ORGANIC NONPROFIT: FEET FIRST

Aiden Roberts and Mason Fielder have been best friends since kindergarten. Raised in an upper-middle-class community, the boys enjoyed a rather idyllic boyhood. Every afternoon after school and most weekends were filled with some sort of sporting activity, usually soccer or baseball. Their families enthusiastically supported their efforts and enjoyed cheering them on from the stands. In their freshman year of high school, both Aiden and Mason were selected to play on the junior varsity soccer team.

Later that same year, they worked together with a local Rotary Club where Mason's father was a member, on a service learning project to help raise money to build clean water drinking wells in rural African villages. They enjoyed their work on the project and became interested in visiting Africa. The opportunity came in their junior year when they were offered the chance to participate in a 2-week-long Rotary International sponsored exchange program with one of the villages. In a letter home to his parents, Aiden described how incredibly friendly the people were and how it felt really good to help them. "The kids loved the school supplies we delivered. You should have seen their faces. When we had some free time we played soccer with them. They don't have nets or really any sports equipment here, but we made it work," he wrote. The trip not only raised their awareness about the needs of the villagers in rural Africa; both boys were also struck by "how good we have it," as Mason put it.

Discussing it on the long trip back to the United States, they both agreed that they wanted to do more to help the kids they had come to know. "We can really do something to help those kids. We know so many people who would be willing to give them something," Aiden said. Before the plane landed, they had come up with an idea to collect used sports equipment and donations of new shoes and to send them back to the villages they had visited. "I think this is something people can really get behind, plus it connects all the things we love to do," Aiden commented.

"It won't look bad on a college application either," Mason kidded.

True to their word, the boys launched their program within days of getting home. They called it Feet Forward. They started with friends and family, collecting donations of used equipment and asking for money to buy some new pairs of shoes. They hosted a couple of small fund-raisers to raise the cash needed to purchase some new items and to cover the cost of shipments. Through Rotary, they connected with a missionary group that agreed to receive and disperse the equipment. Overall, getting the first shipment delivered took quite a bit more effort than either of the boys originally thought, but when they received some photos of the kids playing with the new balls and wearing the new shoes, they were both deeply satisfied. "We need to keep going with this," Mason said.

By the end of their senior year, the boys had coordinated two more shipments of donations. Although they did not have the time or money to return to Africa in person, they had received heartwarming letters back from people working on the ground, letting them know their goods were being dispersed to kids in need. The boys used their knowledge of social media to promote the work of the organization through Facebook pages, and one of their friends produced a YouTube video to share their story.

The local paper ran a story about their work, and they were presented with a leadership award by a local news station.

As their reach broadened and they found themselves getting larger donations from people they didn't know personally, Aiden's mom, Jeanne, suggested they set up a nonprofit so people could get a tax deduction for their donations to Feet Forward. Jeanne was a bookkeeper for a local insurance company and was growing concerned about the boys keeping accurate records of their donations. Using a template from the Internet, Jeanne helped them get the paperwork together. They wrote a mission statement: The mission of Feet Forward is to take a team approach to provide, through charitable contributions, used and new sports equipment and supplies to children with limited resources.

Aiden was listed as president and CEO, and Mason was named chairman of the board. "Who knew I would be a CEO at 18?" Aiden ribbed Mason. They listed Jeanne as the treasurer, and they also named Mason's girlfriend, Brianna, and Aiden's brother, Jack, as members of the board of directors.

In the fall, Aiden and Mason went their separate ways with Aiden attending a small Jesuit school in the Northwest and Mason enrolled in an engineering program at a large southern university. They left the work of Feet Forward in the hands of Jack and some of his friends for the time being; however, they vowed to figure out a way to continue their work.

Aiden, a business major, was particularly interested in learning more about how he could combine his passion for Feet Forward with his interest in business ownership and corporate social responsibility. He was excited to be admitted to an incubator program for social entrepreneurs, and he enrolled in a spring course called Leadership and Social Enterprise. On the first day of the class, he was quick to share the story of Feet Forward with the group. A student named Sydney raised her hand to ask a question. "How do you know you are helping these people?" she asked. This kind of project seems like a handout not a hand-up."

Aiden was taken aback by the question. "Well, we were there, we saw that they needed these things, and so we sent them, simple as that. People really want to help, and we get good reports back from people on the ground," he answered.

"Yes, I'm sure you do, but how do you know they don't need other things more? You say it is simple, but I think you underestimate the complexity of the underlying issues. I've lived in Africa and seen how those kinds of donations just pile up because what people really need is a way to make a living so they can buy stuff for themselves. Do you have anyone from the villages on your board or advising you?" Sydney challenged Aiden.

"Well, logistically, that is sort of hard," Aiden began.

Sydney interrupted him. "In a way, what you are doing is really insulting," she proclaimed. "Projects like this don't help communities to develop; they just make people like you and your friends feel less guilty for having so much when others have so little."

Aiden couldn't help but feel defensive, but before he could respond, their professor intervened and suggested they use Aiden's group as a case study throughout the semester.

Case Questions

1. In your opinion, what are some things that motivate people to form nonprofits? Are some motivations better or nobler than others? Are good intentions enough?

2. How would you have approached launching Feet Forward? What kinds of information would you have gathered before engaging in such an endeavor? How would you plan it?

3. Do you think it was necessary for Aiden and Mason to form a nonprofit, or were there other organizational structures or strategies they could have considered?

4. Are there any things about the way the nonprofit was formed in the case that concern you? What, if anything, would you have done differently?

5. What are the ethical dimensions presented in the case? What are some of the issues that are unique to leading and managing in an international setting?

WHEN DONORS DON'T WANT TO FUND OVERHEAD: IN OVER HER OVERHEAD

Mercy Akoth was worried. Raising money was something that she didn't think much about when she worked for World IMPACT, a renowned international relief and development organization. Now it seemed that money was all she thought about. Forming her own NGO seemed like such a wonderful idea 18 months ago; nowadays, she wasn't at all sure how she would keep it afloat.

Mercy had loved working for World IMPACT. She believed deeply in the mission of the organization, admired the dedication of its staff, and knew that her country, Kenya, had been profoundly changed for the better by its work. World IMPACT had had an active presence in Kenya since the 1980s, working with local residents on a variety of vital programs to deliver improved health care, clean water, education, disaster relief, and food and to provide material and technical support for agricultural activities, economic development, and child protection.

The organization had hired Mercy 3 years ago to help with a primary school building campaign in West Pokot County that would serve the tiny town of Chepareria and its surrounding areas. Although the county was known as home to the Turkwel Hydro Power Plant that fueled the national grid, its energy did not reach many of the local the residents. Mercy was originally from Kapenguria, the county's capital. She had met representatives of World IMPACT at an employee recruitment event that was held at the University of Nairobi, where she had received a degree in education (made possible by a beloved aunt who lived in Nairobi). She was thrilled to be hired by the organization to work on an effort that would empower children from her home area to give them what she envisioned would be a quality education.

The Kenyan government had announced with great fanfare universal free primary education in 2003, although *free* was still a relative term; families were still required to pay for school supplies including uniforms, books, and pens, as well as lunch. The reality was that despite this major push on the part of government to prepare its young citizens to be active contributors to the economic health of the country, only 85%

of Kenyan children attended school (admittedly a much higher figure than in prior years). Those attending schools found themselves studying in crowded classrooms as construction and the availability of teachers still lagged behind the demand for education.

School attendance was particularly problematic in the more rural areas of the country, where poverty was rampant, which made it difficult for parents to afford to send their children. Not only did these parents struggle to pay for school supplies; many of these children were also needed to help tend the house, take care of younger children, and generate income to support the family. In addition, some parents saw education as an unnecessary luxury. Girls, in particular, were less likely to attend school than boys because most parents saw the role of a girl as being more closely tied to the care of home and family. The primary "job" for girls was seen as preparing themselves for marriage.

In 2010, the government's National Assessment Centre office worked in collaboration with the NGO Uwezo to assess the basic literacy and numeracy skills of children 6 to 16 years old throughout the country. The study found that 85% could not read a paragraph in English, 81% could not read a paragraph in Swahili, and 79% could not subtract one number from another (UWEZO Kenya, 2012). Mercy had her work cut out for her.

During the first 18 months of the campaign, Mercy was tasked with coordinating efforts to build the school alongside World IMPACT staffer, Brian Kilpatrick. She worked with Brian to negotiate with the government for a suitable location for the school, to find reputable contractors to do the building work, to order the desks and school supplies, to screen and hire teacher candidates, and to promote the school throughout the countryside. As a public school, the government would pay for Mercy's time as headmaster and for the teacher salaries. In addition to Mercy, two other teachers would be responsible for educating children in Grades 1 through 8 with each being responsible for 2 to 3 grades (with some of the grades combined) and approximately 60 to 80 children per class. The school opened with much fanfare including a celebration attended by villagers from the surrounding community. World IMPACT made sure the school had everything it needed to open successfully.

As the project neared its launch date, Mercy and Brian discussed the future of the school. "Once we are done with the labor and supplies, the school will be in your hands. There are several donors I want to introduce you to who have told me that they would rather provide direct funding to a local organization than continue supporting the project through World IMPACT. We at World IMPACT think this makes perfect sense, and we have confidence in your ability to shepherd the school for many years to come."

"Thank you for your confidence in me, "said Mercy. "I am humbled by your faith in my ability to serve my community."

During the transition period, Mercy worked to obtain her status as an in-country NGO (a complex and time-consuming process that she was able to achieve with the help of World IMPACT staff) and to meet the donors Brian knew who wanted to fund her work directly. Several meetings took place via Skype, where Brian was able to give donors in France, the United Kingdom, Canada, and Holland a virtual tour of the school site and to tell them about World IMPACT's plan for transitioning control of the school to the NGO that would be headed by Mercy. Most of these online sessions were open to groups of donors from each of these countries that were able to log onto the session. Many of them glowed when they spoke about the anticipated return on investment of their charitable dollars.

After each of these Skype meetings, Mercy wrote a formal thank-you letter to the major donors identified by Brian expressing her appreciation for their gift to her community. She was also introduced, via e-mail, to other donors who Brian told her expressed support for the project. Mercy was sincerely grateful for their support of the school and excited about taking on the responsibility of leading it as head mistress and lead teacher.

At the start of the first semester, things seemed to be proceeding smoothly. The children were happy, and her fellow teachers seemed to be engaging the students. The students were attentive with their instructional drills and gave each teacher their undivided attention.

As the months went along, she noticed that an increasing number of students were missing class. To get to the bottom of what was occurring, she travelled to the students' homes to find out what had happened and to discuss the situation with their parents. This was a big undertaking requiring hours of travel on unpaved roads leading to homes that were scattered great distances from one another. What she found, more often than not, were situations like these: a student had torn her uniform (or soiled it) and could not go to school because her parents could not afford a new uniform; female students whose fathers felt they would not be good marriage candidates if they were overeducated; parents who were embarrassed to send their children to school without lunch, and so they did not send them at all; children who were sick and needed worm medication; and children who were needed to work in order to support other members of their families.

Each of these situations required additional resources that Mercy did not have—money for additional uniforms, money to provide lunch to those students who could not afford to bring lunch, money for medication, and money for her time and expenses to travel to meet with these families. She also needed money for someone to provide her with administrative support. Mercy needed time not only to oversee the other teachers but also to act as a substitute when need be (it seemed she was needed in this capacity at least once every 2 weeks), to handle all of the administration required by the government, and to raise money for the school. She had not even begun to administer annual exams, the results of which would need to be reported to the government. Although the international donors were generously funding books, pens and paper, and one uniform per child, these contributions were not enough to cover the full costs of operating the school. Moreover, donations to the school had dropped off significantly once the building had been built. It seemed as if the donors thought that their job was finished when Mercy knew that it was just beginning.

Mercy was worried. She was working 15 hours a day, 6.5 days a week (she took time for church on Sundays) and didn't know how she was going to keep the school going without additional funding and additional help. She had been trained as a teacher, not an administrator. She decided that she needed to communicate with her international donors to give them an update on what was going on but wasn't sure how she should approach the situation. She felt the donors would want to hear that the school was succeeding—not that it was having trouble retaining students. She was concerned that she would sound like the failure she felt she was if she reported the reality of what was occurring. Finally, she gathered the courage to write a fund-raising appeal that focused on what the school was accomplishing. She had never written a letter like this before.

Six weeks after her outreach to donors, letters began arriving with checks for the school. Mercy cried with relief when the first pile of donor envelopes arrived; however, after she opened them, she was puzzled. Nearly every check was earmarked: funding for school supplies (some even wrote, "Please do not use any of these funds for overhead"). After a month of contributions, Mercy realized that she had raised four times what she needed for basic school supplies and nothing to help her pay for administrative expenses. She wasn't even sure if she could consider food and medicine school supplies, although she felt they were essential in order for the students to learn.

Case Questions

1. What kind of training, if any, do you think World IMPACT should have provided Mercy on school administration?

2. Is funding for overhead a problem for nonprofits in general, or is it something that is limited to INGOs and NGOs?

3. Do you think donors are reluctant to support the operating costs of a nonprofit organization? What are donors seeking when they talk about return on investment?

4. If you were Mercy, how would you use the donated funds? Would you use any of the funds for administrative expenses? If so, what would be your justification?

5. If you were Mercy, what would you do next? How would you communicate the situation to the donors? Is there anything she could have said or done to increase contributions for general operating support?

REFERENCE

UWEZO Kenya. (2012). *Are our children learning? Summary of key findings: Primary facts on learning levels*. Retrieved from http://www.uwezo.net/wp-content/uploads/2012/08/Summary-Findings-A4-Primary-Facts-FOR-WEB.pdf